Practising Spirituality

Practice Theory in Context series
Series Editor: Jan Fook

Change is rife in welfare organisations but expectations for sound and effective practice continue to rise. More than ever, professionals need to be able to remake ideas and principles for relevance in a range of different circumstances as well as transfer learning from one context to the next.

This new series focuses on approaches to practice that are common and prevalent in health and social care settings. Each book succinctly explains the theoretical principles of its approach and shows exactly how these ideas can be applied skilfully in the pressurised world of day-to-day practice.

Pitched at a level suitable for students on introductory courses, the books are holistic in ethos, also considering organisational and policy contexts, working with colleagues, ethics and values, self-care and professional development. As such, these texts are ideal too as theory refreshers for early and later career practitioners.

Published

Laura Béres
The Narrative Practitioner

Fiona Gardner
Being Critically Reflective

Laura Béres
Practising Spirituality

Forthcoming

Stanley Witkin
Transforming Social Work

Practising Spirituality

Reflections on meaning-making in personal and professional contexts

Laura
Béres

 palgrave

First published 2017 by
PALGRAVE

Palgrave in the UK is an imprint of Macmillan Publishers Limited,
registered in England, company number 785998, of 4 Crinan Street,
London, N1 9XW.

Palgrave® and Macmillan® are registered trademarks in the United States,
the United Kingdom, Europe and other countries.

ISBN 978–1–137–55684–4 paperback

A catalogue record for this book is available from the British Library.

A catalog record for this book is available from the Library of Congress.

Contents

Foreword

The importance of meaning, and of addressing the bigger questions in life, appears to be steadily on the increase. This is understandable given the kinds of social upheavals and increasing conditions of hardship being experienced by many around the globe. In some ways, the people-oriented professions have been perhaps slower to take up an interest in spirituality, and to integrate it into their practice in an articulated way, than might be expected. This book is therefore very welcome in the Practice Theory in Context series.

I was delighted that Laura considered publishing her book in this series, as I think it makes a timely point about the need to revisit these big questions and to put a diverse form of spirituality back on the professional practice agenda. Although 'spirituality' itself is not a practice theory such as others in the series, it is a way of thinking and an approach to living that I believe deserves to be accorded a place at the forefront of how we think about relating to and working with people who, for whatever reason, at whatever time, and in whatever context, need the assistance of professionals. When in a time of need, it is these issues of meaning that also beg to be addressed, simultaneously with more practical or material concerns. In this sense, I do not believe there is necessarily a hierarchy of needs, but that the spiritual is intertwined with the physical, social and emotional aspects of being. All need to be nurtured if we are to truly connect as human beings.

Given that the idea of spirituality does encompass the "big" questions and that, of course, there are many and varied versions of it, I do think it is an idea and concept which does need to be translated into specific principles and guidelines for practice. For this reason, the authors in this volume have been carefully selected by Laura to represent a range of experiences, from different contexts and backgrounds. It is a fitting approach for the series. On another level it is also fitting, as authors have been asked to approach their topic in a reflective manner, drawing on their own experience and illustrating how they have interpreted the workings of spirituality in their own practice. I find that this approach grounds and makes real the individuality and thoughtfulness of the authors' work. This is very moving reading. Authors speak with their own voice, and the many different styles are a testament to what we each bring to the professional encounter as individual people and human beings. For me it makes professional practice itself a much more meaningful experience. It leads me to reflect further on what it means to be human and to care for each other. I do hope that it enriches your own professional practice in the way it has done for me.

Jan Fook
Series editor

1 What Is Spirituality and How Does It Relate to Professional Practice?

Laura Béres

Introducing spirituality

For several years I have been incorporating the topic of spirituality in direct practice courses I teach in a university social work programme. I do this despite the fact that when I was a social work student I was only taught how to conduct biopsychosocial assessments rather than biopsychosocial-spiritual assessments. The three-dimensional model continues to be the norm in many programmes that aim to educate practitioners within the helping professions in the United Kingdom, Canada, the United States of America and Australia. Yet Cook, Powell and Sims (2009) of the Royal College of Psychiatrists in the United Kingdom suggest it is necessary to add the fourth dimension, that of spirituality, to this biopsychosocial model. Cook's definition of spirituality, which the authors use for their argument, is the following:

> Spirituality is a distinctive, potentially creative and universal dimen-
> sion of human experience arising from both within the inner subjective
> awareness of individuals and within communities, social groups and
> traditions. It may be experienced as relationship with that which is inti-
> mately 'inner', immanent and personal, within the self and others, and/or
> as relationship with that which is wholly 'other', transcendent and beyond
> the self. It is experienced as being fundamental or ultimate importance
> and is thus concerned with matters of meaning and purpose in life, truth
> and values. (Cook, Powell and Sims, 2009, p. 4)

If, in fact, spirituality is related to that which is of ultimate importance to people, providing them with a sense of meaning and purpose in life, then it is necessary for practitioners in health care and social services to develop comfort with, and the skills required for, addressing the area of spirituality in their work with people. Just as the biological/physical, psychological/emotional and social aspects of people's lives might be involved in both the problems and potential solutions/resources related to the situation which results in them accessing health or social services, so might the spiritual aspect play either a problematic or supportive role (Canda, 2006; Pargament, 2011). Practitioners should not ignore any of these four areas of a person's life in the process of assessing, intervening or evaluating outcomes.

Pargament (2011) provides an overview of how the field of psychotherapy in particular has reached its current state of unpreparedness when it comes to dealing with the area of spirituality, yet his remarks are relevant for all the social and health care disciplines. He points out that one of the 'founding fathers' of psychology, William James, took quite seriously that '*psyche* (soul) and *logy* (study of)' (p. 7) would involve the spiritual and mystical. However, Pargament goes on to highlight the impact of positivism in the early twentieth century and the manner in which 'psychology moved quickly to ally itself with the natural sciences and thereby distinguish itself from its embarrassingly close disciplinary kin, philosophy and theology. [...] religion came to be seen as an impediment to the scientific search for enlightenment' (p. 8). He argues that models of personality and psychotherapy, and therefore those trained in the resulting approaches, have become quite separate and different from the people they are meant to be serving. In support of this contention, Pargament cites statistics indicating that in the United States about 58 per cent of the population considers religion to be an important aspect of their lives, whereas this is true for only 26 per cent of clinical and counselling psychologists. Similarly, although a belief in God is held by 90 per cent of the population, among clinical and counselling psychologists, the figure is 24 per cent. 'When it comes to religion, therapists and their clients come from different worlds' (Pargament, 2011, p. 9). Holloway (2007), in the United Kingdom, in much the same way, says 'the evidence base is growing for the significance for large numbers of people of a dimension which they term "spiritual", and a set of issues whose existential source remains untouched by standard psycho-social therapeutic techniques' (p. 275). She also suggests that the majority of social work practitioners are less religious or spiritual than the general public and those people with whom they will work.

In order for practitioners to be ethical, competent and culturally sensitive, they need to learn how to integrate spirituality into their professional practice. For the small percentage of professionals who do have their own spiritual and/or religious beliefs and practices, this means ensuring that they do not impose their beliefs on others in any way. For the majority of professionals who identify themselves as not being spiritual or religious it means needing to reflect on what spirituality means for other people and developing ways of working that take into account the spiritual aspect. This is important not only so that an integral part of people's lives is not ignored in the provision of services, but also to ensure that service providers do not unintentionally silence their clients through their own discomfort with the topic of spirituality or, worse, explicitly patronize or disparage their clients' beliefs. For example, Canda discovered the following in a small qualitative study he conducted, which involved in-depth interviews with 16 participants:

> Five people described sceptical, patronizing, and disparaging attitudes and comments regarding their spirituality from physicians, psychiatrists, or social workers. Four people mentioned tensions arising from differences of spiritual beliefs with significant others including family, coworkers, and friends. One person indicated that the pervasive dichotomy between medicine and spirituality in society generally inhibits patients' access to holistic, spiritually oriented health care. (Canda, 2006, p. 67)

Holloway and Moss (2010) describe religion, spirituality, meaning and purpose by representing them as concentric circles: the largest circle describes what gives people a sense of meaning and purpose; a smaller circle within that contains spirituality; and the smallest circle in the centre contains religion. Some people are religious, spiritual and engaged with considering what gives them meaning and purpose. Others are not religious but would describe themselves as spiritual and interested in what gives them meaning and purpose. Finally, some would not describe themselves as either spiritual or religious but do search for meaning and purpose in their lives.

Canda's extensive work in the area of spirituality has been influential in the social work field internationally, and he defines it as 'the human quest for personal meaning and mutually fulfilling relationships among people, the non human environment, and, for some, God' (Canda, 1988, p. 243). This provides a broad and general description of spirituality that can be inclusive for the majority of people, whether they believe in God or not and whether they attend organized religious gatherings or not. Most people want fulfilling connections with others and are looking for meaning and purpose in their lives, and professional practitioners can support them in these quests. This will involve engaging with people beyond merely attempting to solve presenting problems but will necessitate a curiosity about what motivates people to carry on towards their preferred ways of being: their hopes, dreams and values.

Introducing myself

Having been born and lived in England until I was 17 years old, I was raised participating in services in the Church of England. My involvement with organized religion remained important to me to varying degrees over the years but diminished in importance during my early adulthood and throughout the majority of my university education in Canada. My first degree was in psychology, and consistent with Pargament's observations, I was influenced by Freud, on the one hand, who thought religion provides a sense of security which is merely 'illusory' (Pargament, 2011, p. 9), and Skinner's behaviourism, on the other hand, which analysed the manner in which religion controls people's behaviours (ibid, p. 8). It was only much later that I was introduced properly to the work of Carl Jung, 'who wrote that, of his patients over 35, "there has not been one whose problem in the last resort was not that of finding a religious [spiritual] outlook on life"' (ibid, p. 14), or to Irvin Yalom's existential psychotherapy. Both Jung and Yalom offer a psychological framework and approach to working which are much more sensitive to the spiritual aspects of people's lives.

After my second degree, which was a graduate social work degree, I was employed by a Catholic Family Services (CFS) agency. Family service agencies in Canada primarily employ social workers who provide individual, couple, family and group counselling to a range of people with a multitude of presenting problems. Over the 15 years that I was an employee there, I worked with women who had experienced intimate partner violence, child witnesses of intimate partner violence, men who had perpetrated the violence, adult survivors of childhood sexual abuse, and individuals and couples wanting to improve relationships or their own personal emotional states and functioning in the world. Neither the social workers employed nor the people requesting counselling were required to be Catholic in order to be involved with the agency. During that time, although I had never been educated to deal with spiritual or religious issues, people would sometimes raise topics related to God, the Church or their own personal beliefs. I struggled with how to respond because I wanted to respect others' beliefs and was unsure of how to engage in helpful conversations about these areas of concern. My clinical supervisor at the time, whose own faith was important to him and who was qualified in both social work and theology, suggested that people's experiences with their own fathers often shape their images of God as father, and that it was appropriate and helpful to explore this idea with people so that they could see the impact of their childhood and family experiences on their expectations of religion and their image of God. With hindsight I now consider this as having been a pivotal moment in my thinking about spirituality and professional practice. I had previously hindered myself when attempting to respond to religious or spiritual topics in practice; through my wish to be respectful of others' faith and beliefs about God, I had somehow reified their notions of God: I had not allowed myself to consider the social construction of God. Allowing myself to think about the social construction of God did not mean I was forced to think of God as false and merely a human construct, but rather I was able to imagine that there could be such a vast and immense Divinity that humanity could not understand or describe it fully. Each one of us can only begin to consider the Divine/God from our own personal vantage point that has been shaped by our own experiences and social location. As Sheldrake also points out,

> Spiritual traditions do not exist on some ideal plane above and beyond history. The origins and development of spiritual traditions reflect the circumstances of time and place as well as the psychological state of the people involved. They consequently embody values that are socially conditioned. [...] This does not imply that spiritual traditions and texts have no value beyond their original contexts. However, it does mean that to appreciate their riches we must take context seriously. (Sheldrake, 2013, p. 12)

While employed by CFS and during the time that I was working primarily with women who had experienced assault and abuse, one of the women I was counselling told me she liked to read romance novels so she could try to learn how to behave like the heroines in those novels in order for her husband not to beat her. This comment significantly influenced my ongoing career as I soon afterwards began studies towards a PhD in critical pedagogy and cultural studies. Although I had been taught in my social work degree to consider the biopsychosocial aspects of a person's situation, the social part had lacked any acknowledgement of the power of popular culture in people's lives. Popular culture is another form of education that many of us are engaged with and negotiating all the time (Béres, 1999, 2001, 2002). While I was attempting to understand the impact of popular culture in the lives of my clients/service users I was becoming more familiar with social constructionism and post-modernism.

As I continued to work at CFS while completing my PhD, I also attended a workshop facilitated by Michael White about narrative therapy/practice for the first time (White, 1995). Narrative practices provided me with a method of working with people which involved assisting people in uncovering the influence of culture on the development of some of their meaning-making behaviours. Having taken up a full-time academic position after completing my PhD (at a Catholic university in Canada), I continued to pursue further education in narrative therapy at the Dulwich Centre in Australia. I found that although I had originally struggled with how to hold onto, and respect, others' belief systems when using a social constructionist lens, I began to appreciate the manner in which narrative practices provided a method of doing so. For example, White's (2007) description of the use of conversational maps provides an approach which focuses not only on the social construction of attitudes and behaviours but also on peoples' hopes, dreams, values and what gives them a sense of meaning and purpose (see particularly chapter 7 in Béres, 2014).

Although I had never heard White talk explicitly about spirituality, when I asked him about this area, he directed me to a short interview about the 'little sacraments of daily living' in a collection of his essays and interviews (White, 2000). In that interview he quotes Malouf, an Australian author, as saying: 'the little sacraments of daily existence, movements of the heart and invitations of the close but inexpressible grandeur and terror of things [… are] the major part of what happens every day in the life of the planet, and [have] been from the very beginning' (Malouf in White, 2000, p. 145). I particularly like the way in which White emphasizes the 'little sacraments of daily existence' and stresses the need to be open to, and curious about, those otherwise mundane moments and experiences in people's lives which can evoke a sense of significance and meaning, or of the sacred.

At about the same time as I was becoming more interested in narrative practices I was also becoming curious about Celtic spirituality. I have written extensively about Celtic spirituality in other places (Béres, 2012, 2013, upcoming), so will only say here that Celtic spirituality suggests there is only a thin line between the physical and the spiritual and that there is also a spark of the Divine in all of Creation. This shares something in common with Indigenous and First Nations spiritualities, and also resonates with this idea of the 'little sacraments of daily living'. One image that was given to me was of someone sweeping the hearth or putting on the kettle and all the while engaged in worship of the Divine through these activities; religion, spirituality, even prayer, do not need to be separate and removed from the everyday activities of life.

I audited a module about Celtic Spirituality which was part of the MA in Christian Spirituality offered at Sarum College in the United Kingdom, due to my desire to understand Celtic spirituality academically as well as through the myriad of popular books available on the subject. Having done so, I realized how much more there was for me to learn more generally about spirituality, and so I am now also pursuing formal studies towards an MA in Christian Spirituality at Sarum College.

When I look back in order to explain the influences on the development of my curiosity in spirituality for both personal and professional practice, I find it fascinating to see through the reflecting process how the variety of seemingly different interests has woven together seamlessly over time. However, this is only one of many paths towards an interest in spirituality, and as I began to consider writing a book about the importance of spirituality in professional practice, I realized that such a book would be far more engaging and useful if it brought together a collection of reflections from other professionals and academics as well. This would offer a greater range of insights from different professions and from different spiritual perspectives.

Reflecting upon meaning-making practices in both personal and professional lives, and highlighting the integration and congruence between those two areas of practice, is a method that is particularly suited to Jan Fook's Practice Theory in Context series. Jan had previously asked me to contribute to her series, explaining that her aim for the series was that people should write about their experiences of actually putting theory into practice rather than write in such a way that would create another standard textbook. The initial request resulted in me writing *The Narrative Practitioner* (Béres, 2014). In thinking about this particular edited book about spirituality, and talking with Jan about it, we realized that it could make another contribution to her series. We hoped that authors would not only present theoretical descriptions of spirituality but would also consider the implications of how they make meaning in their personal spiritual practices and how they negotiate these personal values and beliefs as they take up the concept of spirituality in professional practice. The overall purpose of this book, therefore, is to support readers in reflecting upon what gives them a sense of meaning and purpose in their own lives, to realize and respect the potential range of spiritual practices in others' lives and finally to consider developing assessments and interventions which take into account the spiritual aspects of those people to whom they provide health and social care services.

Introducing the contributing authors

To say that I am pleased to be able to introduce the contributing authors in this edited book would be an understatement. I would prefer to say, 'I am thrilled' to introduce them, but that seems a little less academic and even a little less professional. However, because this book is another in Jan Fook's Practice Theory in Context series, and the books in this series are intended to offer something a little different, I am going to throw caution to the wind and say I am thrilled to be able to offer this edited book and to introduce a remarkable group of contributing authors!

I asked contributing authors to consider how spirituality might be integrated into professional practice, but also to reflect upon how their own meaning-making behaviours have shaped their professional and academic work. This was a broad request and has resulted in a fascinating range of responses in the chapters in this book. Some of the chapters are more personal; some, more professional/academic; and some provide an equal balance of the two. I have not asked authors to adjust their work in order to make the chapters more consistently similar, but rather I suggest that it is partly the range of approaches and styles which makes this edited book so interesting. I am assuming that some readers will be more naturally drawn to one type of chapter over another but will be able to reflect upon and learn from all the different chapters. I have also thought it important not to interfere with the particular 'voices' of the authors, again allowing for a range of styles that speak to what is important to each author. We need to recognize the unique differences and celebrate the rich diversity of experiences of both service users and professional colleagues.

A few years ago Jan Fook, Kate Bowles and I had a conversation about our work in critical reflection of practice, cultural/communication studies and narrative therapy, respectively (Béres, Bowles and Fook, 2011). During our conversation, and later while we were transcribing and writing for publication, we talked about the wish to facilitate working groups and conferences one day where we could just invite people with whom we might like to have a drink and chat about ideas. Although we have not yet managed to arrange such a conference (an annual gathering of 'Global Partnerships for Transformative Social Work', which Stanley Witkin organizes, is certainly similar to what we imagined, however), I have begun to think of this group of authors who have contributed to this book as just those sorts of people that it would be lovely to 'hang out with' to talk about ideas, and I am fairly confident readers will feel the same way. Although I may have met these authors through academic channels, some have become valued friends over the years, whereas others I have only just recently met through the writing of this book and hope will become friends over the coming years. I invited them to contribute chapters to this book either due to their expertise and interest in the area of spirituality in professional practice, or because of the thoughtfulness with which they reflect upon meaning-making aspects of their work. I was also keen to ensure a range of voices and social locations would be represented in these chapters. Unfortunately, Gus Hill, who was planning to contribute a chapter about one view of Indigenous spirituality in Canada from his position as an Anishinaabe man and social work academic, was unable, due to a variety of reasons, to complete a chapter at this time. However, it is possible to read his earlier work in this area (Hill and Coady, 2003; Hill and Cooke, 2014).

Most of the chapters share some common interests and themes with other chapters, so I have presented them in an order so that they build upon one another for readers who read from the front to the back of a book. I have also grouped them in short sections so that readers can see which chapters might have a common focus of interest. All of the authors have provided some background about themselves in their chapters, but I also provide a brief introduction for each of them here.

I have titled the first section 'Critical Reflection and Spirituality' and have included Jan Fook's and Fiona Gardner's chapters there.

In Chapter 2, Jan Fook provides a description of the development of her model of critical reflection of practice over the course of her academic career, giving consideration to her growing realization of how her model touches upon spirituality through the manner in which it uncovers people's underlying assumptions and values. She has realized the ongoing process of developing critical reflection of practice not only assists others in becoming clearer about what gives them meaning and purpose but has also given her greater meaning and purpose in her own life. I appreciate the manner in which Jan reflects back on her upbringing and how this pushed her away from all things religious, yet how she has slowly become more interested in spirituality. I think this is especially helpful for readers who may not consider themselves particularly religious or spiritual. It also provides an implicit and useful proviso for people with deep commitments to their own faith traditions, pointing out that professional practice cannot involve proselytizing. Jan also touches on her social and cultural location and how this has further contributed to her ways of thinking and being.

Chapter 3 follows very nicely from Jan's chapter on critical reflection and meaning-making, since Fiona Gardner, who has written with Jan about critical reflection previously (Fook and Gardner, 2007), presents a lovely reflection on how her interest in Quaker spirituality, critical reflection of practice and critical spirituality have all developed alongside one another in congruence with the values she holds most dear. Fiona models critical reflection of practice as she structures her chapter by reflecting upon an incident/memory of the first time she realized that spirituality was more important to her than organized religion.

I have titled the second section of this book 'Holistic and Indigenous Spiritualities'.

In the first chapter of this section, Chapter 4, Rose Pulliam describes the organic integration of spirituality into her daily living as being a spiritual heritage from her African and Native American roots. I met Rose at the same conference where I met Jan Fook and Fiona Gardner (one of the annual gatherings of the 'Global Partnerships for Transformative Social Work' group), so I had a sense she would provide a deeply moving reflection of her practice as a social work academic in the southern United States. She comments that even reflecting and writing about her spirituality feels like a transgressive and dangerous act, as she also describes the tensions inherent with discussing spirituality in a classroom setting in the Bible belt of the United States.

In Chapter 5, Karlo Mila focuses on the way that spirituality permeates therapeutic and restorative health practices and beliefs in Indigenous cultures of the Pacific region, illustrating how spirituality is deeply intertwined with health and well-being within those cultures. Through her chapter, she provides an example of how important it is to be aware of culturally distinctive understandings of spirituality and well-being, broadening our knowledge of how humans all over the world have constructed and approached health and spirituality in different cultural contexts. She explains that she came to this area of interest as she grew up in New Zealand, the daughter of a Pasifika migrant father, and came to realize the much higher incidents of mental disorders experienced by Pasifika peoples, and the need for culturally sensitive practices. I am grateful to David Epston for suggesting I invite Karlo to contribute to this book.

In Chapter 6, Cassandra Hanrahan passionately presents a core dimension of her spirituality, which influences both her personal and professional selves: human–animal interactions (HAI) and bonds (HAB). She describes these as informing a sense of interconnectedness to all, which in turn impacts her understanding of social work and social justice. I have included her chapter in this section because she is making an argument for honouring the sacred in all living creatures and creation, which I believe is consistent with Indigenous spiritualities. I have had the privilege of meeting Cassandra a couple of times at the Canadian Society for Spirituality and Social Work conferences and am grateful she was able to make the time to contribute to this book.

I have titled the third section 'Eastern Influences in Spiritual Practices' and have included Maria Cheung's chapter regarding Falun Gong and Lisa McCorquodale's chapter about mindfulness.

In Chapter 7, Maria describes Falun Gong as a body-mind-spirit practice, describing how she became interested in this approach personally and also providing examples of working with immigrants in a manner which respects their spiritual practices. She demonstrates how her commitment to these spiritual practices has led her, and many other Falun Gong practitioners, to become involved in social justice activities. I also met Maria at a Canadian Society for Spirituality and Social Work conference where she facilitated a workshop in which participants could experience some of the body-mind-spirit practices she describes in her chapter.

In Chapter 8, Lisa McCorquodale describes mindfulness practices, how these have assisted her personally in her own life and also how they have offered many benefits to those professionals who have integrated these ideas in their professional practice. As an occupational therapist, she has focused her research primarily in health-care and occupational therapists' use of mindfulness, yet her reflections are relevant for all of us who wish to be a little more present to others in our work, focusing just as much on 'being' as 'doing'. I recently met Lisa when she asked me to be a member of her PhD dissertation committee.

The fourth section is titled 'Celtic Spirituality and Monastic Influences'.

In Chapter 9, I discuss the concept of hospitality, which at first glance may appear rather mundane and merely a skill to offer guests in our homes but which overlaps with my interest in Celtic spirituality, having a rich tradition in the monastic 'Rules'. These 'Rules' are guidelines for living in monastic communities and I focus particularly on the *Rule of St. Benedict* and what professional practitioners might be able to learn from that Rule about creating safe, welcoming and hospitable spaces for others while also maintaining balance in their lives.

In Chapter 10, Melanie Rogers describes her own spiritual path and her involvement with The Northumbria Community, which is a dispersed Celtic Christian monastic community with its mother house based in Northumberland, United Kingdom. She focuses on the concepts of availability and vulnerability which are aspects of The Northumbria Community's 'Rule of Life'. As an advanced nurse practitioner in England, she reflects on her practice and her research with other nurses about how availability and vulnerability can enhance professional practice. I first met Melanie at a British Association for Studies in Spirituality conference, and we have continued to work together since then.

The final section of the book is titled 'Looking Back to Move Forward'.

In Chapter 11, Bruce Rumbold presents his reflections on over 40 years of practice with spirituality and palliative care. What I find particularly fascinating about his account is his observations about how 40 years ago people working in palliative care would have naturally integrated the topic of spirituality into their work with patients, but now, as there is growing interest in developing a more mainstream acceptance of generic spirituality in all health and social care, there is a risk of an oversimplification and managerial approach to it. He worries that even if spiritual care practice continues to be reflexive, the scope of spirituality could become overly narrowed and 'little more than pop-psychology'. He reminds us as we move forward that it will be essential that 'spiritual care providers develop and maintain a broader, multi-disciplinary, integrative perspective'. I am grateful that Allan Kellehear suggested I invite Bruce to contribute to this book.

Finally, in Chapter 12, I provide some concluding remarks regarding some of the broader themes I have noted that bridge many of the chapters. I reflect upon common descriptions of spirituality and implications for practice which I have drawn from the contributions to this book.

Although each chapter can be read independently of the others, I hope that readers will engage with the whole book in order to be able to reflect on the range of spiritual practices offered here and the manner in which they have influenced professional practices. The section headings and groupings are somewhat arbitrary as I did not ask authors to contribute to particular categories, but rather I have positioned chapters due to themes that I was drawn to. Readers may find they are drawn to different themes and ideas but will nonetheless have the opportunity to enrich their own practices by learning from the diverse examples offered here. For example, even though particular social and health-care providers may never work with Indigenous people in the Pacific Rim or provide occupational therapy to patients in Canada, they can still consider the potential benefits of integrating holistic or mindful approaches in their personal and professional lives. I hope readers will both enjoy this book and find it helpful.

References

Béres, L., 1999. Beauty and the beast: the romanticization of abuse in popular culture. *European Journal of Cultural Studies*, 2(2), pp. 191–207.

Béres, L., 2001. Romance, suffering and hope: reflective practice with abused women. Unpublished PhD thesis. Toronto: University of Toronto.

Béres, L., 2002. Negotiating images: popular culture, imagination and hope in clinical social work practice. *Affilia: Journal of Women and Social Work*, 17(4), pp. 429–447.

Béres, L., 2012. A thin place: narratives of space and place, Celtic spirituality and meaning. *Journal of Religion and Spirituality in Social Work: Social Thought*, 31(4), pp. 394–413.

Béres, L., 2013. Celtic spirituality and postmodern geography: narratives of engagement with place. *Journal for the Study of Spirituality*, 2(2), pp. 170–185.

Béres, L., 2014. *The narrative practitioner*. Basingstoke: Palgrave Macmillan.

Béres, L., forthcoming. Celtic spirituality: exploring the fascination across time and space. In B. Crisp, ed., *The Routledge handbook of religion, spirituality, and social work*. New York: Routledge.

Béres, L., Bowles, K., and Fook, J., 2011. Narrative therapy and critical reflection on practice: a conversation with Jan Fook. *Journal of Systemic Therapies*, 30(2), pp. 81–97.

Canda, E. R., 1988. Spirituality, diversity, and social work practice. *Social Casework*, 69(4), pp. 238–247.

Canda, E. R., 2006. The significance of spirituality for resilient response to chronic illness: a qualitative study of adults with cystic fibrosis. In D. Saleebey, ed., *The strengths perspective in social work practice*, 4th edn. Boston: Pearson Education. Ch. 4.

Cook, C., Powell, A., and Sims, A., eds., 2009. *Spirituality and psychiatry*. Glasgow: RCPsych Publications.

Fook, J., and Gardner, F., 2007. *Practising critical reflection: a resource handbook*. Maidenhead: Open University Press.

Hill, G., and Coady, N., 2003. Comparing Euro-Western counselling and aboriginal healing methods: an argument for the effectiveness of aboriginal approaches to healing. *Native Social Work Journal*, 5, pp. 44–63.

Hill, G., and Cooke, M., 2014. How do you build a community? Developing community capacity and social capital in an urban aboriginal setting. *Pimatisiwin: A Journal of Aboriginal and Community Health*, 11(3), pp. 421–432.

Holloway, M., 2007. Spiritual need and the core business of social work. *British Journal of Social Work*, 37(2), pp. 265–280.

Holloway, M. and Moss, R., 2010. *Spirituality and social work*. Basingstoke: Palgrave Macmillan.

Pargament, K. I., 2011. *Spiritually integrated psychotherapy: understanding and addressing the sacred*. New York: The Guilford Press.

Sheldrake, P., 2013. *Spirituality: a brief history*, 2nd edn. Oxford: Wiley-Blackwell.

White, M., 1995. *Therapeutic conversations as collaborative inquiry*. Two-day training sponsored by the Brief Therapy Training Centres International (a division of the Hincks-Dellcrest, Gail Appel Institute), Toronto, Canada. 22 and 23 March.

White, M., 2000. *Reflections on narrative practice: essays and interviews*. Adelaide: Dulwich Centre Publications.

White, M., 2007. *Maps of narrative practice*. New York: W.W. Norton.

SECTION

I

Critical Reflection
and Spirituality

2 Finding Fundamental Meaning through Critical Reflection

Jan Fook

My own background in spirituality

I have come, somewhat shamefully I feel, to appreciate the role of spirituality in peoples' lives rather late in my own life and career. As I say this, I realize this is not entirely true. I was actually raised as a devout Seventh-day Adventist, and this did colour the way I viewed spirituality. This was from the perspective of organized religion, and looking back on it now, I fear I mistook much fundamentalist culture and dogma for spirituality. In my early twenties, I forsook my religion in favour of just thinking for myself and experienced this as entirely novel and not a little bit liberating. I had developed a severe suspicion of organized religion, especially of the fundamentalist kind. In some ways it meant I gave up thinking about explicitly spiritual matters. This stance was never challenged within the social work program I studied in the mid-1970s, when much social work education was very secular in orientation. (Indeed, I recall in my first year of study how I failed an essay on personal values because I wrote about my Christian values.) Despite an ongoing suspicion of organized religion, however, I have had an interesting relationship with both spirituality and religion since that time. In some ways perhaps, given my early negative experiences, this was more of a relationship than I care to acknowledge. It is challenging to reflect back on this now.

Over the course of my life, I have had the good fortune to have very close friendships with people who both espoused and practised a quiet yet substantial spirituality. In some cases this was coupled with a formal religion and the churchgoing that entailed. Their religion provides a circle of like-minded people, and a framework from which they contribute to and try to make our world a better place. I have great affection for these friends, since their religiosity and faith was never made explicit unless I initiated a discussion. Yet I could always sense it and benefit from its operation in their lives. There was none of the proselytizing which I had come to despise from my fundamentalist background. For others, their spirituality was embedded not so much in churchgoing, but in their understanding of the deeper meaning this entailed not just for themselves, but for others. It came with an embedded sense of personal ethics. This ability to separate religious practices and beliefs from the cultural trappings associated with the way religions are organized and superficially interpreted has been important in my recent interest in spirituality, both for myself and for the professionals with whom I work.

Lastly I should say that my life partner works in end-of-life care. This means we have shared many discussions about the bigger questions in life and the many difficult-to-explain psychic phenomena which occur surrounding the end of one's life. What do we know of an afterlife, and what are the implications of this for how we live in the here and now, what we do with our time, and how we care for those around us? What guidelines for living do we develop as a result of believing in an afterlife? So in some ways I have been long surrounded by the important questions which for many people their spirituality attempts to address.

My work with critical reflection and its meaning in my life

This interest in spirituality has been particularly piqued by my work in critical reflection. Very briefly, my way of practising critical reflection began with Donald Schön's (1983) relatively simple call to uncover the hidden assumptions on which our professional practice is based, in order that practice might be improved by bringing tacit assumptions more in line with thinking which is consciously espoused. Again I am ashamed to admit that I did very little reading about reflective practice at that time, despite designing a master's level course in advanced practice based on this approach. I simply enjoyed and learnt from engaging with social workers in reflection and seeing the kinds of changes which took place in their thinking and actions through uncovering the tacit thinking involved. I remember being particularly moved and surprised by the power of the reflection process. One person – I will call him Shane – particularly stuck in my mind. He began the critical reflection process by talking about an incident which indicated possible corruption by senior members of his organization, but which he was reluctant to report to the board of governors. He ended the whole process by deciding to resign his social work position to pursue a career with the trade unions. Of course there were a lot of steps along the way in this journey of discovering what I shall term his 'political calling', and we will return to them later.

At the same time, when I was witnessing what seemed like momentous realizations in peoples' lives, I was also frustrated by my own inability to explain, or even describe, how the changes were brought about. I finally did turn to reading further, only to find that the various definitions and understandings of reflective practice, critical reflection, reflection and reflexivity were so varied that they still did little to enlighten me about what I was seeing taking place. I determined that I would attempt to research the process, and the changes which occurred, in order to provide some more clarity and certainty about the outcomes which could be expected. That was some years ago, and I am still engaged in that effort! That is me speaking as an academic.

As a person, I was totally riveted by what I experienced in critical reflection sessions with my colleagues. I found the process both humbling and fascinating. I was humbled by peoples' honesty and vulnerability, and the unwavering compassion they held for human beings in social plights. I was fascinated by the integrity which they displayed in the face of great odds, and by their ethical determination. I was amazed that a process so simple, instituted by me, could uncover and develop experiences of such importance. I remember declaring that for the first time in my then 20-year-long career, I felt like I was actually doing social work: I was effecting some change in people. In a sense I had found my own meaning in doing critical reflection with practising professionals. This realization prompted me to further explore the meanings which became revealed when professionals reflect. This is the main topic of this chapter: I explain the critical reflection process in more detail shortly, so you will gain an understanding of how the process allows people to create deeper meaning for themselves.

Before I do that, however, I need to say a little more about my very recent past and now present professional situation. The meaning of critical reflection in my life slowly began to dawn on me about 20 years ago. I mentioned earlier that when I engaged in critical reflection with my practitioner colleagues, I experienced the power and personal satisfaction of feeling like I had made a tangible difference in people's lives. This was something which I suppose I had always felt that social work should be about, but which I had rarely felt in all my (up till then) 20 years of a career as a social worker and educator. I began to reflect further on why the critical reflection approach was so attractive to me and why it gave me such a sense of fulfilment. It is easy in hindsight to recognize that the negative influence of my early fundamentalist upbringing might have pushed me towards the freedom I felt in being able to question the taken-for-granted almost unrestrainedly. Engaging in critical reflection with colleagues also had a therapeutic aspect, something I was very cautious about in earlier days. I admit I had first entered the social work profession with the intention of becoming a counsellor but gave this up when I encountered community development which appealed to me on a more political level. However, there was still a part of me which yearned to engage with individual people, to understand and to try to heal wounds through an empathic way of relating. Critical reflection, whilst definitely not being therapy, allowed that engagement albeit through a more political lens. In my critical reflection sessions, people often experienced being liberated from old ways of thinking and the emotions which often held them back, through coming to an understanding of how they had learnt and conformed unwittingly to taken-for-granted ways. My critical reflection model, the way I theorized it, facilitated personal understanding within a social and political context, and, in my view, paved the way for more empowered thinking and behaviour in the everyday contexts in which people lived and worked. So a lot came together for me: the personal engagement with individuals, but in order to bring about social changes. I felt like I was finally using all of me, my own peculiar biography and my own chosen theories in making a contribution to both my profession and to individuals within it. I was duly excited and contented. I experienced an excitement about my professional life which I had not felt before. I had (almost) always loved my profession, and I had truly enjoyed making an academic contribution through my work on critical social work. However, when I came to understand the significance of critical reflection to myself, and to others in the profession, I realized I had developed the potential for a much more vital and encompassing framework to guide the rest of my life's work. Critical reflection, developing and researching it further, became a clear inspiration and challenge. In some ways it gave me new and deeper meaning about 'what I was put here to do'. I had used phrases like this for some time, always sensing that living was meant to be more than about just finding something you could be good at, making a success of it and being happy. I guess, at the risk of sounding clichéd, I had constantly been searching for some greater meaning or purpose in life, and with critical reflection I felt I had found it.

The social justice mission and its meaning for me

There was still more to be learnt however. I can remember very clearly a critical reflection workshop session about five years later, when I had reflected on a personal experience of mine, and realized that social justice came out strongly as one of my core values. This should not have been a surprise, as social justice was certainly something I went around talking about all the time. Certainly most of us with a critical persuasion in social work did this, so it was really a 'taken-for-granted'. What took me by surprise, however, was that it seemed that social justice principles were also firmly ingrained into the way I saw the world. My reflection showed me that my interest in social justice, and in living it, could be traced directly to my own experiences of being marginalized, discriminated against and sometimes excluded.

At this point I should explain to you that I am a third-generation, Australian-born Chinese person by birth. I grew up in post–World War II Australia with its racist tendencies. Since I also grew up as a Seventh-day Adventist, eschewed from mixing with non-Seventh-day Adventists (over 99.999999 per cent of the rest of the world), and from a lower-middle-class background, you will see that I had plenty of reason to see myself as different from the mainstream. Since then I have lived in both Canada and the United Kingdom so I have a sometime migrant identity as well. It will perhaps seem obvious to you that my life experiences should have made me especially attuned to my social difference, and especially the negative effects of this. However, the norm for young people of Chinese appearance, growing up in 1960s Australia, was to deny racism and try to avoid trouble by fitting in as closely as possible – and certainly not challenging dominant groups. My mindset for much of my life has therefore been not to acknowledge racism or discrimination directed towards me. But because of my commitment to social work, I have always found it easier to recognize the wrongs directed towards other marginalized people.

So, with this realization that social justice was both something I espoused but also lived, I felt renewed in the important mission this entailed.

My life has taken odd professional twists and turns, and so it is that I have moved and changed jobs perhaps more than I would have chosen. However, I now have the very fortuitous opportunity to work in a new Catholic University where social justice is explicitly espoused as part of the university philosophy. In some ways this is rather ironic: that it should be a university, affiliated with an organized religion, which has made my more explicit commitment to social justice possible. I am Professor Higher Education Pedagogy with a brief to lead research in higher education teaching and learning across the university from a social justice perspective. This has given me new freedom and credibility to pursue social justice through my actual paid employment. What a bonus! I now actively develop and research pedagogical initiatives across different disciplines, including education, business, social care, religious studies, psychology, theology, history, English, sport education, media studies and journalism. This means I need to understand social justice and its implications in many different disciplines, professions and fields of employment. I am happily re-engaging with what critical reflection might mean in all these different arenas.

To have a meaningful approach to critical reflection which is relevant in more universal ways, I have had to return to the basics of what critical reflection is about, rather than focus on its use in specific professional settings. How does critical reflection actually relate to social justice, and how can critically reflecting actually contribute to one's spirituality? Next, I outline my approach to critical reflection and its practice in order to draw out the responses to these questions.

Critical reflection, social justice and spirituality

I mentioned earlier that my own approach to critical reflection was initially based on Schön's reflective practice, the process of unearthing hidden assumptions. What I found, however, was that when people did this, and especially when they unearthed deep assumptions which they had not articulated or thought about much beforehand, this brought about very radical changes. Often people unearthed thinking or early experiences which they had either forgotten about or whose significance they had not realized. This, of course, partly accounts for a therapeutic aspect of critical reflection.

I define critical reflection as a way of learning from experience, using a framework based on understanding how we both create and are created by power relationships and arrangements in society. The emphasis on power provides the critical aspect of reflection and also underpins the interest in social justice. Because there are many different definitions and approaches to critical reflection, I attempt to combine and integrate them into one broad approach (Fook and Kellehear, 2010). The idea of 'learning from experience' is taken from Dewey (1933), and the understanding of power and how it operates is classic critical theory (Fook and Gardner, 2007). However, there are other concepts which contribute to an understanding of critical reflection. For instance, Schön's work (1987) provides useful guidelines on how to begin the reflection process (unearthing tacit assumptions). The concept of reflexivity illuminates how, as human beings, we are both active and passive in creating and accepting what is regarded as legitimate knowledge, and therefore how we have a role in shaping our worlds. Postmodern and post-structural thinking adds to this perspective by filling out our understanding of how knowledge is constructed, and how power is exercised through this process. More recently I have added the concept of spirituality to underscore the meaning-making aspect of critical reflection. Even more recently I have returned to the Socratic idea that the purpose of reflection is for more 'ethical and compassionate engagement with the world and its dilemmas' (Nussbaum, 1997). This puts a broader context around why we learn from experience: namely, in order to be better citizens and members of a community. To become more ethical and compassionate is certainly a tall order, but it is the stuff of what it means to be human, which hopefully good education should equip us for. Some writers have referred to this fundamental goal of critical reflection as contributing to 'human flourishing' (Ghaye, 2010). So you see we are dealing with the big and fundamental issues here.

There is beginning to be quite a bit written about the connections between spirituality and critical reflection. One strand is the usefulness of some Eastern philosophies and related concepts in relation to reflection (Johns, 2005; Humphrey, 2009; Béres, 2009). Others discuss the potential overlap or integration of reflection with spirituality (Hunt, 2016) or the congruence of critical reflection with critical spirituality (Gardner, 2011; 2014). Allen (2013) goes another step and discusses the use of critical reflection in researching spirituality. A theme that most of these authors share is the idea that there is much congruence between the *ethos* of critical reflection and spirituality, and that the *methodology* of critical reflection can also assist in accessing peoples' sense of spirituality. In this chapter I am primarily focusing on the latter, that is, I am interested in how a process of critical reflection can assist people to rediscover and articulate the deeper meaning of their experience. So my understanding of spirituality, in this chapter, is a relatively straightforward focus on fundamental values and their meaning. In this sense, I often speak about critical reflection as a process which enables going to the heart of an experience in order to re-engage with the fundamental values which provide a bedrock for all of life's activities. Towards the end of the chapter, I examine different meanings of spirituality from the literature and how these relate to the changes which occur through critical reflection.

The critical reflection process

I have designed a process for engaging in critical reflection based on this approach (see Fook, 2002, 2012; Fook and Gardner, 2007). I normally provide training sessions for critical reflection in workshop formats with small groups. All members of the group are asked to choose a critical incident (something which happened to them, which they feel is significant to their learning and that they would like to learn from). They are asked to write this down in as raw descriptive form as possible. Each person then takes a turn presenting this incident to the small group, and the group then engages in dialogue to help the person unearth the basic assumptions which underlie his or her thinking, as it comes across in the 'story' of the incident. The dialogue involves members of the group asking the presenters questions which help them reflect on their incident by making them aware of their hidden assumptions. The process is framed by a group culture which enables 'critical acceptance', that is, creates a learning environment which enables risk-taking for better learning. In this learning culture, views should not be imposed on the person reflecting: the climate should enable the person to reflect and learn for him- or herself. This is difficult to achieve, as often the traditional learning cultures are based on the idea that there is one 'right' way of thinking, which is predetermined, and learning simply involves being led to this way of thinking. With the critical reflection process, there is no certainty about what issues will arise and how learners will respond.

The process takes place in two stages. In the first stage, participants reflect on their experience (incident), aiming only to unearth the deeper assumptions of which they were unaware. They are asked not to make judgements of their assumptions at this stage, but just to sit with them and get a feel for whether these ideas do seem to be congruent with how they believe they think. At the end of this stage-one reflection, they are asked to try to sum up what they will take away to reflect on further; what has stood out for them about their main assumptions; and where they feel they have gotten after this first stage of reflection. They are then asked to reflect further on these main ideas which have arisen, after they leave this first session.

In the second stage of the reflection, all participants present their further reflections on the main assumptions which arose from the first stage. The purpose of this stage is to remake their understanding of their experience, given their new awareness, and to turn this learning into a new framework including new guidelines for action. It is in this stage that I think that the links with spirituality are made, as this is the stage in which participants remake the fundamental meaning of their experience. They are able to do this because in the first stage of reflection they became aware of really deep or taken-for-granted beliefs or values. Once they become aware of these, they are often led to reframe or reinterpret earlier experiences in line with these values.

Some examples of critical reflection and the changes which occur

In this section I detail some different examples of what has happened in the critical reflection process and how the experience has assisted in discovering some fundamental meanings for these people.

The first is Shane, as mentioned above. Shane's critical incident involved becoming aware of what he thought might be some corruption on the part of senior people in his organization, and the conflict he felt about whether or not to report this to the board of governors. He described his fears about 'sticking his neck out' and the power he felt he didn't have. However, as a result of engaging in critical reflection with his colleagues, and possibly being able to air these fears and examine them in more detail, he decided to write a letter to the board of governors, outlining his concerns. When he came back to undertake his stage-two reflection, he had already done this and had a positive response from the governors. This reminded him of his lifelong interest in the politics of work and led him to decide to resign his social work position and seek work in the trade union movement.

The second story is of Adrian, a very well-respected social worker of about 20 years' standing. Adrian presented an incident from long ago, the first time he had been required to remove a child from the care of that child's parents. He described the trauma he felt at the time and indeed the distress he still felt. His reflection unearthed some of his major assumptions about professionals needing to be unaffected by personal emotion and being more resilient than he felt. Through the reflection process, he came to accept that being distressed did not make him a bad professional, and he managed to remake his own sense of himself as a caring professional.

The third story is Jane's (Fook, Royes and White, 2016). Her incident involved a client dying in a house fire some years earlier. Jane felt directly responsible for this, even though at the time she only supervised the worker of the client and so was only indirectly responsible. She was racked with guilt and distress and could not find any release from these emotions, even though she attempted to discuss them with colleagues many times. When she reflected on the incident, she realized there were deep-seated assumptions about being a manager and the inherent control this involved. She blamed herself for being a 'bad' manager, which was evidenced by the fact that she had not prevented the fire and the client dying. When she examined these assumptions about what it was possible for a manager to control, she realized how she had been unwittingly taken in by the 'form-filling' bureaucratic culture of her organization. In a way, she was finally able to see, in a symbolic sense, that there was no form for preventing a fire or a death. This realization freed her from her sense of guilt, as she was able to acknowledge the uncertainty of many situations which cannot be controlled. She also became aware of (and able to resist) the subtle culture of management which implied that everything could be controlled (and that you were a bad manager if you didn't).

What do these stories say about the process of critical reflection and the kinds of changes which take place? And how do these changes relate to our understanding of spirituality?

Shane was able to uncover what he felt was really important about the way he wanted to contribute to his world. This allowed him to take direct action and make very specific changes in his life's work. Adrian also was able to remake his sense of himself as an inadequate professional into a notion of a caring professional, one whose feelings of distress made into a more complex and holistic human being. And Jane no longer thought of herself as a 'bad' manager, but rather recognized the limits of bureaucracy and management. This allowed her to also remake her sense of herself as a good manager, despite not being able to control everything. In the latter two cases, there is also an acceptance of some aspects of personal experience and an ability to integrate these into a current (more acceptable) sense of self. These three examples provide illustrations of some of the major changes which can occur.

Below I have tried to describe and summarize overall the main types of changes which can occur through the critical reflection process.

First, as illustrated in the case of Shane, it is possible to develop a sense of integrity. By integrity here I mean an ability to act upon fundamentally held values. Through a critical reflection process, people are often able to find a way through what they have perceived as a dilemma (usually a conflict between fundamentally felt values and what actions they believe are possible). Sometimes they realize the dilemma has simply been their own construction (creating only two mutually exclusive options, neither of which are acceptable). By creating a third way, they are sometimes able to find a way to act which is in keeping with their conscience. In Shane's case, he was able to examine more closely his own assumptions about what might happen, or what he feared might happen, if he wrote a letter. He decided he wanted to choose to write the letter regardless, once the choice was more clearly exposed.

The second change which happens involves remaking a sense of self. Adrian did this by being able to examine his assumptions about 'good' professionalism, and accepting his own emotional reactions. Jane did this by coming to understand her own assumptions about 'bad' management, and realizing it was unrealistic to expect to control every situation. There is something in these types of changes about remaking a sense of self in relation to three aspects: (1) accepting negative emotions and finding a place for them; (2) reaffirming deeply held values and being able to find a way to act on them; and (3) remaking a sense of self as more powerful. Elsewhere I have categorized these changes in much more detail and in relation to an explicit critical framework (Fook and Askeland, 2006), and I will discuss briefly below how these might overlap with how the changes could be characterized in terms of spirituality. Overall, however, there is a sense of also remaking the self as a whole person, one who acknowledges deep values, accepts oneself and is able to act and influence in a way one chooses.

There are other changes which accompany these bigger ones. There is an affirmation of complexity and uncertainty, and an ability to live with these. This was especially the case for Jane. This type of change goes hand in hand with an ability to tolerate not always knowing, to accept different points of view and to seek to make changes through open dialogue.

Some specific responses from participants in critical reflection workshops (see Fook and Gardner, 2007) will give another sense of changes as they perceived them.

Turning 'pain' into 'gain' is one aspect of a 'meaningful' process and the 'transformative nature of new meaning'. For some this involved helping them to integrate 'macro/micro' and 'head/heart' matters, and ultimately to find 'satisfaction and direction'. The quote below, from a workshop participant, illustrates an overall sense of critical reflection:

> Critical reflection is a process which allows for the deep reflection and questioning of one's previously unexamined assumptions and values, but which provides strategies to evaluate one's core integrity and remain not only intact but also respected. (Fook and Gardner, 2007, p. 141)

Critical reflection and spirituality?

How does the experience of critical reflection sit with our notions of spirituality? Obviously in broad terms as I have defined it, people do manage to make deeper and greater meaning from their experience through engaging in critical reflection. Indeed, whilst most writers are agreed that there is no one simple definition of spirituality, meaning-making seems central to most notions. The idea that spirituality is associated with the 'transcendent' aspects of life, such as 'meaning, purpose and hope' (White in Gardner, 2013, p. 28) is also commonly shared. Hunt (2016) mentions the focus on 'ultimate questions' involving meaning and values: who am I, why am I here, and what am I supposed to be doing? Rumbold also notes a political aspect in that using the term 'spirituality' can be seen as a way of resisting the scientific neglect of the more 'subjective, relational and transcendent aspects of identity' (Rumbold, 2002, p. 9). Hunt (2016) also notes the more immaterial and mystical aspects of spirituality, which she likens to her own experience in trying to fathom her experience of 'community'. This does have some parallels with my own experience in trying to outline and discuss some of the deeply moving changes I have witnessed in my own critically reflecting colleagues.

Sheldrake (2013) draws our attention to another way of conceptualizing spirituality as an integrating factor in life. In this sense, 'spirituality' is best understood not so much as one element among many in human existence, but as a stance of attending to 'life as a whole' (p. 3). This also has some resonance with my own experience in finding that most elements of my life have come together in the quest to develop critical reflection for professionals.

Indeed, these connections have been reinforced for me through new writing which links spirituality with social justice (Sheridan, 2014).

At the end of the day, both critical reflection, as I have conceived it, and the moves towards spirituality are concerned with the big questions in life. From this point of view, of course, they come up against the same problems: difficulties of definition and of 'evidence', as would be expected of any endeavour concerned with questions which perhaps remain big because they are ultimately unfathomable using just one methodology and one frame of reference. It has been my small hope only that the process for critical reflection I have introduced might provide one way of practicing spirituality for some people. Certainly for myself it has reintroduced me to the big questions and the continued desire to keep asking them, even in an academy which seems increasingly concerned with smaller and smaller questions (and the ability to fund the research to answer them). It is heartening that we at least live in a world where some people are still asking the big, ultimate questions.

References

Allen, J., 2013. Using critical reflection to research spirituality in clinical practice. In J. Fook and F. Gardner, eds., *Critical reflection in context.* Abingdon: Routledge. Ch. 14.

Béres, L., 2009. Mindfulness and reflexivity: the no-self as reflective practitioner. In S. Hick, ed., *Mindfulness and social work.* Chicago: Lyceum Books. Ch. 4.

Dewey, J., 1933. *How we think.* Boston: Heath.

Fook, J., 2002. *Social work: critical theory and practice.* London: Sage.

Fook, J., 2012. *Social work: a critical approach to practice,* 2nd edn. London: Sage.

Fook, J., and Askeland, G. A., 2006. The 'critical' in critical reflection. In S. White, J. Fook and F. Gardner, eds., *Critical reflection in health and social care.* Maidenhead: Open University Press. Ch. 3.

Fook, J., and Gardner, F., 2007. *Practising critical reflection: a resource handbook.* Maidenhead: Open University Press.

Fook, J., and Kellehear, A., 2010. Using critical reflection to support health promotion goals in palliative care. *Journal of Palliative Care,* 26(3), pp. 295–302.

Fook, J., Royes, J., and White, A., 2016. Critical reflection. In M. Chambers, ed., *Psychiatric and mental health nursing: the craft of caring,* 3rd edn. Abington: Routledge.

Gardner, F., 2011. *Critical spirituality.* Farnham: Ashgate.

Gardner, F., 2014. *Being critically reflective.* Basingstoke: Palgrave Macmillan.

Ghaye, T., 2010. In what ways can reflective practices enhance human flourishing? *Reflective Practice,* 11(1), pp. 1–7.

Hunt, C., 2016. Spiritual creatures? Exploring an interface between critical reflective practice and spirituality. In J. Fook, V. Collington, F. Ross, G. Ruch and L. West, eds., *Researching critical reflection: multidisciplinary perspectives.* Abington: Routledge.

Johns, C., 2005. Balancing the winds. *Reflective Practice*, 6(1), pp. 67–68.

Nussbaum, M., 1997. *Cultivating humanity: a classical defense of reform in liberal education*. Cambridge: Harvard University Press.

Rumbold, B., 2002. *Spirituality and Palliative Care*. Melbourne: Oxford University Press.

Schön, D., 1983. *The Reflective Practitioner*. New York: Basic Books.

Sheldrake, P., 2013. *Spirituality: a brief history*, 2nd edn. Chichester: Wiley-Blackwell.

Sheridan, M., ed., 2014. *Connecting spirituality and social justice*. Abingdon: Routledge.

Spiritual Influences on Practice: The Interaction between Being a Quaker and the Development of a Critical Spirituality

Fiona Gardner

Introduction

My current social work practice is as an academic, including provision of training and supervision in critical reflection and critical spirituality. This is both a theory and a process which 'requires workers to use all of themselves, to take into account the emotional, social, mental, physical and spiritual. This process is one that includes recognizing and working with emotions and thoughts, recognizing the influence of social context and the physical world and the impact of what is meaningful' (Gardner, 2011, pp. 70–71). What I hope is that for both practitioners and their clients this opens up possibilities for working holistically, including the spiritual, in the sense of what is meaningful for them, in practice. This critical reflection process asks practitioners to work with a specific experience of significance to them in two stages, first to unearth its meaning and secondly to articulate how to put this new understanding into action (Fook and Gardner, 2007). Central to the training I offer is first having the group work with an experience of mine so that they can see how the process works. Before the training, when I am trying to decide what experience to use, I picture the group and then sit with that image and allow an experience to arise into my awareness.

I hadn't thought about using that practice in writing this chapter, but when I was thinking about how to write it, I remembered a spiritual experience I had when I was about ten years old. Initially, I was surprised that so distant a memory had surfaced, but the more I thought about it, the more it illuminated the changes in my interests in religion and spirituality over the years and in some ways also how these linked to being a social work practitioner and an academic interested in critical reflection and critical spirituality. I found it fascinating to see how many parallel processes reinforced the connections between these different aspects. So I have chosen to use this experience to ground my exploration of how my spiritual self connects to my experience of practice and in the process to highlight how critically reflective practice can provide useful theory as well as processes to foster understanding of spirituality.

So, the experience: when I was nine I immigrated to Australia from Scotland, where my family had been strongly connected to the Presbyterian Church, and we continued to attend the Presbyterian Church in Australia. Our local church annually offered a small scholarship to students in their final year of primary school, to help with the costs of transferring to secondary school. The recipient had the best marks in a written test that explored his or her understanding of biblical texts covered in a series of classes. When I was ten, I agreed somewhat reluctantly to go to the classes and undertake this test, but as the classes went on, I found myself feeling increasingly uncomfortable about what felt like a way of thinking that threatened my experience of the spiritual (although I couldn't have put this into words at the time!). One day when I was walking through the local park on my way to play with a friend, I suddenly felt a deep understanding of the strength of my inner experience of God or spirit, a transcendent and immanent sense of union with the world, and a conviction that no amount of more formal studying of the Bible could undermine this.

So what did this experience mean for me? Of course, I am naming this now in retrospect: at the time, I felt simply upheld and comforted. Having said that, it's fascinating to see how what emerged for me in thinking about this experience connects to my journey as a social worker. Firstly, the experience validated the strength of my own inner subjective experience of the spiritual, recognized as my own, individual and acceptable, at least to me and to the Spirit. I felt deeply affirmed in my experiential understanding of the spiritual and of the power and authority of my individual experience. Linked to this was a sense of 'this is what really matters'; that in being open to this essentially silent and deep way of being and connecting to the transcendent, clarity and meaning would emerge. It was significant too that this happened in the park, in nature, not in a church. Next, it generated a sense of being able to stand against what I perceived as the dominant culture, what might be expected from more formally theological ways of knowing and my perception of the institutional Church. My way of experiencing the spiritual then was validated as being equally powerful. Then, in what might be seen as a contradiction but was rather experienced as a workable and helpful paradox, I also felt that I could still be part of that community in a positive and engaged way, accepting shared values, mutual support and active enjoyment of the church community. Essentially, it seemed that there was more than one way to be in this spiritual community: my way was equally valid, and I could assert my way against a more dominating way of being.

Given this experience, it makes sense that in my early twenties I felt increasingly drawn to Quaker (Religious Society of Friends) spirituality. Over several years, in Australia and then in the United Kingdom, I frequently met Quakers, who were very welcoming, inviting me to their Meetings for Worship, to eat with them and to other Quaker-related activities, often peace-activist and anti-nuclear related. I was by then a social worker, trained in a secular university where spirituality was not mentioned in the curriculum, as was generally the case in Australian social work (Lindsay, 2002). I had worked for several years in Australia and then in the United Kingdom. Sometime after I returned to Australia, I made contact with Quakers here and eventually became a member. Over this time and since, I found that, often unconsciously or intuitively, what was important to me about being a Quaker contributed to, but was also mutually reinforced by, my experience of being a social worker and later as a social work academic in engaging with critical reflection and eventually critical spirituality.

So what were the connecting threads?

Perhaps the first and most obvious aspect of Quaker spirituality that links to my earlier experience as a child is the emphasis on validating each person's inner experience of the spiritual as well as the connection to the external world. Typically, Quakers would say, 'Our authority is the Spirit. This is a huge and exciting challenge for us. We need to practise our faith by learning to let go of our burning passions and our daily concerns; learning to get to that place within us where we are centred, where we listen to the Spirit' (Spinks, 1995, p. 4). The Quaker movement arose in the seventeenth century in reaction to the institutionalized church which considered that a priest was the only path for communication between God and the community. Instead, Quakers believed that it was their own direct and mystical experience of the Spirit that was important. Implicit in this was the view that a priest's perspective was not necessarily 'better' or 'right', and Quakers then differed from most other religious traditions in not having priests or religious leaders. The expectation was that people would each need to find their own way, supported and sometimes challenged by their Quaker community but guided by their own inner spiritual experience. The implication is that each takes responsibility to do this and to live from that place of deeper meaning. As Johnson, a Quaker, writes, 'It is possible to be in touch with the Spirit, so that this Spirit will lead you both internally to a deeper life spiritually, and also externally into a life in which your work is led by the Spirit' (Johnson, 2007, p. 2).

This resonated for me with my social work experience in working with individuals and families perceived as being at risk in various settings (child protection, juvenile justice, prisons) as well as in mediation and working with consumers to advocate with the health system. Individuals, families and community members often had their different perceptions of what was right for them to do, what fitted best with their values and beliefs.

They were often struggling to articulate their subjective and experiential knowing against other family, community, and sometimes organizational expectations. Similarly, people interested in social work training articulate many different reasons for this, from their religious or spiritual beliefs to a desire to 'make a difference,' or come to understand more deeply, or to redeem an aspect of their or their family's experience. Practitioners using critical reflection processes also validated the power of working with specific experiences to understand underlying meaning and the implications for their practice.

This sense of validating the experiential, combined with a sense of relative theological freedom in Quakers, echoed my childhood desire to value my own experience and not to have this undermined by the expectations of the institutional church (while appreciating the wisdom of at least some theological teachings). Heelas and Woodhead (2005) call this valuing of subjective experience as 'subject life-as' which from a spiritual perspective focuses on the inner authority of the self as opposed to external authority. This links also with the next connecting thread: noticing and valuing underlying or deeper meaning, finding what really matters. Ideally, then, returning to this place of spiritual connection, of deeper meaning or what some might call integrity or fundamental values, became my reference point for clarifying how to make decisions, particularly what mattered in a given context. Taber (1984), a Quaker, names this as 'the living stream' which is always present but which we don't always pay attention to. Quakers would name this sense of decision or direction as a leading or 'the way forward'. This leads of course to asking how can I or how can others be sure that this sense of leading or discernment does come from this place of the spirit or this place of integrity and not from ego or some kind of confused desire to please others or some other unhealthy motive. Quakers do have processes that can help with testing discernment in the faith community, partly encouraging each person to sit with, to be patient with, to wait with a decision to see whether this sense of rightness continues over time, which I will come back to later.

This remembering fundamental meaning was, of course, also part of what I saw as essential in my social work practice. Much of my work was with people who were in danger of losing something vital to their well-being: their children, their liberty, their cultural heritage, their relationships. Being in prison, for example, was a place where many men contemplated what they had lost. In a prison in rural Australia, I ran a small group with men interested in exploring why it is that I keep returning to prison. What really matters to me that would enable me to make a change? When I moved to teaching social work, the question of what really matters also emerged: students often feel challenged by their learning, (which can question their fundamental values and beliefs) and by their capacity to respect the values and beliefs of others. Similarly, in critical reflection the process encourages identifying underlying fundamental values which are often expressed very simply, such as, 'I believe in the worth of all human beings' or 'My spirituality is part of all of my life, including work.'

What seems to combine with valuing experience and seeking underlying meaning is the third strand from my initial experience: acknowledging that more than one way is possible, or more fundamentally valuing both what is similar and what is different. Lartey, writing about spirituality, says, 'Every human person is in certain respects: 1. Like all others, 2. Like some others, 3. Like no others' (Lartey, 2003, p. 34). Although I was initially clear about Quakers valuing individual experience, the similarities and differences among Quakers gradually also became clear to me. Quakers were explicit about not being a unified group in the sense that they all expected to experience the spiritual in the same way or to have completely shared beliefs about their religious practice. The most obvious division superficially was between those who saw themselves as Christian Quakers, primarily influenced by Christian theology and understanding, and those who saw themselves as Universalist Quakers, those relating to a range of religious and spiritual traditions. Internationally, there was also the significant difference between my experience of unprogrammed meetings in the United Kingdom and Australia, with no formal minister or priest and with essentially silent worship, compared to those from programmed meetings found in some parts of the United States and in other parts of the world, with a minister or pastor and more formal spoken and sung worship. However, there were also vast variations within those groups, such as those who saw themselves as more contemplative compared to those who saw themselves as primarily social activists. The emphasis was on actively exploring your own spiritual experience and that you would recognize the validity of the different experiences of others.

Of course, in practice, people struggled with this: many Quakers had come wounded from other faith traditions and found it hard to accept someone who seemed to have similar values to those from that painful place. However, for me, it was affirming to find a group whose expectation was of validating such experience and of, at least in principle, valuing difference. A frequent Quaker quote, from one of the originators, George Fox, reminds Quakers to respond to that of God in every one. Hilken says for Quakers, the Spirit or Light 'is in everyone, of any religion, age or gender, though not everyone pays attention to it. It is universal and omnipresent. We believe that we can recognise the workings of this same Spirit in secular literature, in poetry, art and music and even in some scientific writings' (Hilken, 2007, p. 4) – and others would add in nature and in relationships.

Again this reinforced and was reinforced by social work values of actively valuing and celebrating diversity: taking seriously respecting the essence of each person even if not his or her status or behaviour. The postmodern aspect of critical reflection theory further supported this belief in affirming and celebrating difference and articulating the multiple selves most of us experience. However, it is also one of the challenges for social work: students often wrestle with how to respect the 'essence' of someone whose behaviour they find abhorrent, such as people who have perpetrated violence or abuse. Practitioners in critical reflection express their frustration with those whose way of being or acting seems to oppose theirs.

Practice example: that of God in everyone

Mediation was one of the places that most clearly brought this home to me. In mediation, I worked initially with couples who were thinking about separation or divorce. We saw each person in the couple separately first, then the two together, with the aim of enabling them to come to agreement firstly about separating or divorcing and, if so, what that would mean: how to manage the process. In the first meetings, it was relatively easy to convey empathy but also to be respectfully challenging about why a partner might see some behaviour as unreasonable. In the joint sessions, it was crucial to be able to maintain this in a neutral or balanced way so that each person continued to feel respected even if his or her partner was disagreeing with the person's perception. If I lost the sense of equal respect for or valuing the inherent goodness in each person, rapport was eroded and the possibility of enabling an agreement significantly reduced. Here too the centrality of experience was relevant: acknowledging that people frequently experienced their relationship completely differently and that what was comfortable and supportive to one might be alienating to the other. Again, as the worker, it was key to affirm the legitimacy of these different perceptions and to work to enable each to understand where the other was coming from.

Much of this example connects with the next strand in my experience: the importance of community and being able to continue to engage with others in mutually supportive ways while experiencing spirituality differently. Of course, this is the nature of community life as well as organizational life: how do we manage the tensions of difference in practice? For Sneed, a black, gay Christian, the key question is 'What makes for human happiness and fulfilment? [and he suggests] Human fulfilment and flourishing is to be found in the recognition and appreciation of human difference' (Sneed, 2010, p. 181). Inevitably, this raises questions about how and what happens when difference leads to conflict? The Quaker community, with its valuing of individual experience, has to confront what this means when shared decisions are needed: for example, simple decisions about where and how often to meet, more complex decisions about what social and political projects to engage in and decisions about the buying and selling of property. This is epitomized in the contrasting theories underlying critical reflection: the postmodern valuing of subjectivity and individual choices compared to the expectations of socially just practice embedded in critical social theory. This is also one of the frequent tensions in social work practice: how do we – or is it even possible – come to an agreement that suits everyone and remains true to social work values?

Quakers do have processes for engaging in these: a formal 'Meeting' or worshipping group has Meetings for Business as their formal decision-making body which operates in the same spirit as a Meeting for Worship. Quakers don't vote, as the aim is to reach a spirit-led agreement: to hear from those who want to speak on a particular issue (who are hopefully speaking from a sense of openness and clarity about what really matters) and then to see if there is a shared sense of agreement about the movement of the Spirit. If not, 'Quakers would rather defer action if they are unable to reach a united decision. This may slow the pace but it does help to ensure that when decisions are reached they will command the respect and loyal support of everyone' (Gorman, 1981, p. 46). Similar processes are used in 'clearness meetings', which any individual may request: the opportunity to meet with a small group of Quakers to help them understand more deeply an issue or concern they have and to discern how to act. Each listener tries to pay attention to the Spirit to try to hear, understand, cajole from the person, their feelings, thoughts and confusion in a way that helps them reach, at least, greater understanding or, ideally, clarity about direction. I've seen this process used for people uncertain about a work decision that had implications for family and other relationships, but also used by those concerned about a political issue and whether they should be more actively involved in seeking change. The emphasis here, as it is in critical reflection or good social work practice, is to enable the people to come to their own understanding and decisions about what to do. Interestingly for me, there are many parallels here with a critical reflection process, with the expectation of participants being reflective and reflexive: identifying deeply held underlying assumptions and values and the influence of history and social context: 'to consider how we impact others, how we present to others, how we are perceived and that includes the context within which we engage, as well as our role and specific mandate' (Walsh, 2012, p. 192). The process also enables practitioners to move from exploring and understanding a particular experience more deeply, to clarifying what it is they want to change or affirm – internally, their own attitudes, assumptions or values; externally, specific actions.

The other question implicit here is 'When are there limits to accepting people's individual experience?' Much of my social work practice was with clients who were subject or in danger of being subject to some kind of statutory order. This meant I was confronted with the limits to acceptance of diversity and with what behaviour was acceptable to the community/social context in which the agency operated. This raised for me the tension between Quaker acceptance of each person's own journey, with necessary limits to this and how this would be determined. The Quaker processes outlined here can act as a check on someone's own preferences: a way, or ways, of testing the 'rightness' of what feels like a clear direction or 'leading'. Jane, for example, called a clearness meeting about her desire to leave her current school and go teach in Uganda. As she was asked about her feelings, her thoughts about what would change for her, what her promptings were to go, it became clear that this was more about escaping what she was finding to be a very undermining environment. Gradually, she moved from exploring why it would be good to be 'helpful' in Uganda, to acknowledging underlying meaning: her desire to be useful and valued. She could see that her skills were not likely to be useful in Uganda and that she might not be appreciated there either. She ended by exploring ways to be supported to seek change in her current school.

These examples perhaps link most clearly to the strand from my experience of wanting to stand against the dominant way of being while remaining a constructive and participating member of the community or organization. There are clear parallels here with all three ways of being: Quakers, social work and critical reflection. Valuing each individual and his or her way of being is, of course, not the norm in our culture and not necessarily expressed in our social structures. Quakers have a strong and active desire to promote social justice, being involved historically in prison work, the antislavery movement and promotion of women's and children's rights. Some of these continue, and Quakers generally seek to actively engage with human rights whatever that might mean in a particular context. Social work values clearly challenge practitioners to do the same, the current international definition concluding, 'Principles of social justice, human rights, collective responsibility and respect for diversities are central to social work' (International Federation of Social Work, 2014). The use of critical social theory underpinning critical reflection also encourages thinking about the broader social context and the need for socially just change, even if, as Brookfield (2005) suggests, we can't know exactly how that will look until we try it. Critical spirituality affirms combining 'a postmodern valuing of the individual's experience with all its diversity with a critical perspective that asserts the importance of living harmoniously and respectfully at an individual and community level' (Gardner, 2011, p. 77). Perhaps the more subtle aspect of this is remaining aware enough of the dominant ideology to be able to stand against it. It's easy to be seduced by organizational or societal ways of doing things: to become acculturated so that we no longer see what is taken for granted. Combating this can be as simple as asking why things are being done a certain way rather than assuming things have to be as they are.

Practice example: what is the way forward?

Within the Loddon District Health Council, I was the Executive Officer (and only full time worker) for a small agency overseen by a committee of management, with the aim of enabling the consumer voice to be heard in the health system. The committee was made up of three main groups: consumers of health services, health service providers and community members, with varying degrees of understanding and significantly different perspectives about the health system. Initially, the committee emphasized quick decision making, but as it became clear that different people needed different lengths of time to understand and engage with issues, we moved from a 'let's vote' mentality to 'let's wait and see if we can reach consensus' perspective. Given there were more projects than we could manage quickly, there were rarely decisions that couldn't wait for a meeting. Without me being conscious of using them, I noticed that Quaker language and ways had spread: we were all talking about finding 'a way forward', waiting till we reached agreement and being prepared to sit with uncertainty until we reached unity. The three initially sometimes hostile groups became more integrated so that people appreciated more one another's positions and wisdom.

Finally, the last strand I want to draw out is about being open to, and allowing, opportunities for hearing from what I will call the Spirit, that part of you that offers wisdom. As a child, I obviously wasn't seeking this but was simply open to hearing it, as children often are. Quaker processes reinforced for me the need to return to that quiet and open space, to be reminded of what really matters. This was reinforced by the Quaker form of worship: sitting in silence together seeking the Spirit, usually for an hour. If people are moved to speak they do, and what they say is simply heard, but not responded to directly. If what is said resonates for some people, then they take what meaning there is for them; if it doesn't, they just let it go. Experiencing a meeting like this for the first time felt both liberating and grounding for me. I suddenly realized that what I had found increasingly challenging for me about traditional church services was that there was so little time of silence in which to experience your own sense of connection with the transcendent. This Quaker style of worship for me validated and strengthened my desire to live from a place of connection with that experience.

Seeing silence as central, or even acceptable, is very contrary to much of how we experience life now. The expectation in our culture is that there will be something happening audibly for most of the time. Open plan offices lessen opportunities for quiet, to sit and think, and the culture discourages simply sitting and being, so individuals feel guilty if they aren't doing. Finding a place that nurtures spiritual connection can also help (Crisp, 2010). The current appeal of mindfulness can be seen as a helpful reaction to this, encouraging the capacity to be and to be present. Related to this is the capacity to wait, and particularly to wait in uncertainty, with the faith that the Spirit will move and lead to clarity, even if not immediately. Religious and spiritual traditions demonstrate there are rarely quick and easy answers. This is helpful in reminding me in social work practice that sometimes you simply have to wait and to support others in the discomfort of uncertainty. This can clearly apply to clients, but also to students or practitioners in critical reflection groups who need people to wait in silence while they become clear. Particularly for us in the West, this is a painful place. We like to know and to have decisions made; we want to be in control and keep things moving along. Those who work in fields of practice like palliative care know particularly well that you often just have to wait and see what happens. More generally, though, it is often in being with and allowing people time that they are able to become clear for themselves. A social worker in a health setting found that using critical reflection in supervision helped her move from 'trying to push them (clients) somewhere without actually trying to listen' to creating 'the space to think' (Gardner and Taalman, 2013, p. 101).

So what does this mean about how I express this in my work and what I'd want to encourage or advocate for others?

Before I outline this, I do want to acknowledge that integrating spirituality in professional practice can be challenging. I have been somewhat alarmed, in working with practitioners from many different organizations, to see how, more and more frequently, working with fundamental meaning gets lost. Practitioners using critical reflection often say how difficult it is to think about issues of meaning for their clients when they, both practitioners and clients, feel overwhelmed by organizational expectations, focused on specific and measureable outcomes within restrictive time frames. Sturgeon suggests that in many organizations 'measurement and outcome are considered the most important indicator of quality' (Sturgeon, 2010, p. 1049); the danger is that the more intangible but essential aspects of effective practice, such as compassion, are forgotten. For practitioners, engaging in critical reflection offers some sense of possibility of managing such dilemmas. For example, one practitioner, wrestling with issues of how to manage redundancies, was able to implement a more respectful and affirming process. A related challenge is discomfort in naming and engaging with spiritual and/or religious meaning. Weinstock's (2015) study of non-Catholic social workers in social work organizations indicated that some social workers see it as inappropriate to engage with religion in practice, even though for some clients this is fundamental to their sense of meaning (Ni Raghallaigh, 2011).

So specifically, what are the implications of what I'm saying for other practitioners?

Awareness of who you are and your own spirituality

I am making an assumption, partly influenced by Quaker spirituality, that everyone has their own spirituality: at its simplest an understanding of 'that which gives life meaning, in a way that connects the inner sense of meaning with a sense of something greater' (Gardner, 2011, p. 9). Awareness of what this is for you is crucial in first being able to actively engage with this for your own well-being. Working from what matters is generally about connecting with fundamental values and a sense of integrity, which is key for professional practice (Banks, 2010). Some writers connect this to morality or moral distress: 'the sum of the nicks in one's moral integrity and the self-punishment inflicted when one does not do the right thing' (Epstein and Delgado, 2010, p. 9) and what Gustafsson, Eriksson, Strandberg and Norberg (2010) call 'perceptions of conscience'. Whatever language you use, articulating your own spirituality, your religious practice and belief, sense of integrity, or fundamental values helps with being clearer about how you want to be and act and how to use these in engaging with the inevitable challenges of practice.

Ensuring that you are aware of your own spirituality also means that you are less likely to impose your own assumptions about spirituality onto others. This can happen in many forms: not understanding the importance of religious beliefs, feeling uncomfortable about how some else's religious beliefs confront your own, reacting from your own negative experiences. It is useful here to ask, What are the experiences that have formed you? What is your equivalent to my experience of walking through the park? What continues to influence you? What do you want to keep and what do you want to let go of? How can you be open to learning from your clients?

Actively valuing holistic practice including the spiritual

Genuinely holistic practice includes all aspects of a person related to his or her well-being including the social, emotional, physical, psychological and spiritual. My hope here is that all practitioners would include the spiritual in their practice, being interested in what underlies life for their clients/

communities. This has implications for all of practice from assessment to acting with clients for change.

Inextricably linked with this is affirming and relishing diversity, taking seriously that there is that of the Spirit in everyone and developing your capacity to be positively interested in what this means for a particular person, even if it is very different from your own preferences. This also implies not overgeneralizing or assuming that people from a particular tradition, or using a particular approach, will be the same. Two practitioners in a critical spirituality workshop reacted uncomfortably to each other's spirituality: one to what she perceived as 'convenient spirituality', a practitioner combining mindfulness mediation with yoga; the other to what she saw as conservative, patriarchal Christianity. It was only when each explored underlying meaning for the other that both could let go of their initial unhelpful judgements.

The implication here is that in the broader social context, social workers will be actively promoting acceptance of spiritual and religious diversity. Given the influence of the current attitudes, this might mean actively advocating for the capacity to express spiritual preferences. Examples might include supporting shared space for meditation in an organization, allowing staff flexible hours to attend their own religious observance, encouraging dialogue between different groups using a community centre or supporting the disputed building of a mosque. A small Centre for Spirituality, in my country community, began a monthly 'conversation hour' where the community was invited to hear local people be interviewed about their spiritual journey, which fostered mutual understanding.

Actively practising awareness of including the spiritual

What I mean here is taking seriously the value of developing your own processes for (at least) awareness of what matters for you and how to engage with this in your practice. Clearly, from what I have written, I'm suggesting that using critical reflection processes can help. Being critically reflective helps with this: having 'an attitude to life in general, the desire to approach all aspects of life in some spirit of enquiry; seeking to understand more deeply the underlying values and reactions to the everyday as well as to professional practice' (Gardner, 2014, p. 3). Using specific critical reflection processes can help with this, either on your own, such as through journaling, or with a friend, colleague or in supervision, either individually or in groups. It's important to tease out what will work for you: I meet every four to six weeks with a colleague and friend, and we each take turns critically reflecting on a particular experience that is bothering us.

What also seems to help is having some kind of practice that engenders connections to your spiritual self or to deeper values, which also has benefits for self-care and remaining positive in the workplace. Another way of putting this is to actively practise what restores or regenerates you. My experience from workshops is that this is completely idiosyncratic, though informed sometimes by traditional religious practice: people have identified having a morning walk at sunrise, weekly morning tea with friends, walking in the forest or on the beach, meditation or prayer using silence, a focus on breathing, using a mantra, gardening and spending time with family. What they say is most challenging is giving themselves permission to have this time.

Conclusion

For me the artificial divisions of spiritual life and secular professional life are more arbitrary than they appear. In practice there are many connections: attitudes and practices complement and reinforce one another. Each also reinforces the other in the dilemmas of professional practice, both supporting and challenging me to remember to act from fundamental values.

References

Banks, S., 2010. Integrity in professional life: issues of conduct, commitment and capacity. *British Journal of Social Work*, 40, pp. 2168–2184.

Brookfield, S. D., 2005. *The power of critical theory: liberating adult teaching and learning*. San Francisco: Jossey-Bass, a Wiley imprint.

Crisp, B. R., 2010. *Spirituality and social work*. Farnham: Ashgate.

Epstein, E. G., and Delgado, S., 2010. Understanding and addressing moral distress. *The Online Journal of Issues in Nursing*, 15(3), pp. 1–12.

Fook, J., and Gardner, F., 2007. *Practising critical reflection: a resource handbook*. Maidenhead: Open University Press.

Gardner, F., 2011. *Critical spirituality: a holistic approach to contemporary practice*. Farnham: Ashgate.

Gardner. F., and Taalman, E., 2013. Critical reflection and supervision: an interdisciplinary experience. In J. Fook and F. Gardner, eds., *Critical reflection in context: applications in health and social care*. Abingdon: Routledge.

Gardner, F., 2014. *Being critically reflective*. Basingstoke: Palgrave Macmillan.

Gorman, G. H., 1981. *Introducing Quakers*. London: Quaker Home Service.

Gustafsson, G., Eriksson, S., Strandberg, G., and Norberg, A., 2010. Burnout and perceptions of conscience among health personnel: a pilot study. *Nursing Ethics*, 17(1), pp. 23–38.

Heelas, P. A., and Woodhead, L., 2005. *The spiritual revolution: why religion is giving way to spirituality*. Oxford: Blackwell.

Hilken, R., 2007. *Reason, faith and experience: an introduction to 21st century Quaker-ism*. Exeter: Exeter Fairway Publications. Available at: www.qcea.org/wp-content/uploads/2011/02/hilken-en.pdf. [Accessed 20 July 2015.]

International Federation of Social Work, 2014. *Definition of social work*. Available at: http://ifsw.org/policies/definition-of-social-work/. [Accessed 26 July 2015.]

Johnson, D., 2007. *The Quaker way: serious religion without priest, creed or Eucharist*. South Australia: Religious Society of Friends Inc. (Quakers).

Lartey, E. Y., 2003. *In living color: an intercultural approach to pastoral care and coun-selling*, 2nd edn. London: Jessica Kingsley.

Lindsay, R., 2002. *Recognizing spirituality: the interface between faith and social work*. Crawley: University of Western Australia Press.

Ni Raghallaigh, M., 2011. Religion in the lives of unaccompanied minors: an available and compelling coping resource. *British Journal of Social Work*, 4(3), pp. 539–556.

Sneed, R. A., 2010. *Representations of homosexuality: Black liberation theology and cultural criticism*. New York: Palgrave Macmillan.

Spinks, J., 1995. Experiences of the spirit. In Australian Yearly Meeting, 2003. *This we can say: Australian Quaker life, faith and thought*. Canberra: Australia Yearly Meeting of the Religious Society of Friends (Quakers) Inc., p. 4.

Sturgeon, D., 2010. 'Have a nice day': consumerism, compassion and health care. *British Journal of Nursing*, 19(16), pp. 1047–1051.

Taber, W., 1984. *The prophetic stream, Pendle Hill pamphlet 256*. Wallingford: Pendle Hill.

Walsh, T., 2012. Shedding light on the expert witness role in child protection work: the value of social constructionism. In S. Witkin, ed., *Social construction and social work practice interpretations and innovations*. New York: Columbia University Press. Ch. 8.

Weinstock, J., 2015. *The experiences of non-Catholic social workers employed in Catho-lic social service organisations*. Unpublished honours thesis. Bendigo: Latrobe University.

Holistic and Indigenous Spiritualities

4 What Spirituality Can Contribute to Social Work Education: Reflections on Teaching and Living

Rose Pulliam

Introduction

I am a social work educator. The classroom is the primary setting of my professional practice. Students are not individually my clients, but their education is my client. The future clients that they will serve are, by extension, my clients. Although my spiritual practice is rarely formal or associated with organized religion, it is nearly always organic and integrated into my daily living and professional practice. My spirituality, whether revealed and shared, or concealed and obscured, provides me, as social work educator, with centring and support for the difficult work of teaching, as well as providing a foundation that is useful for developing and maintaining professional relations, including student engagement. However, the institutional situation, professionalization and ongoing struggle for the legitimacy of social work education as manifested by an emphasis on evidence-based practice and a positivist outcomes-centred approach creates dissonance and dilemmas where my spirituality is concerned.

In this chapter, I discuss the dilemmas and dissonance that my spirituality creates in my professional work as a social work practitioner teaching in a university setting and how spirituality supports and affirms my success as a teacher. This chapter utilizes examples from my personal and professional experience to illustrate the importance and impact of spirituality to my professional social work practice.

Never before in my professional life have I been asked about my spirituality. To write about it feels transgressive and dangerous. There lies a boundary here that once voiced and crossed could serve to separate me, again and more, from the many. What lies on this side of the boundary is a sense of safety that requires invisibility of that which makes me authentic and whole, whereas on the other side of the boundary is perhaps a form of liberation. To speak of myself and to name my connections to purpose and spirit is a necessity and a burden. The disinterest that I have experienced, that approaches prohibition, of speaking about the practice of spirituality in the professional realm leads to my difficulty in writing this piece. The burden seems huge, excruciatingly so. It requires me to frame and name my practices for myself and to make them visible here for the scrutiny of others. This requires that I uncover the aspects of my spirituality that I obscure to myself and others, thinking it a protection. This revealing also requires me to name the painful aspects of the dilemmas that I face in my work related to my spirituality. Yet, it is necessity born of the yearning to name myself to myself and the resulting liberation that that affords, a hope that my thinking and writing has potential value for others, and the knowledge that the increased self-awareness that comes from this naming will serve to make me a better teacher. These possibilities give me the courage to begin my narrative.

The frame of my spirituality

Definition

Canda and Furman's (2010) definition of spirituality as a process of human life and development resonates closely with me. They describe spirituality as focusing on the search for a sense of meaning, purpose, morality and well-being, and situate spirituality broadly in relationship with self, other humans, other beings, the universe and ultimate reality, however that is understood. Canda and Furman's definition includes that spirituality is oriented around centrally significant priorities and engages a sense of transcendence (p. 75). This definition recognizes that spirituality is not necessarily associated with religion and that one's spirituality shifts and changes over a life course.

Integration

Organic integration of spirituality into my daily living is certainly a spiritual heritage from my African and Native American roots. Though my family history serves to disconnect me from specific knowledge about my ancestors, I do know that I have African and Native American ancestry. The remnants of this ancestry and ancestral spiritual practice make themselves known in practices that have been passed down to me most notably from my maternal great-grandmother, grandmother and mother but also by my paternal grandfather and grandmother. I learned to 'talk out fire', 'moan as prayer' and 'pray incessantly' from observing them. I saw them integrate their spirituality into every aspect of their life. Mbiti (1969), an African American scholar, discusses this integration as follows:

> Because traditional religions permeate all departments of life there is no formal distinction between the sacred and the secular, between the

religious and non-religious, between the spiritual and material areas of life. Wherever the African is there is his religion: he carries it to the fields where he is sowing seeds or harvesting a new crop: he takes it with him to the beer party or to attend the funeral ceremony; and if he is educated, he takes religion with him to the examination room at school or in the university; if he is a politician he takes it to the house of parliament. (Mbiti, 1969, p. 2)

The integration of spirituality in my life manifests itself into my performance of spiritual and ritualistic practices in every aspect of my life, with little distinction between settings. For example, it manifests in my gardening and in my teaching.

I am a sometimes gardener. I have little experience, less expertise and immense passion for the process, which I perform in a somewhat ritualistic manner. I prepare the soil meticulously while in prayerful concentration, experiencing it with my multiple senses, until I know that it is ready for its work. When I plant a seed or seedling in my little garden, I whisper a prayer of gratitude to the seed, the earth, the sun and the water. As I close the earth around the seed and give it a first soak with water, a libation, a prayer of release from expectation comes forth as a sigh of exhalation. I am always surprised and ecstatic when the seed sprouts and shows itself above the soil and when the first flower and the buds of produce emerge. I am exquisitely grateful and happy when I can pick, prepare and eat the produce.

I come from a long line of farmers. My maternal and paternal families are rooted in rural Alabama and were subsistence farmers for as far back as memory remains. Though my parents did not farm for subsistence, they farmed any patch of land available to them because that is just what was to be done. Despite this legacy of planting and spending many hours of my childhood in farming processes with my grandparents and parents, the process of prayerful planting, care and harvesting was not taught to me, nor do I recall ever experiencing it with anyone.

I experience teaching in much the same way as I experience gardening. I prepare for classes meticulously and with prayerful awareness. When I enter the classroom, I whisper a prayer of gratitude for the privilege of engaging in a profession that I love. In a ritual of preparation, I arrive a bit early, lay my materials out, power up the computer console (whether I plan to use it or not) and set my bottle of drinking water near at hand. As I watch the students enter the classroom, I notice their countenance, and a prayer of release from expectations comes forth as a sign of exhalation. I am always surprised and ecstatic when students embrace the possibility that I have so carefully prepared, and flower, bud and make fruit. I do not get to experience the entire fruition of their work in their practice, but I send each student from my class with my hope and faith that they will be instruments of justice, sustenance, restoration and healing for others.

I don't know why I pray and perform ritual when I garden or teach, but my guess is that many before me have also done so. And although I was not taught to pray and perform ritual in these ways, and have not shared with my children or grandchildren that I do it, I expect that when they come to their gardens or their classrooms, as they inevitably will, their instinct will be to do something similar. This integrated and intuitive spiritual practice, I think, is a spiritual heritage.

Spirituality construction

I was raised in a Southern Baptist household. I have studied and practised organized religion. I have identified at different times as a Southern Baptist, a non-denominational Christian, a Jehovah's Witness and a secular Buddhist. My search for religion was an intellectual and spiritual exercise that I thought would bring me to the one religion that honoured my authentic self and exemplified some absolute truth. When I found this search for an absolute truth futile and abandoned my search for religion, I thought that I could create something new for myself; something solely my own that honoured my authentic self. What I discovered, however, is that I bring elements of all of the religions I studied and practised and something more inexplicable to my current spiritual practice. My spirituality constitutes an ongoing discovery and construction process which is reflected in this statement by Audre Lorde:

> [T]here are no new ideas still waiting in the wings to save us as women, as human. There are only old and forgotten ones, new combinations, extrapolations and recognitions from within ourselves, along with the renewed courage to try them out. (Lorde, 1984, p. 36)

In my spiritual practice, I attempt to diminish intellectualism and enhance discovery of old and forgotten ideas, intuitions and ways of knowing. My practice is one of extrapolations and combinations of spiritual practices, some known and seen before and others emanating from my intuition. I am in a constant state of spiritual formation and reformation. My spirituality discovery and construction process informs and influences how I approach personal and professional life as well as how and what I teach.

My spirituality is grounded in an ethic of love, compassion, loving kindness, service and peacemaking. My spiritual values include gratitude, hope and authenticity. My spirituality is grounded in belief in some things/ones transcendent and great, and a universal connectedness of living beings and things that transcends time and space. This mirrors Boone, Fite and Reardon's (2010) idea about spirituality, which they state

> concerns individual belief in and experience of a higher power or purpose that reaches beyond our own limited existence. Spirituality encompasses such things as a recognition of the presence of a transcendent purpose or being; an awareness of the self as more than material; and an appreciation of the impact of the self on the lives and well being of others. (Bonne, Fite and Reardon, 2010, p. 45)

My spiritual practice includes meditation, prayer, dance, discussion with friends, music and immersion in nature.

Ways of knowing, spirituality and the art of education

Acceptable ways of knowing are defined by those with the most power (Tangenberg and Kemp, 2002). Bordo (1986) characterized the predominant Western viewpoint as one of abstract masculinity which separates the knower from emotions, culture and other contexts that might influence conceptualizations of knowledge. The brand of knowing that I ascribe to would likely fall outside of this predominant acceptable ways of knowing. My way of knowing is relational (Palmer, 1998) and includes the context of culture and emotion. It includes a relationship to self, others and the world. In my scheme, knowing is formed from the process and product of experience, analysis coloured by emotion, a cultural lens framing the current and past in context, and indelible, inexplicit and inexplicable spirit. Knowing in this way may be conscious or unconscious, and very often manifests itself in my body as physical discomfort, energy or heightened awareness. It is a supra-perception, a knowing that transcends perception of the senses, of measurement, of boundaries of science. That adults create knowledge and meaning through the use of spiritual understanding has been discussed in the literature (Vella, 2000). The inclusion of emotion, culture and spirit in this way of knowing conflicts with the legitimized ways of knowing in social work, where the validity of evidence is based on the extent to which it can be quantified/qualified, measured, replicated and transferred. Consequently, what I know and how I know it may be invalidated in the social work education environment by faculty and students alike. This is marginalization of other ways of knowing that can also serve to invalidate the multiple ways that students know and the ways that our knowledge is shared with one another.

I often use a sort of pantomime, euphemisms or photographic and visual imagery to initiate students' access to the kind of knowledge that includes spirit. I tell students to 'dig deep' while moving my hands from my head to my stomach and simulating pulling something out, to 'use your heart and your mind' while cupping one hand to my chest and the other to my forehead, to 'develop and trust your social work gut' while patting my belly and to use 'your whole being' while framing my whole body. I sometimes simulate brushing off my arms, chest and back to indicate release of difficult or hurtful emotion. I also show them pictures of nature and beauty to stimulate emotional response and connection. I use these methods because some of what I am trying to communicate is inexplicable and inexplicit and is knowable only through supra-perception, but also, if I am to tell the truth, because I sometimes lack the skill for, and fear the result of, explicit narration. I think the skill for narration of supra-perception is art. I define art as the manifestation through some type of expression of what we know at any level for the interpretation of others. When I make what I know accessible through any medium and encourage students to access and express what they know, we are producing art. Consequently, for me social work education is art. Like most art the practice and product, particularly as it connects to spirituality, is subject to interpretation and laden with dilemmas.

Dilemmas, dissonance and impact of spirituality

Culture of religiosity

I live in the southern region of the United States. This region has a long history of religiosity that has resulted in it being called the Bible belt. It is noted for high levels of fundamental Christianity (Pew Research Center, 2015) and social conservatism in politics and culture. The consequence is that religion has influence from the courthouse to the schoolhouse. Although in my experience there is an attempt to make the higher education environment totally secular, religion still permeates the environment, and Christianity is centred, accepted and validated. Consequently, there is an acceptance of spirituality if it is Christian in origin and concern about the expression of other spiritual practices both at the institutional and interpersonal level. For example, in an undergraduate class session on self-care, I introduced the concept of affirmations. One student asked me if I knew whether affirmations were religious and if participating in affirmations would be against her Christian faith. The expectation was that I should know the tenants of a supposed universal Christian faith and perhaps protect her from exposure to other forms of spirituality. This seems to me to be a sort of spiritual entitlement that is demonstrated in an assumption of normality for Christian religion and an assumption of difference of all other religious or spiritual practices. This constitutes an 'othering' that then supports tolerance of other spiritual practices, rather than acceptance, as the best that can be expected.

Social work is secular

While the overall culture in the southern United States is highly Christian, conversely, the culture of social work education is that the classroom must be entirely secular, and professional social work practice is devoid of spirituality. This may create the impression for faculty and students that any mention of their spirituality is unprofessional. Recently, in a diversity course, the students and I were discussing a module on religion. The topic resulted in robust conversation. One student seemed to gather her courage and proclaimed that she was Christian. She articulated, with trepidation, that she feared that her Christian values had no place in social work. Other students agreed that they shared this concern. Another student said that she was agnostic and that she feared that there was not a place for her in social work. Using a show of hands, I polled the students to see how many of them thought that expression of their religion, absence of religion or spiritual practice might be a problem for their social work education or practice as a social worker. In a class of 36, all but three hands were raised. I asked them why they felt this way, and one student, with the agreement of many others, said that any such expression would be perceived as unprofessional. It was only because there was a specific module designed to discuss diversity of religion in this course that this conversation was raised.

The idea that social work values are characteristically separate from spiritual values underplays and obscures the historical underpinnings of social work (Todd, 2012, p. 126). The secularization of social work, from its previous grounding in spiritual/religious roots, was related to the quest for legitimacy as a profession based on science and objectivity. Todd argues that this secularization was incomplete and that spirituality and religion still shape the world views of social workers through the institutionalized values and ethics upon which social work practice is centred. The secularization of social work is dissonant to acknowledging and considering the wholeness of clients, including spiritually, which is a relatively accepted aspect of social work practice (Canda and Furman, 2010; Canda, Nakashima and Furman, 2004; Gotterer, 2001). Although there has been value placed on the integration of the personal and professional self (Shulman, 2009), never during my own social work education did I experience guidance about how to do this. Social work education, in this regard, is like a house with no foundation. The expectation that social workers in practice should be able to assess and acknowledge the strengths that spirituality can provide for clients and acknowledge the impact that their own spirituality has on their own life and work, without having seen it modelled or taught to them, provides really shaky ground for practice. Yet, there is the expectation that after leaving the social work education environment, students will be able to effectively include spirituality of the client into social work practice with a client. It makes little sense that we would think that we can help clients to identify the support or impact of spirituality in their lives, when as students and teachers we have had a virtual prohibition about talking about how it affects our work and our lives.

This fear of expression of spirituality in a teaching and learning environment inhibits exploration and reflection about spirituality and the impact that it has on our biases and decision making. Consequently, teaching students to practice social work with diverse clients is hampered by the silence that surrounds the function and impact of spirituality on students and teachers. Helping students to decentre their own religion or spirituality in the context of this silence is difficult.

As the discussion in the classroom described above continued, one student said that in her volunteer work with abused children, when faced with difficult behaviour of a child, she often did not know what to do, so she retreated and privately prayed for the child. She indicated that she had not spoken to her supervisor about this for fear that she would be asked not to come back. I asked her, if she was afraid that she could be dismissed for her actions, why did she continue to retreat and pray? She said that prayer was the best that she could do. When I asked her how she thought prayer helped, she indicated that it kept her from feeling helpless and perhaps provided spiritual benefit for the child. I asked, if she had more skills related to engaging with difficult behaviour, how that would change her practice? The student said she would use her skills in the moment and pray later. She agreed that she had failed to seek to improve her skills because she could retreat to prayer, but now she understood that as a social worker she needed to use both. I took this conversation a bit further by asking what it would mean for her if she understood that some people might not like her to pray for them. After some thought, the student said that maybe she would pray for them anyway. This developed into a discussion by students about religious entitlement and arrogance, which ended with this student saying that perhaps she could use her social work skills with the client and pray for herself. It was clear that for this student, many others and myself, spirituality will be manifested in practice. In this case, it was only because there was space and safety for revealing her practice that the student could analyse her practice and decentre her own spirituality. Hopefully, this also is an example of what hooks (1994) describes as a way of teaching essential for the creation of an environment conducive to initiating deep and intimate learning 'that respects and cares for the souls of our students' (hooks, 1994,

p. 13). To create this environment, like my student, I need to exercise skill along with allowing my spirituality to support and guide me. One or the other alone is insufficient for the job.

Power and influence

I do not want to impose my spirituality on students or inhibit their spirituality. I desire to, by my openness, give permission to others to bring their spiritual self to the work. However, my experiences in churches where, more times than I like to acknowledge, I saw power abused, and at work, where lip service is given to collegiality while in practice quests for power are so common as to be expected, leave me fearful of my ability to use power well. My experience has been that power and the quest for power are like sandpaper: rough and wearing over kindness, compassion and love. I am left questioning how to practice my spirituality as it is constituted, including the lack of separation in my daily life, without unduly influencing students or employing bias.

Certainly self-awareness is central to the analysis necessary to prevent, expose and mitigate undue influence and bias. Through self-awareness I understand, to some degree, who I am and how I construct reality in any given context. Although important, I would suggest that it is not enough. My self-awareness is limited by my construction of reality and my ability to perceive reality. I need also to employ reflexivity, similarly described by White (2001, p. 102) and Fook (1999) as a knowledge production process that uses reflection directionally focused inwardly and outwardly that makes connections to cultural and social knowledge. While self-awareness takes into account context, reflexivity takes into account how I produce knowledge based on relationship and prior conceptions of knowledge. And yet, while this complexity adds dimension, it still fails to make room for active relational exchange and knowledge generation: for that, accountability is necessary. Accountability, by which I mean to expose my thoughts and actions for assessment by others, allows possibility for adopting, abandoning or transforming some conceptions of knowledge; however, just as in the example of the student removing herself to pray, I find accountability about use of power hard to create in the social work education context. It would take a sense of safety that does not exist in the setting where I work, tremendous courage or both. There seems to be little space to talk and think about power in social work education, and without this discourse, accountability for power and influence is hard to imagine. This of course complicates the difficulty of overt spirituality. If I cannot fully attend to the dilemmas of power and influence, is it possible to responsibly bring my spiritual presence into my teaching space? The answer, of course, is that I have to do the best that I can because the idea that I can hide my spirituality is an insult to the presence and perception of my students and peers. Spiritual is what I am, not what I do. The best that I can do, as I have constructed it thus far, is to actively practice self-awareness and reflexivity routinely and seek accountability as possible. I designate specific time and space in my work-day for self-awareness and reflexivity. I practice accountability by talking about power and my expressions of spirituality, not with my social work education peers, but with my students and with a small group of activists and educators in other fields. Once each year I attend a gathering convened by the Global Partnership for Transformative Social Work group, where I have had many conversations about power and spirituality in practice with other social work educators and practitioners.

Groen (2012) indicates that 'the overt presence of spirituality in teach-ing and research is still greeted with some caution and hesitation' and that 'venturing into this arena as an academic can be risky business' (p. 78). I admit that I am fearful that something I say or do will be interpreted by a student or other faculty member as an imposition of spirituality, and complaints will be made about me to the administration. As a non-tenured faculty member who is reappointed annually and may be dismissed without cause, this is a great concern and sometimes inhibits my narration of my own spirituality and my teaching students about how to assess their own or clients' spirituality. I also acknowledge that this living spirituality is difficult to implement given the power and influence that I, as a teacher, have with and over students. Yet with conscious awareness of the influence and power I have with students, mindful implementation of lessons and a bit of cour-age, I am able to be my authentic self in the classroom in ways that examine and honour my spirituality, and by example give permission and opportu-nity to students to examine and honour their own spirituality.

With-ness

While I am aware of the power and influence that I have with students, I also have an awareness of my lack of control in the classroom. Individually, students come into the classroom in differing states of distress, engagement and physical health. They come with experiences that impact their ability or desire to focus, varied foundations for the learning that is to take place on any day and different levels of trust or distrust of me as a guide to their learning experience. Spirituality impacts how I view and manage this lack of control. My experience with birth, birthing and death has tutored me in how to think about this. I have attended many births, given birth four times and been present at several deaths. Each birth and death that I have witnessed or experienced has been a privilege. The predominant memory of each is of a relational experience with the labouring one, the one coming in or the one going out. I could not control the coming or going, neither hurry it nor delay it nor determine the outcome. All I could really do with each was abide. This abiding is a spiritual 'with-ness' that I characterize as bearing witness through deep presence, complete acceptance and profound connection.

Most recently, I was privileged to be with my mother as she transitioned into death. I performed an absurd drama with her where, knowing that she was a very private person and likely not to want to make her exit with anyone watching, I announced to her that I was going to sleep, went to a corner of the room where she lay comatose preparing to die, and there I pretended to sleep. I continued to peek at her with one eye. I could see her respirations decreasing and finally stop, and immediately I jumped up and ran to her bed and called her. She promptly began to breathe regularly again. We preformed this drama three times until I went to her and asked her permission to stay with her. Only then, when I was fully present, had the permission of my mother and could sit with a patient open heart could I abide with her in 'with-ness' as she made her transition. I remember thinking, as I sat those few minutes with my mother as she made her exit, 'I am here. I love you. Do whatever you need to do.'

I attempt to bring a level of this 'with-ness' to my teaching. In the classroom, as my students struggle to grasp a concept, grapple with self-awareness, tentatively practice a skill, or sit with ambiguity, the presence and acceptance that I can offer them is much the same as with my mother. While the love that I felt for my mother was born of a lifetime of connection with her, the love I feel for my students is born of acknowledgement of their humanity and their potential. The degree to which students give me permission to be with them, however, is totally in their control, but, as with my Mother, I believe that my 'with-ness' with students helps to ease the way.

Love and dialogue

Like Svi Shapiro (2006), who references love as an integral part of teaching, and his faith as foundational to his pedagogy, love is central to my spiritual and teaching practice. Freire asserted that 'love is an act of courage, not fear [...] a commitment to others [and] to the cause of liberation (2000, p. 78). Freire's conceptualization of love, which emphasizes the centrality of dialogue and the power of language, matches well with the conceptualization of love that I apply in the classroom. He insisted that

[d]ialogue cannot exist [...] in the absence of a profound love for the world and for people. The naming of the world, which is an act of

creation and re-creation, is not possible if it is not infused with love. Love is at the same time the foundation of dialogue and dialogue itself. (Freire, 2000, p. 89)

So, love and dialogue are indelibly linked. Love as a tool and the impetus for dialogue, and dialogue as a function and expression of love.

Dialogue serves as my primary method for engaging spiritually and with spirituality in the classroom. Freire believed that, '[f]ounding itself upon love, humility, and faith, dialogue becomes a horizontal relationship of which mutual trust between the dialoguers is the logical consequence' (Freire, 2000, p. 91). Consequently, dialogue 'cannot exist in a relation of domination' (Freire, 2000, p. 89). Dialogue, then, is an important tool in undermining power arrangements that have potential to privilege one form of spirituality over another, or the spirituality of the teacher over that of the student. I use the power that I have in the classroom to create an expectation and culture of dialogue as a process with rules of engagement that stress curiosity, enquiry, reflection and non-judgement. These rules of engagement are meant to create a relational and conceptual safe space. This use of power in process, in turn, protects me and my students from undue exercise of power and influence in relationship to concepts, ideas and beliefs.

I am supposed to be here even if I don't belong here

The first time I was on the campus where I now work, I travelled from a nearby city where I lived and worked as the executive director of a large national non-profit social service organization. I had travelled to the university to see an acquaintance perform in a stage play. When I stepped out of the car, I turned to my partner and said, 'Someday I am going to work here.' We both laughed and she asked me if that was a prophesy. At the time, I was in a job that I intended to stay in, had not earned a PhD and did not intend to become a professor. Still, I somehow felt I belonged at that university – that it was the site of some partial realization of my purpose. Five years later, despite very long odds, and many seemingly coincidental convergences, I took a job at the very university where my intuition had insisted I belonged. A fairy tale ending would demand that everything be happily ever after, but of course that is not the case. There are challenges of culture and bureaucracy that often result in my feeling that I am out of my element, but because of this sense of spiritual impetus to be at this institution, I am led to have an optimistic outlook, make the most of what is here and when what I need does not exist, create what I need to stay there. I have purpose here beyond any hardship or lack of sense of belonging.

Fear and courage

I am afraid much of the time in my work. I have experience that supports that fear. I have had experiences where my race, gender or sexual orientation made me the subject of routine microaggressions (Pittman, 2012). In the jobs where I experienced microaggression, I often felt insecure. I am black and queer in a culture that often problematizes race and sexuality. In addition, I am relatively new to academia and teaching. This means that I often really do not know what I am doing in a setting and culture where there seems to be little room for less than full competence or failure. I am afraid that if I fail to teach effectively, students will graduate into the profession of social work and not work well with, or do harm to, clients. I believe that I am most effective when I am fully authentic, but I fear the consequences. And I am embarrassed to say this, but I am afraid that my co-workers and students will not like me and that I will fail to have community in my work. My experiences of struggle, much like the experiences of women of colour social work faculty included in the qualitative study conducted by Vakalahi and Starks (2010), include the impact of white privilege and surveillance. Also, like the participants in this study, I use spiritual forces to sustain me. I am not paralyzed with fear. My spirituality provides me with the strength and resilience to practice courage. I am able to trust that I am neither omnipotent nor powerless – that I will be alright regardless of the outcome and that in my attempt to practice love in all aspects of my life, I will do right, recover from hardship and help others.

Conclusion

In this chapter, I have provided an overview of the frame and constitution of my spirituality. I have discussed dilemmas, dissonance and some impacts of my spirituality on my social work practice as a social work educator. I had intended to write a different chapter: one that was intellectual, impersonal and (initially) focused on reflections about racism and my spiritual practice in social work education. But as I attempted to make use of the exercise of writing to expand my own understanding of my spiritual practice in the context of my social work practice what emerged was an unwillingness to focus much on race and an inability to write something particularly intellectual and impersonal. I think that instead, the overarching need to explain myself to myself overshadowed my desire to write a brilliant piece for others. This chapter perhaps exemplifies my spiritual practice: it is infused with love, authenticity, gratitude and hope. I hope this chapter generates questions, discussion and perhaps opens a small window of insight about what spirituality might contribute to social work education and practice.

References

Boone, M., Fite, K., and Reardon, R., 2010. The spiritual dispositions of emerging teachers: a preliminary study. *Journal of Thought*, 45(3–4), pp. 43–58.

Bordo, S., 1986. The Cartesian masculinization of thought. *Signs: Journal of Women in Culture and Society*, 77, pp. 439–456.

Canda, E. R., and Furman, L. D., 2010. *Spiritual diversity in social work practice: the heart of helping.* New York: Oxford Press.

Canda, E. R., Nakashima, M., and Furman, L. D., 2004. Ethical considerations about spirituality in social work: insights from a national qualitative survey. *Families in Society*, 85(1), pp. 27–35.

Fook, J., 1999. Reflexivity as method. *Health Sociology Review*, 1999, pp. 11–20.

Freire, P., 2000. *Pedagogy of the oppressed.* New York: Continuum.

Gotterer, R., 2001. The spirituality dimension in clinical social work practice: a client perspective. *Families in Society*, 82(2), pp. 187–193.

Groen, D., 2012. Kindred spirits? Challenges and opportunities for the faculties of education and social work in the emerging teaching focus on spirituality. In J. Groen, D. Coholic and J. R. Graham, eds., *Spirituality in social work and education: theory, practice, and pedagogies.* Waterloo: Wilfrid Laurier University Press. Ch. 5.

hooks, b., 1994. *Teaching to transgress: education as the practice of freedom.* New York: Routledge.

Lorde, A., 1984. Poetry is not a luxury. In A. Lorde, *Sister outsider: essays and speeches* Trumansburg: Crossing Press.

Mbiti, J. S. 1969. *African religions and philosophy.* New York: Praeger.

Palmer, P., 1998. *The courage to teach: the inner landscape of a teacher's life.* San Francisco: Jossey-Bass.

Pew Research Center, 2015. Religion and public life. Available at: www.pewforum.org/religious-landscape-study/region/south/. [Accessed 21 October 2015.]

Pittman, C., 2012. Racial microaggressions: the narratives of African American faculty at a predominantly white university. *The Journal of Negro Education*, 81(1), pp. 82–92.

Shapiro, H. S., 2006. *Losing heart: the moral and spiritual miseducation of America's children* Mahwah: L. Erlbaum.

Shulman, L., 2009. *The skills of helping individuals, families, groups and communities*, 6th edn. Belmont: Brooks/Cole.

Tangenberg, K. M., and Kemp, S., 2002. Embodied practice: claiming the body's experience, agency, and knowledge for social work. *Social Work*, 47, pp. 9–11.

Todd, S., 2012. The ties that bind and unwind: spirituality in the secular social work classroom. In J. Groen, D. Coholic and J. R. Graham, eds., *Spirituality in social work and education: theory, practice, and pedagogies.* Waterloo: Wilfrid Laurier University Press. Ch. 7.

Vakalahi1, H., and Starks, S., 2010. The complexities of becoming visible: reflecting on the stories of women of color as social work educators. *Affilia: Journal of Women and Social Work*, 25(2), pp. 110–122.

Vella, J. K., 2000. *Taking learning to task: creative strategies for teaching adults.* San Francisco: Jossey-Bass.

White, S., 2001, Auto-ethnography as reflexive inquiry. In I. Shaw and N. Gould, eds., *Qualitative research in social work.* London: Sage. Ch. 7.

5 Mana Moana: Healing the Vā, Developing Spiritually and Culturally Embedded Practices

Karlo Mila

Introduction

To be in life is to be in relationship. For centuries among the atolls, islands and archipelagos across the Pacific Ocean, the quality of your relationships was understood to be synonymous with the quality of your life and health. 'Vā', or 'wā', is a word that is Austronesian in origin, still spoken in 22 languages in Oceania. Vā means relationships. However, it also means space – the space between us. Albert Wendt, the Samoan writer, tells us, 'Vā is the space between, the between-ness, not empty space, not space that separates, but space that relates, that holds separate entities and things together in the unity-in-all, the space that is context, giving meaning to things' (Wendt, cited in Refiti, 2002, p. 185).

This is the space that we 'feel' as opposed to 'see' (Mila-Schaaf, 2006). Health and well-being is associated with the quality of our vā: the quality of our interconnections with land, with sea, with sky, with family and other people and with spirit. It is not possible to leave spirituality out of the health and well-being equation.

In this chapter, I focus on the way that spirituality permeates indigenous Pasifika therapeutic and restorative health practices and beliefs, illustrating how spirituality is deeply intertwined with health and well-being within Pasifika cultures. This provides an example of how important it is to be aware of culturally distinctive understandings of spirituality and well-being. It also provides an opportunity to broaden the scope and understandings of how humans all over the world have constructed and approached health and spirituality in different cultural contexts.

Background and context

Growing up in New Zealand, the daughter of a Pasifika migrant father, I came to this subject area drawn to the challenge of the much higher burden of mental disorders experienced by Pasifika peoples, especially Pasifika youth (Foliaki et al., 2006). Pasifika youth have disproportionately high rates of suicide attempts (Helu et al., 2009; Mila-Schaaf et al., 2008), and evidence also shows higher rates and a higher frequency of admissions for psychotic disorders in both the Pasifika adult and youth populations (Craig, Taufa and Yeo-Han, 2008; Pulotu-Endemann, Annandale and A, 2004). This is met with service trends of low utilization (Davis et al., 2005; Foliaki et al., 2006; Craig et al., 2008), late presentation (Pulotu-Endemann et al., 2004), high rates of emergency referral (Davis et al., 2005), longer stays (MoH, 2005) and the highest average cost of adult inpatient and community episodes (Pulotu-Endemann et al., 2004).

Solving these challenging problems as a Pasifika community has required all sorts of innovative responses and efforts; the desire for more culturally responsive services, a strengthened Pasifika workforce, the development of cultural models of care and Pasifika-centred solutions (Le-Va, 2009; Minstry of Health, 1997, 2005, 2008, 2014).

My own role to play in the challenges facing the well-being and health of the young people in the Pasifika community was to embark on a four-year postdoctoral research project exploring 'What is healing in a Pasifika mental health context?' The core question of this research endeavour was, 'What is healing in a Pasifika mental health context?' If we were to turn to how our Oceanic ancestors had healed and treated and practiced therapeutically, what would we learn? How did they do what they did? What could have continuing energy in contemporary contexts? The aim was to develop a culturally responsive intervention.

This began with over 30 face-to-face interviews with Pacific service users, Pacific clinicians and practitioners and Pacific traditional knowledge holders, to explore what they believed was healing in a Pacific mental health context. This was supplemented with an explorative literature review of archetypes, mythical motifs, psyche and healing traditions in indigenous Pacific cultures. The project aimed to bring together cultural, historical, linguistic, anthropological, indigenous and cultural research about the Pacific, identify what would resonate in an applied context of contemporary New Zealand diasporic living and mobilize that knowledge into applied clinical and community contexts, testing it for feasibility and acceptability.

This research journey was inspired in part by living in Aotearoa, New Zealand, whereby the cultural renaissance of the indigenous Polynesian Māori population and their commitment to vitalizing indigenous knowledge has created a context that is ripe and encouraging for the process of 'appropriation by cultures of their own rich genius' (Okere, Njoku and Devish, 2005, p. 1). This kind of research endeavour is understood to be 'the gateway to re-acquiring cultural dignity and self confidence', but it is also an opportunity 'to positively contribute to the commonwealth of world knowledge' (Okere et al., 2005, pp. 1–2). Conducting this kind of research is part of a movement of reclaiming indigenous knowledge throughout the region of Oceania:

> The awareness among growing numbers of Pacific academics of the need for a genuine and far-reaching contextualization – acknowledging the relevance and applicability of indigenous cultural values in contemporary settings. Second is the success of communities whose initiatives have followed the ways they know and understand, reaping many rewards. (Huffer and Qalo 2004, p. 108)

In this chapter, therefore, I am able to provide insight into knowledge possessed by the people of Oceania as 'potential treasure trove for the global expansion of knowledge horizons' (Hviding, 2003, p. 6). This recognizes that all of our ways of knowing are constructed in culturally distinctive ways, via 'an endless sequence of mediators' and 'discontinuous transformations' in which 'verified reference circulates through constant substitutions', and eventually we can come to 'link ourselves' to an 'aligned, transformed, constructed world' (Latour, 1999, pp. 78–79). Just as the world is linguistically and geographically diverse, so there are also multiple ways of knowing and interpreting what is seen. In other words 'the epistemological diversity of the world is immense' (de Souza Santos, 2007, p. xix).

Existing research shows that effective Pasifika approaches are holistic (Anae et al., 2002; MHC, 2007) and spiritual (Pulotu-Endemann et al., 2007; Suaali'i-Sauni et al., 2009; Tamasese Efi, 2002; Tiatia, 2003; Vaka et al., 2009) in orientation. A range of Pasifika researchers have showed that relationships and relational spaces (*vā*) are critical to understandings of health and well-being (Autagavaia, 2001; Bush et al., 2009; Ka'ili, 2005, 2008; Lilomaiava-Doktor, 2009; Mila-Schaaf, 2006; Poltorak, 2007; Thaman, 2003, 2004). Effective Pasifika practice also relies on practitioners who empathize and engage as if they are family (Mafile'o, 2004), with deep compassion (Malo, 2000), and who are willing to go above and beyond professional expectations (Agnew et al., 2004).

Mana Moana

Mana Moana is the intervention approach developed during my postdoctoral fellowship. A framework developed by Paulo Friere was selected as a process for developing a culturally responsive intervention (Cajete, 1994). This recognizes that words themselves are the building blocks of world views, are connected to a whole way of seeing the world and illuminate, in their entirety, a whole cultural context, an entire version of reality. By focusing on these words, it is possible to 'begin with the way a group communicates about itself, their world, their experiences, in their own social contexts' and identify 'generative words', metaphors, proverbs, 'words that evoke thoughts, feelings, or reveal a historical perspective that has an intrinsic meaning to a people and their cultural way of life' (Cajete, 1994, p. 216).

With Mana Moana a matrix of generative, or power, words, based on common Pasifika language and concepts, relevant to health and well-being, were collected, and over 250 associated proverbs and narratives. Mana Moana organizes an indigenous canon of archetypal words and concepts arranged into the categories: *atua* (spirit), *fenua* (earth), *moana* (sea), *langi* (sky), *kainga* (family and home) and *vā* (relationships). Dr Johnson Witehira, a Māori/Samoan designer transformed many of these concepts into visual images. As well as bringing together this resource, one of the outcomes of the research process was the clarity about 'traditional'/indigenous Pasifika cultural constructions of health and well-being. An aim was to be able to articulate a research-based clear and coherent understanding of indigenous Pasifika ecological, holistic, and cyclical framing of health and associated rationales for aetiology and treatment. These shared understandings of health and well-being, and how to restore health from illness embedded within philosophical and cultural worldviews, informed by core cultural values, ideas, and beliefs across Polynesian-language speaking parts of the Pacific are widely shared although not identically reproduced.

The approach developed was then shared with over 100 experts: cultural, clinical and community, for refinement and feedback. Two retreats were conducted. Focus groups with young people, service-users, Pacific elders, Pacific mental health services and practitioners were held to ensure cultural credibility and face validity. In partnership with a Pasifika clinical psychologist, Dr Evangelene Daniela, this intervention was operationalized and delivered successfully with a group of young Pasifika people.

Moana, meaning 'ocean', is a Polynesian word that can be found in 35 contemporary Pacific languages, and it often evokes the deep sea and the great depths in relation to the shallows or tides. It is the sea that we have in common, all of the distinctive cultures of Pasifika, shaped by a continuous engagement with, and adaptation to, the largest ocean in the world. The sea, as the writer and philosopher Epeli Hau'ofa pointed out, has never separated us. Descending from great seafarers, the sea has always been our pathway to one another (Hau'ofa, 2008).

Mana is an Oceanic word that can be found in 26 languages. The anthropologist Bradd Shore (1989) writes, 'It is not by chance, that Western observers have so often sought the soul of Polynesia in the concept of *mana*' (p. 137). It is the embodiment and harnessing of power, of energy and authority. Collocott (1921) explains that 'manifestations in the seen world of the unseen world are *mana* [... and] traced to its ultimate source, it was ever the gift of the gods' (p. 436).

Maori Marsden (2003) writes that *mana* refers to spiritual authority and means 'that which manifests the power of the gods' (p. 4). *Mana Moana*, then, is about the power, energy, vitality and gifts sourced to an Oceanic existence and cultures. It is the empowerment found in being who we are, where we are from and how we have come to be.

Atua/Otua/Akua is the word across Pasifika cultures (Malayo-Polynesian in origin) that it is used (in 33 languages) to denote God, gods or the realm of the Spirit. When researching *Mana Moana*, the role of spirituality as an essential and non-negotiable aspect of healing emerged very quickly. As one of the research participants said, 'Our ability to be aware of the spirit and the transcendent, it's precious and we have to hold onto it. It's the piece that Western society lost when they began the age of enlightenment. I think that was in the eighteenth century. When Descartes began to use the head only, you know, Cogito ergo sum (I think, therefore I am). So we have to bring this back into the equation, we have to bring the whole together: the spirit of the soul, the transcendent.'

Figure 5.1 Atua / 'Otua/Akua – spirit by Dr Johnson Witehira.

Spirituality is a fundamental component of well-being among many indigenous peoples (Valentine, 2009). There is growing insistence that the realm of spirit, the unseen, the unknown, the metaphysical, must be factored into the healing and health-seeking process.

While researching what was considered healing according to the ancient, ancestral and cultural knowledge of Polynesian peoples indigenous to the Pacific, the more fundamental spirituality appeared to be. Perhaps the question was not, 'What was spiritual?' but rather, 'What was not considered spiritual?'

The more I tried to reduce the spiritual aspects of healing into one component of a processes or intervention, the trickier it became. My difficulty in articulating the deep pervasiveness of spirituality associated with both health problems and solutions was solved by someone else.

Timote Vaioleti, a Tongan scholar, had observed one of the most successful and widespread indigenous therapeutic models in Aotearoa, New Zealand. Sir Professor Mason Durie, one of the most eminent leaders and academics, had very successfully introduced a model called '*te whare tapa whā*' – this very simply translates as 'the house of four walls' (Durie, 1998).

The model acknowledges that all kinds of health must be in balance in order to be a whole person: *whanau* (family health), *tinana* (physical health), *hinengaro* (mental health) and *wairua* (spiritual health) – a four-dimensional approach to well-being (Durie, 1998). If one of these aspects of a person is out of balance, a person or a collective may become imbalanced and/or unwell.

Because of Sir Mason Durie's credibility and cultural leadership, his many positions of influence and lifetime of dedicated scholarship, the model of *tapa whā* spread widely into almost mainstream usage, affecting many fields, including nursing, social work, medicine, care and protection, youth work and in the prisons. This had the effect of opening up the conversation about spiritual well-being in predominantly secular well-being contexts.

Recent research on Maori traditional healing and well-being also now emphasizes the ecological (environmental) component of the natural world and adds this to the dimensions in the *whare tapa whā* model (Ahuriri-Driscoll et al., 2012).

Timote Vaioleti's insights are also valuable. He acknowledges the significant contribution of the *whare tapa whā* model but shifts us towards an aesthetic that is found in all Polynesian cultures. The *manulua* pattern (also known as the vane swastika) motif is found throughout Polynesian art and art forms (Vaioleti, 2011). The pattern dates back to Laptita pottery – a shared, ancestral source of culture origins – and is called *manulua* in Tongan – two birds – stylized as two sets of wings flying.

Figure 5.2 Manulua (two birds) Pasifika pattern.

Drawing on the *tapa whā*, Vaioleti suggests that all four dimensions are indeed critical. However, the *manulua* image (see Figure 5.2) illustrates the importance of spirituality and how the nature of the seen is actually shaped by the unseen, in crucial ways. According to our indigenous epistemologies and beliefs, the role of spirituality cannot be reduced to simply one side of the whole. He writes that the realm of the intangible, invisible, which consists of 'energies' and 'spirit', permeates and shapes the 'seen' present (Vaioleti, 2011, p. 102). The unseen may represent many things: 'the past, ancestors, church matters, old religious obligations, unrecorded knowledge, other relatives both in the home country and elsewhere as well as possibly their future' (Vaioleti, 2011, p. 102).

What is useful about this conceptualization is that it illustrates clearly how the unseen actively shapes the tangible world. The *manulua* is an evocative visual motif for societies that have believed for centuries that aspects of the divine penetrate the human world and that, interchangeably, humans may take on divine qualities associated with the spirit world (Huntsman and A, 1996, pp. 1–2).

Pasifika knowledge is often encoded within stories, described as deliberate constructs by seers and visionaries, that were created to contain and pass on memories, knowledge and vital information (Marsden and Henare, 1992). This is a story from Mangaia:

Thousands of years ago, a young, strong Polynesian man sailed his outrigger canoe through the bluest waters of the largest ocean in the world. His name is Rangi. Leaving behind everything that he knew, he searches for new land, hoping to begin afresh with the rich resources of a new island. He dreams of being chief in this new world he wants to create for himself. With much to lose but more to gain, he sails for days, seeing only blue. He follows a celestial star path that he has dreamed, knowing that it has not yet been navigated. Finally, he sees the movement of land birds break the blue of the skies. Excited, he sails toward these birds, and it is not long before a lush island appears before him.

He pulls his travelling vessel onto the beach, seeing and hoping that the island before him is uninhabited. Climbing a coconut tree, he peers around the island, and seeing no one, he begins to explore the island. He walks around the coastline, through the dense bush, and then finally across the rocks and around the caves. He declares himself the ruler of this new land.

As soon as he does this, he hears a women's voice.

'What are you doing here?' this strange feminine voice asks him. He can see no one. Her voice appears to emanate from the rocks themselves.

'I am Rangi,' he cries out. He is bold and foolhardy enough to say, 'I am ruler of this land.' Then, 'Who are you?' he asks.

'I am Tumu-te-ana-oa; I am Echo. I am she who everywhere inhabits the rocks of Mangaia, who always has and always will.'

The story of 'Echo', as William Wyatt Gill (1876), the narrator, named her, and Rangi was collected and documented well over a century ago from Mangaia. Rangi, the Polynesian human adventurer, encounters a non-human spirit of the land, Tumu-te-ana-oa. Rangi tries to settle the island on his own terms. Tumu-te-ana-oa unsettles him.

With typical human arrogance, Rangi underestimates Echo. Yet she operates on another more ancient dimension of the Polynesian multi-verse. She cannot be beat. He has no power over her. They eventually come to the conclusion that neither of them will willingly leave. They make their way towards an uneasy alliance, characterized by begrudging but mistrusting, cautious respect for one another.

On many levels this is not a remarkable story. But when I first read the story of Rangi and Echo, in William Wyatt Gill's collection, something about this story stayed with me. Who and what was Echo? Why was this story remembered? What was the significance?

Much later I came across a scholarly article by a New Zealand academic whose career has specialized in Mangaia. Michael Reilly (2009) notes that this story was not neatly categorized by Gill in 1876 but appears towards the end of his collection of stories under the section 'Miscellaneous'. He too was similarly intrigued by the story of Rangi and Echo.

After much thought, he realized that it was not so much its unique-ness, but the way it captures the essence of something that is widespread and fundamental. Reilly posits that this small story about uneasy alliance between the first human settler and the ever-present spirit realm that already inhabits the land captures the Polynesian understanding of the spiritual world and spirituality.

The realm of the unseen, non-human, spiritual others, who are essential, eternally connected and ever-present is interrupted by this human inter-loper. The unknowable and uncontrollable commands respect and the rules of engagement. Beings from the spiritual realm are not passive, but active. Echo has a hand in shaping the world of humans, appearing at will or disap-pearing. Rangi, the human protagonist, emerges with an understanding that he must acknowledge Echo's existence and authority, and avoid disturbing or upsetting her. She is not to be dealt with on human terms. She exists. She is not to be trifled with, but not necessarily feared.

A symbiotic relationship between the human and spiritual realm was and remains highly desirable and is woven into the fabric of many Pacific ways of behaving, knowing and being (Vaioleti, 2011). Eventually there would be a *tapu* around things associated with Echo and her kind, ways of arrang-ing the relationship to avoid future error – the avoidance of certain caves perhaps, a ritual of acknowledgement – a set of agreements that would be respectfully observed.

The word 'taboo' in the English language is traced etymologically back to the Oceanic word *tapu*, spoken widely in the region of Polynesia and found in at least 38 languages. *Tapu* is a generative concept, one that holds intrinsic meaning to a people and their cultural way of life (Cajete, 1994). *Tapu* always refers to that which is beyond human control in one way or another. It can be translated in many ways – as referring to that which is sacred or holy, or simply out of bounds or prohibited. The Samoan cultural elder, indigenous philosopher and Head of State, Tui Atua Tamasese Ta'isi Efi, describes *tapu* as the sacred essence that underpins humanity's relation-ships with all things: their gods, the cosmos, environment, other men and self (Tamasese Efi, 2007, p. 2).

To observe *tapu* is to honour relationships, particularly those beyond the human realm. A Maori proverb says, '*Ko te tapu te mana o nga atua*', which translates as '*Tapu* is the *mana* of the spiritual powers' or spiritual realm, or gods, or God (Shirres, 1982, p. 51).

Mana refers to all that is empowered, authoritative, energy-imbued, vitalized and powerful. To observe *tapu*, to acknowledge, respect and abide by it – its rules, its regulations and requirements – is to uphold the harmony of an interconnected system much larger than yourself. It is to humble yourself, and restrain your own individual desires for the greater good of an already established ecology, that is multidimensional in orientation. In this system gods are 'the guardians of *tapu*' (Tamasese Efi, 2008b, p. 6).

Vā tapuia refers to the sacred relationships among all of creation, which are constructed as genealogically linked in an evolutionary sense, interconnected and ultimately ordered, so that we all find ourselves part of the greater family of things (Tamasese Efi, 2008a). Being bound genealogically to all other parts of creation, as elder or younger sibling, is associated with rights and responsibilities, duties and roles to perform.

Although there is strong scientific evidence that all living organisms on earth are descended from a common ancestor (Dawkins, 2004), this sense of being interrelated and operating as part of a genealogically connected whole, does not have a strong emphasis in prevailing Western constructions of society or psyche. In contrast, as the anthropologist Craig (2004) notes, 'All Polynesian creation narratives involve forms of (pro-creative) union, conceive of evolution within a genealogical frame and for the most part, "they" (Polynesians) "were a part of it"' (p. 41).

Tui Atua Tupua Tamasese Efi explains it this way: The Samoan word, *vā tapuia*, includes the term *tapu* within it. The term literally refers to the sacred (*tapu-ia*) relationship (*vā*) between man and all things, animate and inanimate. It implies that in our relations with all things, living and dead, there exists a sacred essence, a life force beyond human reckoning. The distinction here between what is living and what is dead is premised not so much on whether a 'life force', that is, a *mauli* or *fatu manava*, exists in the thing (i.e. whether a 'life breath' or 'heartbeat' exudes from it), but whether that thing, living or dead, has a genealogy (in an evolutionary rather than human procreation sense) that connects to a life force. 'The vā tapuia, the sacred relations, between all things, extends in the Samoan indigenous reference to all things living or dead, where a genealogical relationship can be traced' (Tamasese Efi, 2007).

When we understand ourselves as a part of a genealogically linked, interdependent ecology, the quality of our interconnections with all others comes to the fore. The way that we language these relationships is through the *vā*. *Vā* as space is 'fundamentally different from the popular western notion of space as an expanse or an open area' (Ka'ili, 2005, p. 89). *Vā* is imbued with energy, memory, history, essence and interactions. It is a repository of what has been, what is and what can be. It carries and holds the to and fro of interpersonal energy, attraction and repulsion. Everything is possible in the *vā* (Carmel Peteru in personal communication). *Vā* is relationship, connection, space, distance, responsibility, obligation, state of being, position, standing and so much more (Le Tagaloa, 2003, pp. 7–8).

The *vā* is the space where the reciprocal flow of relating occurs. It is within the context of relationship and interconnection that health or illness is experienced. We are never understood to be individuals separate from our woven universe of interconnectedness (Marsden, 2003).

When we see ourselves as fundamentally interconnected and when we take the relational space between all others and ourselves seriously, this

Figure 5.3 *Wā/Vā*: The space that relates – by Dr Johnson Witehira.

requires a focus on what kind of energy and impact we have on all that is around us. How are other people, plants, all life, all dead, the seen as well as the unseen, the spiritual and the secular – how are all affected by our attitudes and our behaviour?

A word used to mark in many Pasifika languages that which comes from us is the Oceanic word '*atu*' or '*aku*', found in 32 languages. The '*atu*' movement is perhaps best theorized by Durie's (2002) construct of an 'outward flow of energy' which is characterized visually by centrifugal movement. A focus on *atu* is a focus on that which flows from us, our lived intentionality from self towards all others.

In contrast, '*mai*' is an Austronesian term, found in 28 contemporary languages. *Mai* enables an opportunity to reflect on what comes towards us, what flows our way, what impacts and influences us. A focus on *mai* invites reflection on what we are on the receiving end of. This 'inward flow of energy' can be understood as characterized by centripetal movement.

Figure 5.4 *Atu/aku*: what flows from you in the *vā* – by Dr Johnson Witehira.

Mai provides a language for what we are taking on board, what we are open to and are actively engaging with. This is considered to be on multiple levels – spiritually, ecologically and interpersonally. To acknowledge *mai*, as well as *atu*, is to recognize that energy flows between us in the *vā/wa*, and that we impact upon one another in multidirectional ways.

Health and well-being, given this broader, multidimensional and holistic understanding of an interconnected system, is defined in a particular culturally specific way. Health, in this context, is equated to healthy relationships and healthy interconnections – the freedom from holding negative feelings, actions and intentions towards others within that system and the freedom from being on the receiving end of negative feelings, actions and intentions (Bloomfield, 2002).

Mental and physical well-being is affected when our relationships (*vā*) are not what they should be, through ignorance or blatant disregard (Bloomfield, 2002, p. 34). This involves either the harbouring of bad

Figure 5.5 *Mai*: what we receive – by Dr Johnson Witehira.

feelings towards others, or being on the receiving end of bad feelings from others, movements across the *vā* – both *atu* and *mai*. Ideally we want clean, contributive, free-flowing *vā*, characterized by love, mutual reciprocity, compassion and empathy.

When relationships are not right with others on all of these dimensions, this is considered to be the major source of illness. In non-negotiable ways, others always refer to 'those of this world and those not of this world' (Bloomfield, 2002, p. 34). 'Others' extends to that which is spiritual or secular, human or non-human. This epistemology extends to all creation – recognizing that all things have the wish to be appreciated. And when the quality of our interconnections is not what it should be, then full health is not realized.

This ability to locate active agency in the spiritual realm in relation to health departs considerably from what is thought possible in Western psychiatry and psychology. Early anthropologists noted that there was widespread belief that *atua* (realm of the gods) was in a position to influence, penetrate and infiltrate the ordinary physical world (Handy, 1927/1971). The presence of gods, spirits and ancestors, and their ability to influence human's lives, recurs consistently in Pacific mythological narratives, whereby gods and goddesses frequently fall in love with mortals, and there are multiple stories of transformations where the supernatural becomes imbued in objects, animals and humans (Kirtley, 1971). However, these are not just fairy stories – they are actually understood to be causative, powerful and influential agents in relation to a person's health.

Good relationships – the ability to give and receive love freely – translated as *aroha atu, aroha mai*, or *ofa atu, ofa mai*, or *aloha aku, aloha mai*, or *alofa atu, aloha mai* (and the list goes on), is the flowing and mutually reciprocal guide to well-being, to health, to healthy life itself.

When someone is unwell, there is something in the *vā* that is unhealthy, that is not life-giving, that is out of balance. There is some kind of block that involves something which is causing pain or anxiety or disturbance. On the feelings, thoughts, intentions level, something, somewhere is wrong, and it is blocking the reciprocal flow of *aroha atu, aroha mai* through the *vā* of cooperative mutuality.

Mary Kawena Pukui, a Hawaiian knowledge holder and elder, suggests that the negative breach can be visualized as similar to a cord: 'It binds the offender to his deed and to his victim. The victim holds on to this cord and becomes equally bound' (Pukui, Haertig and Lee, 1972, p. 71). People become bound in ways that are constraining, restraining and in ways that they are not free.

Illness is frequently interpreted as the consequence of some kind of breach of *tapu*, which is ultimately a breach of ideal and appropriate relationships applied on multidimensional levels that require a decolonization of the time-space continuum as it is currently interpreted (Tamasese et al., 2005). This can be a breach in the past with intergenerational impact. It can be a breach with the living or dead, with the human or ecological world.

To restore health and address relational breaches that cause disruptions, a process must be put in place for restoration and atonement so that 'the offended party (which may be a person or spirit) has been appeased', and then 'the most important part of the cure has been effected' (Baddeley, 1986, p. 141).

Conclusion

These are old ideas that I have shared in this chapter. They have been marginalized, suppressed, considered superstitious, anti-Christian and savage. However, these ideas belong to a beautiful and complex way of being in the world that is indigenous to Pasifika. In a contemporary Pasifika therapeutic context, these ideas can have continuing energy in relation to well-being. Traditional health restoration practices require bringing relationships back into balance.

In Aotearoa, Pasifika practitioners are re-engaging with a body of knowledge, an indigenous reference that has much to tell us about healing, wholeness and aetiology and treatment, if we are willing to search and listen. As a sector of predominantly Western-trained Pasifika peoples, who have been led to healing work in contemporary contexts, drawing on Mana Moana, the knowledge legacy of our Pasifika ancestors, is one way that we can ensure that we are culturally responsive to the people who appear to us, in pain and with problems.

Our rich traditional knowledge bank tells us that if there are problems in the *vā*, and they have not been resolved, they can end in entanglements, which are very difficult to unbind, mend and untangle. Ultimately returning to healthy free-flowing *vā*, of reciprocal free-flowing love and mutual affection with all things, earth, sea, sky, spirit, the seen and the unseen, is the pathway to health and well-being.

As stated in the introduction to this chapter, I hope that by sharing these old ideas and knowledge, I have provided an example of how important it is to be aware of culturally distinctive understandings of spirituality and well-being. I hope this has also contributed to broadening the understandings of how humans all over the world have constructed and approached health and spirituality in different cultural contexts.

References

Agnew, F., Pulotu-Endemann, F. K., Robinson, G., Suaali'i-Sauni, S., Warren, H., Wheeler, A., and Schmidt-Sopoaga, H., 2004. *Pacific models of mental health service delivery in New Zealand 'PMMHSD' Project*. Auckland: Health Research Council of New Zealand.

Ahuriri-Driscoll, A., Hudson, M., Bishara, I., Milne, M., and Stewart, M., 2012. *Ngaa Tohu o te Ora: traditional Maaori healing and wellbeing outcomes*. Christchurch: Institute of Environmental Science and Research.

Anae, M., Moewaka-Barnes, H., McCreanor, T., and Watson, P., 2002. Towards promoting youth mental health in Aotearoa/New Zealand: holistic 'houses' of health. *International Journal of Mental Health Promotion*, 4, pp. 5–14.

Autagavaia, M. , 2001. Social work with Pacific island communities. In M. Connolly, ed., *New Zealand social work: contexts and practice*. Auckland: Oxford University Press. Ch. 6.

Baddeley, J., 1986. Traditional healing practices of Rarotonga, Cook Islands. In C. D. F. Parsons, ed., *Healing practices in the South Pacific*. Honolulu: Brigham Young University – Hawaii Campus in association with the Polynesian Centre. Ch. 7.

Bloomfield, S. F., 2002. *Illness and cure in Tonga: traditional and modern medical practice.* Tonga: Vava'u Press.

Bush, A., Chapman, F., Drummond, M., and Fagaloa, T., 2009. Development of a child, adolescent and family mental health service for Pacific young people in Aotearoa/New Zealand. *Pacific Health Dialog*, 15(1), pp. 138–146.

Cajete, G., 1994. *Look to the mountain: an ecology of indigenous education.* Durango: Kivaki Press.

Craig, E., Taufa, S., Jackson, C., and Yeo-Han, D., 2008. *The health of Pacific children and young people in New Zealand.* Auckland: Department of Paediatrics, School of Population Health.

Craig, R., 2004. *Handbook of Polynesian mythology.* Santa Barbara: ABC.

Davis, P., Suaali'i-Sauni, T., Lay-Yee, P., and Pearson, J., 2005. *Pacific patterns in primary health care: a comparison of pacific patients and all patient visits to doctors.* Wellington: Ministry of Health.

Dawkins, R., 2004. *The ancestor's tale.* Boston: Houghton Mifflin.

de Souza Santos, B., 2007. *Another knowledge is possible: beyond northern epistemologies.* London: Verso.

Durie, M., 1998. *Whaiora – Māori Health Development*, 2nd edn. Auckland: Oxford University Press.

Durie, M., 2002. Is there a distinctive Maori psychology? In L. Nikora, M. Levy, B. Masters, M. Waitoki, N. Te Awekotuku and R. Etheredge, eds., *The proceedings of the national Maori graduates of psychology symposium.* Hamilton: University of Waikato. Ch. 1.

Foliaki, S., Kokaua, J., Schaaf, D., and Tukuitonga, C., 2006. Pacific people. In M. Oakley-Browne, J. Wells and K. Scott, eds., *Te Rau Hinengaro: the New Zealand mental health survey.* Wellington: Ministry of Health. Ch. 10.

Gill, W. W., 1876. *Myths and songs from the South Pacific.* London: Henry S. King and Co.

Handy, E. S., 1971,1927. *Polynesian religion*, 2nd edn. Honolulu: Kraus Reprint.

Hau'ofa, E., 2008. *We are the ocean: selected works.* Honolulu: University of Hawai'i Press.

Helu, S. L., Robinson, E., Grant, S., Herd, R., and Denny, S., 2009. *Youth '07 the health and wellbeing of secondary school students in New Zealand: results for Pacific young people.* Auckland: The University of Auckland.

Huntsman, J., and A., H., 1996. *Tokelau: a historical ethnography.* Honolulu: University of Hawai'i Press.

Hviding, E., 2003. Between knowledges: Pacific studies and academic disciplines. *The Contemporary Pacific*, 15(1), pp. 43–73.

Ka'ili, T., 2005. Tauhi vā: nurturing Tongan sociospatial ties in Maui and beyond. *The Contemporary Pacific*, 17(1), pp. 83–115. .

Ka'ili, T., 2008. *Tauhi vā: creating beauty through the art of socio-spatial relations* University of Washington. Unpublished PhD thesis in social anthropology.

Kirtley, B., 1971. *A motif-index of traditional Polynesian narratives.* Honolulu: University of Hawaii Press.

Latour, B., 1999. *Pandora's hope: essays on the reality of science studies.* Cambridge: Harvard University Press.

Le Tagaloa, F. A., 2003. *Tapuai Samoan worship*. Apia, Samoa: Malua Printing Press.

Le-Va., 2009. *Kato fetu: setting a Pacific mental health and addiction research agenda summary*. Auckland: Le Va.

Lilomaiava-Doktor, S., 2009. Beyond 'migration': Samoan population movement (malaga) and the geography of social space (vā). *The Contemporary Pacific*, 21(1), pp. 1–32.

Mafile'o, T., 2004. Exploring Tongan social work: Fakafekau'afi (connecting) and fakatokilalo (humility). *Qualitative Social Work*, 3(3), pp. 239–257.

Malo, V., 2000. *Pacific people in New Zealand talk about their experiences with mental illness*. Wellington: Mental Health Commission.

Marsden, M., 2003. *The woven universe: selected writings of Rev. Māori Marsden*. Ōtaki: Estate of Rev. Māori Marsden.

Marsden, M., and Henare, T.A., 1992. *Kaitiakitanga: a definitive introduction to the holistic world view of the Maori*. Unpublished manuscript.

Mental Health Commission (MHC), 2007. *Te Haerenga mo te Whakaoranga 1996–2006: journeys of recovery for the New Zealand mental health sector*. Wellington: Mental Health Commission.

Mila-Schaaf, K., 2006. Vā-centred social work: possibilities for a Pacific approach to social work practice. *Social Work Review (Tu Mau II)*, 18(1), pp. 8–13.

Mila-Schaaf, K., Robinson, E., Schaaf, D., Denny, S., and Watson, P., 2008. *A health profile of Pacific youth: findings of youth 2000: a national secondary school youth health survey*. Auckland: University of Auckland.

Ministry of Health, 1997. *Making a Pacific difference: strategic initiatives for the health of Pacific peoples*. Wellington: Ministry of Health.

Ministry of Health, 2005. *Te Orau Ora: Pacific mental health profile*. Wellington: Ministry of Health.

Ministry of Health, 2008. *Pacific peoples and mental health: a paper for the Pacific health and disability action plan review*. Wellington: Ministry of Health.

Ministry of Health, 2014. *Ala moui: pathways to Pacific health and well-being 2014–2018*. Wellington: Ministry of Health.

Okere, T., Njoku, C., and Devish, R., 2005. All knowledge is first of all local knowledge: an introduction. *Africa Development*, 30(3), pp. 1–19.

Poltorak, M., 2007. Nemesis, speaking, and Tauhi Vaha'a: interdisciplinarity and the truth of 'Mental Illness' in Vava'u, Tonga. *The Contemporary Pacific*, 19(1), pp. 1–35.

Pukui, M. K., Haertig, E. W, and Lee, C. A., 1972. *Naanaa I Ke Kumu: look to the source*. Honolulu: Queen Lili'uokalani Children's Center.

Pulotu-Endemann, F., Annandale, M., and Instone, A., 2004. *A Pacific perspective on the NZ. Mental Health Classification and Outcomes Study (CAOS)*. Wellington: Mental Health Commission.

Pulotu-Endemann, K., Suaali'i-Sauni, S., Lui, D., McNicholas, T., Milne, M., and Gibbs, T., 2007. *Seitapu Pacific mental health and addiction clinical and cultural competencies framework*. Auckland: Te Pou.

Refiti, A., 2002. Making space: Polynesian architecture in Aotearoa/New Zealand. In S. Mallon and F. Pereira, eds., *Pacific art Niu Sila: the Pacific dimension of contemporary New Zealand art*. Wellington: Te Papa Press. Ch. 15

Reilly, M. P. J., 2009. *Ancestral voices from Mangaia: a history of the ancient gods and chiefs*. Auckland: The Polynesian Society.

Schulz, E., and Herman, B., 1951. Proverbial expressions of the Samoans (Continued). *Journal of the Polynesian Society*, 60(1), pp. 1–21.

Shirres, M. P., 1982. Tapu. *The Journal of the Polynesian Society*, 91(1), pp. 29–52.

Shore, B., 1989. Mana and tapu: a new synthesis. In A. Howard and R. Borofsky, eds., *Developments in Polynesian ethnology*. Honolulu: University of Hawaii Press. Ch. unknown.

Suaali'i-Sauni, T., Wheeler, A., Saafi, E., Robinson, G., Agnew, F., Warren, H., and Hingano, T., 2009. Exploration of Pacific perspectives of Pacific models of mental health service delivery in New Zealand. *Pacific Health Dialog*, 15(1), pp. 18–27.

Tamasese Efi, T., 2002. *In search of meaning and nuance and metaphor in cultural competencies*. Waitemata District Health Board Pacific Mental Health Competency Training Programme. Auckland, New Zealand. 23 September.

Tamasese Efi, T., 2007. *Keynote address: bio-ethics and the Samoan indigenous reference*. Paper presented at the Regional Pacific Ethics of Knowledge Production Workshop, Wellington, New Zealand. 13 November.

Tamasese Efi, T., 2008a. *Su'esu'e Manogi – in search of fragrance: Tui Atua Tupua Tamasese Ta'isi and the Samon indigenous reference*. Apia, Samoa: University of Samoa.

Tamasese Efi, T., 2008b. *Water and the Samoan indigenous reference*. Paper presented at the Te Au o te Moana: across Oceania, Tofamamao Conference Centre, Le Auvaa, Samoa, 26 January.

Tamasese, K., Peteru, C., Waldegrave, C., and Bush, A., 2005. OLE TAEAO AFUA The new morning: a qualitative investigation into Samoan perspectives on mental health and culturally appropriate services. *Australian and New Zealand Journal of Psychiatry*, 39, pp. 300–309.

Thaman, K., 2003. Decolonizing Pacific studies: indigenous perspectives, knowledge, and wisdom in higher education. *The Contemporary Pacific*, 15(1), pp. 1–17.

Thaman, K., 2004. Tauhi va ha'a: a possible foundation for peace and inter-cultural understanding. *Intercultural Education*, summer, pp. 32–36.

Tiatia, J., 2003. *Reasons to live: N.Z. born Samoan young people's responses to suicidal behaviours*. Auckland: University of Auckland. Unpublished PhD thesis, Public Health, University of Auckland.

Vaioleti, T., 2011. *Talanoa, Manulua and Founga Ako: frameworks for using enduring Tongan educational ideas for education in Aotearoa/New Zealand*. Hamilton: Waikato University. Unpublished PhD thesis in education, Waikato University.

Vaka, S., Stewart, M., Foliaki, S., and Tu'itahi, M., 2009. Walking apart but towards the same goal? The view and practices of Tongan traditional healers and Western trained Tongan mental health staff. *Pacific Health Dialog*, 15(1), pp. 89–95.

Valentine, H., 2009. *Kia Ngawari ki te Awatea: the relationship between Wairua and Māori wellbeing: a psychological perspective*. Unpublished PhD thesis in clinical psychology, Massey University.

6 Being Different with Different Beings: Social Work and Trans-species Spirituality

Cassandra Hanrahan

Introduction

This chapter is about a core dimension of my spirituality that imbues both my personal and professional selves – human–animal interactions (HAI) and bonds (HAB) – and how, in particular, they inform a sense of *interconnectedness* to all, which in turn informs my understanding of social work and sense of justice. HAI and HAB are the threads that weave my professional and personal worlds together into one life guided by the spiritual lessons[1] learned from the daily interactions I have with other species and the natural world.[2] Having the opportunity here, in this designated public space, to delineate these interconnections is welcome and indeed remarkable.

Ironically, although HAI and HAB constitute for many an expectant topic that resonates readily in our diverse everyday lived experiences, increasingly supported by an unprecedented groundswell of popular interest in our relationships to other animals[3] and the natural environment,[4] HAI and HAB are virtually absent from the field of Canadian social work as well as from health care contexts more broadly. With a mere few scholars and practitioners, including this author, advancing HAI/HAB *and* social work in Canada, the topic by comparison enjoys extraordinary attention in the United States.[5] Such scholarship and activism are supported by a developing body of discipline-specific and multidisciplinary scientific literature, and an ever-increasing number of human–animal studies (HAS), university and college programs, legal centres for animal issues, conferences, journals, individual courses, listservs, databases, museums, animal-assisted therapy programs and HAS organizations for collaborative research.[6] The prominent US-based *Animals & Society Institute* provides a long list of such entities that spans an impressive number of countries, including, in addition to the United States and Canada, Australia, Austria, Finland, France, Germany, Israel, The Netherlands, New Zealand, Poland, Spain, Sweden, Switzerland and the United Kingdom. In the United Kingdom, the prestigious Oxford Centre for Animal Ethics, the University of Oxford, has a history dating back to the famed Oxford Group, a cluster of intellectuals at the University of Oxford in the late 1960s and early 1970s who met to discuss the emerging concept of animal rights. Today it is known as the Oxford Centre for Animal Ethics, which 'believes that the rational case for animals is frequently understated within academia and misrepresented in the media'. The Centre's aim is to create a worldwide association of academics from all disciplines who want to pioneer ethical perspectives on animals (www.oxfordanimalethics.com/about-the-centre/welcome/), which ineludibly draws from and extends spiritual belief systems and world religions.

While not altogether absent from the profession of social work, religion and spirituality are similar to HAS, at least in *practical terms*, in being peripheral to the profession of social work. This is the case regarding the education of social workers and practice,[7] wherein spiritually sensitive work is left up to the inclination of individual practitioners, agencies and faculty members. The realm of the spiritual is generally not professionally viewed as a critical dimension of life, additional and complementary to the physiological, psychological and social spheres of a person's development, which make up the scope of professional practice. With that said, however, following an extended period of secularization within the profession, the topic of spirituality and social work has enjoyed renewed interest in North America and the United Kingdom from approximately the mid-1980s onwards (Graham, Coholic and Groen, 2012; Crisp, 2010; Holloway and Moss, 2010; Canda, 2008; Graham et al., 2007; Bethel, 2004; Cascio, 1998; Jacobs, 1997; Sheridan, 2004). Indeed, Jacobs (1997) argued almost 20 years ago that there are 'growing societal and professional trends toward bringing spirituality out of the closet and into both social and academic discourse and clinical practice settings' (p. 172). Proponents of an expanded biopsychosocial-spiritual scope of practice in social work argue that as we adopt more holistic and anti-oppressive models of practice, we can no longer ignore the spiritual dimensions, the heart of a person's sense making (Canda, 1988). According to Clay Graybeal:

> Most persons see themselves as a complex constellation of qualities, with many dimensions, some known, and some not. All humans are influenced by and exist within at least four major dimensions, biological, psychological, social, and spiritual. Most theories of practice, even in social work, emphasize the first two dimensions, and traditional assessment practices, especially the DSM, give little or no credence to the latter two. Interestingly enough, *it is in the social and spiritual dimensions that the substance of persons' lives is played out. That is where meaning is constructed and relationships developed.* (Graybeal, 2001, pp. 235–36, italics mine)

Thus when HAI and HAB form the basis of one's spirituality as a way of life that is brought to bear on her work as a social work educator, and applied as an additional lens through which she envisions social work theory, policy, research, scholarship and practice, recognition of such by way of inclusion in an anthology on diverse expressions of spirituality and the ways in which these have been integrated into professional practice, can be seen as twofold: first, as a manifestation of the growing interest in both spirituality and people's relationships to other animals and the environment in mainstream culture, and second, as an indication of an expanding openness towards diverse forms of spiritual expression within the health professions due to increasing identification of the intensifying diversification among service users, many for whom religion and/or spirituality is a central organizing life feature.

Still, some readers may ask what do animals other than human have to do with social work? With spirituality? And even more to the point, with both? This chapter serves as an introductory discussion to these questions. The first half explores key social work research within the field of human–animal studies (HAS) that emphasizes the theme of interconnectedness, through which, it is argued, the inclusion of other animals and the natural world within social work's mandate would fulfil its greater moral potential. I begin with this because of the moral questions such literature opens up, and think that it provides a solid theoretical background for the reader. It also offers interconnectedness as a spiritual principle for practice. The latter half of the chapter introduces a vision of harmonized well-being and service for the health professions that surpasses disciplinary boundaries and those of the human ego: a spiritual vision that is truly inclusive of *all* beings, not only the human being.

Human–animal studies: raising the moral bar in social work

There is an astonishing absence of consideration for non-human animals in mainstream or institutionally supported social work (especially in Canada) compared to other academic disciplines, notwithstanding a developing core of individual scholars and practitioners who raise the issue of treatment of other animals as a priority value. This gap is all the more surprising given that human–animal interactions (HAI) and human–animal bonds (HAB) inform the fastest growing academic field today, known variously as human–animal studies (HAS) and as critical animal studies (CAS) (DeMello, 2010; Shapiro and DeMello, 2010; Shapiro, 2008; Flynn, 2008; Shapiro and Church, 2000; Marvin, n.d.). HAS draws from virtually all of the academic disciplines, including the natural, health and social sciences;

the humanities; and some professions including public policy and law. As a multidisciplinary endeavour,

> HAS is the only field that directly investigates relationships between human and nonhuman animals and their environment. The forms of bonds, attachments, interactions, and communications under investigation are impressively variable because of (1) the number of species of nonhuman animals, (2) the ingenious (and often exploitative) ways that humans have used other animals, and (3) the ways that humans view other animals. These latter views also have played a critical role in the complex and often contradictory ways that we compare ourselves to them. (Shapiro, 2008, p. 1)

Even though social work is a profession directed towards people and human society, given the paramount emphasis today in structural and anti-oppressive social work on relationship, context, the *places in between* or liminal spaces, and intersectionality, these approaches are remiss in not taking up the relational significance of the animal. In one form or another, non-human life, in realistic or symbolic, practical or theoretical, contemporaneous or historical, individual or collective terms, occupies a role for virtually all. As Shapiro contends,

> [t]hat, at present, HAS defines itself exclusively by its subject matter distinguishes it from many other fields that are 'disciplines' in the sense that they *constrain* research [and practice] to certain *rules* of procedure or methods. That situation may change as HAS scholars modify existing methods from various other fields to encompass the animal side of such relationships and/or develop unique methods for the study of human-animal relationships. (Shapiro, 2008, p. 3, italics mine)

An early challenge to social work's basic 'rules' with HAS information was David Wolf's (2000) groundbreaking commentary published 15 years ago in the American journal *Social Work,* boldly though aptly called *Social Work and Speciesism.*[8] Pointing out the conspicuous absence of speciesism – that is, the discrimination on the basis of species membership – in discussions related to social work, Wolf argued that because attention to marginalized groups is a 'defining feature of the social work profession, we must consider what groups we are not serving' (p. 88). In an unprecedented move, Wolf further argued that because the appreciation and respect for the inherent dignity of all persons is a core social work value (National Association of Social Workers [NASW]; Canadian Association of Social Workers [CASW]), 'it is worth deliberating over whether our treatment of other species, in places such as slaughterhouses [among many others], is associated with our own sense of dignity and self-respect' (p. 88).

Wolf's brief overview of such themes as speciesism, the environment and oppressed populations; slavery, feminism and speciesism; ethics; speciesism and the impact of violence on mental health; and the extensive coverage of speciesism in other academic fields including psychology, sociology, law, philosophy and ethics, to name only a few, makes a powerful case for why animals and animal welfare are relevant to humans, our health and welfare, and thus matter to social work. 'Surely,' writes Wolf, although 'as an expression of personal values some social workers are vegetarians, work against animal experimentation, or participate in other aspects of the animal rights movement […] this article recommends that the issue of speciesism should be incorporated as a basic element of the profession' (p. 90). That is to say, speciesism should be regarded as a *structural oppression* as are, for instance, racism, sexism and ableism – as another form of discrimination and basis of exploitation.[9] The question of speciesism in institutionally based practice and in core curriculum of accredited education programs, however, has been ignored since Wolf's clarion call for an expanded moral and ethical orientation.

Writing a decade after Wolf, social work educator and practitioner Risley-Curtiss also takes up HAS's core theme of *relationship* and submits three pragmatic reasons why animals matter to social work:

Companion animals should be integrated into social work research, education, and practice because of their *interconnectedness* with humans. This inter-relatedness plays out in three ways that are essential for the social work profession and include: (1) Companion animals are usually considered to be family members and, thus, part of family systems; (2) animal cruelty by children or adults is a deviant behavior that is commonly correlated with a dysfunctional home life, indicating a need for mental health services, and is related to many forms of human oppression (for example, violence against women and children); and (3) companion animals can have a therapeutic impact on the functioning of people of all ages. (Risely-Curtiss, 2010, p. 39, italics mine)

By focusing on the ubiquity of non-human animals in Western society and on the multiple forms of interconnectedness with humans, including both negative and positive, Risley-Curtiss emphasizes the *benefits* of including HAB and HAI in social work. Because interconnectedness is a key underlying concept in social work theory and practice from structural and ecosystems perspectives, this strategic approach is perhaps more amenable to the task of introducing animals in social work and to challenging the profession's dominant anti-oppressive and structural approaches that are, while responsive to diversity, nonetheless closely bound within a humanist paradigm. As Risley-Curtiss also argues:

> Given the ever-growing body of evidence supporting the importance of human–other animal relationships in early identification of potential problems and regarding the potential for companion animals to help individuals and families build resiliency, it is incumbent on the social work profession to join other professions and disciplines in efforts to delve into, and build on this bond. If social work practice is to be truly anti-oppressive and ecologically grounded (which requires one to see humans in the context of their environments and as constantly in reciprocal interaction with significant others), then the inclusion of the HCAB [human–companion animal bond] is essential. (Risely-Curtiss, 2010, p. 44)

Indeed, the concept of interconnectedness is generally used as an analytical tool and/or theoretical framework in contemporary critical discourse as a means to identify, investigate and/or articulate issues and experiences of diversity, oppression and privilege. However, in the next section of this chapter, I introduce the notion of interconnectedness as an underutilized *spiritual principle* in social work that would assist in broadening the circle of compassion regarding consideration of oppressed groups (Faver, 2011). Although Risley-Curtiss argues for an extended scope of practice by including and building on HAB to assist the profession to 'maximize its potential' in its core mission to help people 'enhance their well-being' (p. 45), Thomas Ryan's substantive revision (2011) of the Australian Association of Social Work's *Code of Ethics* (1999) (and by implication all contemporaneous codes) advances a moral imperative for the inclusion of individuals other than humans, and the natural world. In an examination of several scenarios taken from casework experience where animal cruelty was present in conjunction with other forms of human violence directed towards people, social workers did not know what to do or even how to think about those situations; thus in all cases abandoning the non-human animals in need is what Ryan calls a 'moral paralysis':

> What is often missed in the linkage between violence to animals and violence to human beings is the fact that a fellow sentient creature has been *directly* harmed; violence towards or neglect of animals is conceptualized *indirectly* (befitting their status as *things*), whilst violence towards or neglect of, human beings, is conceived *directly* (befitting their status as *persons*). (Ryan, 2011, p. 154, italics in original)

The 'species-inclusive code' (Ryan, 2011, p. 153) subverts the dominant worldview's dualistic conception of people as subjects and other animals as objects by 'acknowledg[ing] our terrestriality and our ontological continuity and kinship, and the moral and ethical implications that issue from such recognition' (Ryan, 2011, p. 151). If adopted, the revised code would provide workers with the moral and behavioural framework to attend to all animals, human and other than human, within practice responses, preparing them with a just index of non-exclusive values as well as written or concrete behavioural guidelines. Moreover, in enlarging the definition of *who* is a client, to encompass all sentient creatures, human and other-than-human individuals, as well as the natural world, a revised code would also facilitate grounded inter-professional cross training and reporting with animal welfare and environmental agencies.[10]

To some, a 'species-inclusive code' may seem a radical move, and indeed it is, insofar as 'radical' signifies a departure from present convention. Still others may view such a code akin to certain media portrayals of the animal rights movement; as sentimental, anti-intellectual, or worse, antihuman (Linzey, 2008), indubitably with no place in professional social work or any human services paradigm. However, we are reminded by Reverend Professor Dr. Andrew Linzey, current Director of the Oxford Centre for Animal Ethics, that the origin of the modern animal rights movement is in the nineteenth-century humanitarian movement that was 'concerned with improving living conditions for various oppressed subjects, children, as well as animals' (2008, p. 110). We are also reminded by Watkins (1990) how the early animal welfare movement in North America inspired and supported the development of early child protection agencies. Today, the common basis of animal rights theory is that 'protective rights are owed to all conscious or sentient beings, human or animals [... because] conscious/sentient beings are selves – that is, they have a distinctive subjective experience of their lives and of the world, which demands a specific kind of protection in the form of inviolable rights' (Donaldson and Kymlicka, 2011, p. 24).

These examples of bold scholarship further raise questions about the extent to which HAS has been institutionally accepted by universities and colleges (Shapiro, 2008, 2010), and I would add by extension, health institutions and social welfare agencies. Having created a critical intellectual infrastructure over the past two decades and more, it is helpful, suggests Shapiro (2008), to examine 'the prospects for and barriers to HAS playing a constructive role in changing the ways we as a society *choose* to relate to and treat nonhuman animals' (p. 3, italics mine). In the words of Froma Walsh (2009), clinical psychologist and Co-Director of the Chicago Center for Family Health, there is a 'curious disconnect' between the evidence of the positive mental health impacts of HAB and 'clinical training and research curricula' (p. 476). This is the critical difference between holding knowledge intellectually and knowing it experientially. Indeed, the lack of correspondence between the information produced by HAS and formal health professions' curricula and paradigms has been repeatedly noted by HAS scholars in the health disciplines.

For example, despite the ubiquity of companion animals in the lives of clients, Risley-Curtiss (2010) found in a national US study of 1600 social work practitioners, a significant lack of education and training regarding human–companion animal bonds (HCAB). Likewise, in Canada, a replicated provincial survey of social workers in Nova Scotia (Hanrahan, 2013) found similar results: a lack of knowledge and education, and thus lack of preparedness concerning HCAB, further resulting in a reduced potential to better serve clients. According to Ryan (2011), 'There is absolutely nothing in the curriculum or education of social workers that prepares them to be able to resolve the conflicts, or to negotiate their way through moral dilemmas' involving animal cruelty, 'for there is no linkage made between the maltreatment of human beings and other animals' (p. 154). In other words, the interconnections among humans, other animals and the natural world are not recognized, and thus, the 'connections in suffering'[11] are not easily discernable or far too easily ignored and/or justified.

Notably, not long after the emergence of HAS in the late 1980s, Wolf decried, '[A]s evidenced by its coverage in other academic and social fields, animal rights is clearly a social and moral issue, and its neglect in the social work profession is significant' (2000, p. 89). Such neglect is not surprising, however, when one considers 'the legacy of anthropocentrism that has dominated Western thinking and mental health paradigms' in particular (Walsh, 2009, p. 476). A long history of pervasive *othering* of animals – non-human *and* human, has indeed been the dominant ruse and means for defining and establishing a construction of a 'normative human' as an elevated being. HAS theorists seek to challenge this very construction by disrupting the abiding assumptions that underline the traditions that support, and the very conceptual frameworks that shape, our everyday ways of seeing and doing from the perspective of a normative human; as well as that which is conversely deemed, abnormal, but in this sense, that which is deviant and antisocial, often shunned to the undersides and outskirts of society, hidden from public view (e.g. dog fighting and animal hoarding). In this vein, HAS theorists variously challenge, unpack and seek to reinterpret the language, symbols, customs, histories and beliefs that define the myriad *interconnections* between human (humanity/subjects) and animal (animality/objects), society (community/persons) and nature (wilderness/resources) – first exposing them as false dichotomies, and second, as dyads highly contingent upon a hierarchical taxonomy and anthropocentric bias which has as a purpose the devaluation of the latter entity within the dyad.

The general absence of HAS in social work, except for a developing core of dedicated scholars and practitioners, is partially understandable when we consider how '[c]onventional health thinking and practice are grounded in the liberal individualism and humanism that distinguish the modernist worldview, which in turn privileges rationalism and positivist science over *other* ways of seeing the world' (Hanrahan, 2014, p. 34). To be sure, to recognize the interconnectedness or 'unity of all life' (Faver, 2011) – a spiritual principle as well as a scientific reality, argues Faver (2011, p. 114) – as a moral imperative requires humans to become accountable for *all* our actions regarding other animals, not merely those that are characterized by positive dynamics or that render our culpability in animal cruelty invisible or 'normative'. However, I have noted elsewhere that although there is a history of integrative thinking in both conventional and critical social work that can be traced to systems theory, anti-oppressive practice and, more recently, to intersectional theory, 'the consistent omission of other animals and the natural environment has limited not only earlier systems and later ecological thinking within the profession of social work, but critical anti-oppressive practice as well, to a *person-centred philosophy*' (Hanrahan, 2014, p. 42, [italics mine]).

This particular constriction severely limits the value base of social work, adversely rendering the profession's ethical sensibility, preventing social workers from seeing how the harmful actions of humans have far-reaching consequences for other species and for the universe as a whole. Indeed, such (re)vision, as Faver (2011) argues, would indeed require a 'willingness to seek information about the consequences of potential choices [personal and professional] and to draw a web of connections that includes our own role in the suffering of others, taking into account the likely impact of our behavior on future generations' (p. 122).

Regrettably, the interdisciplinarity of inter-professional education (IPE) (Pollard and Miers, 2008; Romanow, 2002), through which social work has recently begun to extend its knowledge base and scope of practice, is, to the best of this author's knowledge, limited to the human health professions and/or services.[12] Such exclusiveness constitutes ongoing evidence of *anthropocentrism* in what are otherwise progressive efforts to broaden, deepen, enrich client/patient welfare and services. Although beyond the scope of this chapter, an exception worth mentioning is the emerging One Health concept. As a global public health strategy, One Health takes inter-professional health practice to another level as a 'worldwide strategy for expanding interdisciplinary collaborations and communications in all aspects of health care for humans, animals and the environment'

(One Health Initiative, 2013). With a local conservation and global health perspective, I have suggested elsewhere that One Health has the potential to provide a promising template for a much-needed new social work paradigm, provided we are willing to examine hard ontological questions concerning *whose* health within the presumed holism of the concept's qualifier of *One* (Hanrahan, 2014). Significantly, however, social work is egregiously absent from that discourse as well. [13]

Other ways of *being* with other *beings*: trans-species spirituality

The foregoing discussion in light of the ever-expanding field of human–animal studies (HAS) introduced key contributions to social work regarding the absence of animals, highlighting significant limitations in mainstream social work theory and practice, including anti-oppressive and structural approaches. It has been suggested that an important outcome of that literature is that now some attention is given to other animals in terms of their impacts on human well-being (Faver, 2009). Indeed, there is more interest in such topics, including the links between animal cruelty and domestic violence (Arkow, 2003, 1997; Ascione, 2007a, 2007b, 2005; Flynn, 2000); animal-assisted therapies and other interventions (Chandler, 2012; Fine, 2015); and the multiple benefits of animal companionship across the life cycle, thus ostensibly widening the scope of practice. However, this interest is disparately located primarily within the purview of independent HAS research conducted within the scope of one's health profession and/or discipline. Moreover, it is largely ideas-led and except for the popular animal visitation programs, which are conducted outside the scope of established health professions and volunteer driven, still very much on the periphery of public and institutionally based practice.

Concerning the challenges put forth by HAS to the ontological limits of academic disciplines and professions by exposing the human privilege and exceptionalism that infuses them, significantly less attention is given in social work to extending moral consideration (and corresponding actions) to other animals as sentient subjects in their own right. Typically any consideration extended at all to other animals and the natural world in social work is only acknowledged institutionally insofar as it can benefit people. Respect for the inherent dignity of *all* beings within expanded ethical and moral spheres is still lamentably outside the purview of mainstream social work.

In comparison to the benefits of HAB regarding human health and welfare issues, of which sceptics persistently demand quantitative evidence, the link between human spirituality, morality and ethics, *and* other animals, areas that are even more difficult to measure, generate little to no interest. Citing Manes (1997), author of *Other Creations: Rediscovering the Spirituality of Animals*, Faver (2009) writes that this exclusion persists in social work even though '[t]he spiritual significance of animals has been evident throughout history' (p. 363). Indeed, as Faver explains,

> All sacred texts and writings of spiritual leaders of diverse traditions reflect three common themes: (a) the existence of a "divine spark" within all life, (b) the natural world as a source of spiritual lessons, and (c) human responsibility to care for the natural environment, including nonhuman animals. (Faver, 2009. p. 363)

In this final section of the chapter, I introduce *trans-species spirituality* as a lens through which life is understood and experienced, and the implications of this for the social work profession that has by and large ignored non-human animals as well as the environments made and/or manipulated to contain or manage them. My use of the term 'trans-species spirituality' is closely based on the conceptual reasoning behind Dr. Gay Bradshaw's concept of *trans-species psychology*.[14] As Bradshaw explains, '*trans* re-embeds humans within the larger matrix of the animal kingdom by erasing the "and" between humans and animals that has been used to demarcate and reinforce the false notion that humans are substantively different cognitively and emotionally from other species' (Trans-species living: an interview with Gay Bradshaw). Together the terms 'trans' and 'species' designate a new paradigm for Western thinking, including the health professions, in which 'humanity is challenged to re-think almost every aspect of modern culture [...] charged with a re-creation of ethics and reasons and ways of knowledge-making that reflects our understanding that animals are fully sentient beings' (Bradshaw interview). Understood as representing a paradigm shift, Bradshaw purports that as society moves away from the Cartesian frame, 'Even science cannot continue as is because it is still driven by a social-political agenda that legitimizes animal exploitation. Animals remain objectified in the frame of conventional science. We are faced with rediscovery and reinventing human identity' (Bradshaw interview). There is no better place to rediscover and reinvent than the rich topography of spirituality where people strive to make meaning of life's events.

I do not, however, offer a model or formula for trans-species spirituality. Instead, at the time of this writing, trans-species spirituality is conceptualized as a *way of life* involving all aspects of living, including work. It is not something I do part of the time, or merely contemplate. According to American social work scholar and practitioner Edward Canda (1999), recognized for his prolific and trailblazing work regarding the role of religion and spirituality in human development and coping across the lifespan:

> All cultures have systematic ways of compassion, justice, and helping. Traditionally, these were based explicitly on spiritual ways of living. Most cultures do not have a separate word for religion or spirituality. Spirituality is just the way of life; it is the way people find meaning, moral guidance, and proper relationship between themselves, all our fellow *beings*, and the great Mystery that infuses all. (pp. 4–5, italics mine)

The implication of what a spirituality informed by trans-species awareness means for social work more specifically is premised upon the understanding that '[t]he welfare of nonhuman animals and the health of the natural environment are inextricably connected to the well-being of humans' (Faver, 2009, p. 374). Therefore, as Carolyn Faver contends, 'In order to fulfill our professional obligation to promote the welfare of society as well as individuals, social workers must attend to humans' relationships with nonhuman animals and the environment.'

Many people spontaneously feel an innate affinity or mystical connection with other animals and/or the natural world, which they interpret as a spiritual experience. Drawing on the work of Lasher, Faver refers to such experiences as one's 'animal path': 'Defining spiritual development as "a journey of widening and deepening connections," psychologist Margot Lasher (1996, p. 2) maintained that relationships with animals are one way to reach an "awareness of the essential connectedness of all things" (p. 2)' (Faver, 2009, p. 365). For people who have had little exposure to other animals and/or opportunities to experience the natural world, the links between animals and spirituality may seem tenuous, the circle of compassion smaller. Non-human animals are far from the yards and psyches of many because, as Bradshaw explains, 'Western civilization has really broken the backs of animal societies' (trans-species living), and many humans have grown accustomed, even oblivious, to the myriad contradictions characterizing hierarchical and anthropocentric animal taxonomies and our relationships with them. As such, humans who have experienced the sublimity of inspired interactions with other animals are often pathologized, seen to like and care for humans less because of their compassion for other animals, or deemed to be incapable of forming relationships with humans (Ryan, 2011; Serpell, 2008; Bekoff, 2007). Yet despite this, humans like Professor Mary Lou Randour, PhD in human development, and past Chair, Section on Human–Animal Interaction at Society of Counseling Psychology, American Psychological Association, explores the human–animal relationship as a path to enlightenment (Randour, 2000). Elsewhere I discuss my own experiences involving animals and place, referred to as 'environmental epiphanies', and although intrinsic to the growth of my consciousness and my professional development, these have, until my own recent public acknowledgement, been foregone within my advanced education, training and practice (Hanrahan, 2011). In her exploration of the animal paths of social workers, Faver (2009) writes that

> [t]hrough their relationships with animals, they realized their connectedness to all life and subsequently used their professional skills to benefit the larger community of humans and animals. In like manner, clients' relationships with animals may contribute to their spiritual development; thus, social workers can support clients' spiritual development by recognizing and validating the reality of 'the animal path'. (p. 366)

Insofar as theologian Andrew Linzey resolves in his research regarding what the world's major religions say about other than human animals, that 'animal rights philosophy appears to have no obvious religious tradition to which it can appeal and in which it feels unambiguously at home' (2008, p. 111), it shares with 'almost all religious traditions the notion of *empathy* or *compassion* for those who suffer' (p. 113). Notably, the US-based Religious Proclamation for Animal Compassion, which decrees kindness to animals as a key spiritual value, was signed by faith leaders of all major denominations (Best Friends Animal Sanctuary, 2007). And I suggest, just as the realization of interconnectedness is at the heart of compassion, so too is compassion the soul of social work (Canda, 1999). Indeed, compassion in social work is sustained in the profession's foremost ethical standard or moral imperative of *Primum non Nocere*, or 'Do no harm' (CASW; NASW). According to Canda (1999):

> Ways of compassion existed long before professional helping. Spiritually inspired compassion is the source of all genuine helping, whether informal or professional. Social work, medicine, the ministries, and other helping professions do not have a monopoly on helping, though often they try to legislate it, control it, license it, package it, and sell it. (p. 6)

Trans-species spirituality in social work inspires workers to have compassion for all animals, human and non-human, *and* to do no harm to others within the web of life. These tuitions are at once organic and political. They compel one to believe or, one might say, to have faith in social work's core values and principles of respect, justice and service, and at the same time to have the wisdom and strength to renounce the human privilege that characterizes them within the profession's code of ethics (CASW,

Code of Ethics, values 1–3, 2005). The anthropocentric qualifications of 'inherent dignity and worth of *persons*' for the value of respect, of 'social' for the value of justice and of 'humanity' for service involve a power dynamic that limits the value base of the professions' code of ethics to humans and human society. This speciesist dynamic used to privilege humans over non-human animals has deep roots in the professions' historical paternalism that has informed the dividing practice of separating out *deserving and non-deserving* humans on the basis of class, race, gender and abilities for example. Rather than an either–or situation, wherein helping humans precludes helping other animals, or vice versa, trans-species spirituality is a spiritually inspired compassion for *all* species. It is a compassion that stems from both our life-affirming interconnectedness, and the realities of the interlocking oppressions of speciesism, racism and sexism caused by industrialization, imperialism and colonialism.

Conclusion

A discussion about social work and trans-species spirituality inevitably raises questions about animal rights. It is, however, far beyond the scope of this chapter to address such questions adequately, especially due to the complexity of the issues and the multidisciplinarity of the debates comprising animal rights theory (ART). As summarized by Donaldson and Kymlicka (2011) in their groundbreaking political theory of animal rights, suffice to say:

> The assumption of most mainstream contemporary Western political theory is that the community of justice is coextensive with the community of human beings. Basic justice and inviolable rights are owed to all humans by virtue of their humanity, and should be blind to intra-human differences such as race, gender, creed, ability, or sexual orientation. Against this mainstream background, ART poses the question: why just humans? The universalizing impulse to human rights is to extend basic protections across boundaries of physical, mental, and cultural difference, so why should this impulse stop at the boundary of the human species? (p. 24)

Authors of *Zoopolis* (2011), Donaldson and Kymlicka, offer an innovative relational model of *citizenship* as a new moral framework for addressing the current system of animal exploitation in which relationships between and among humans and other animals are conceived beyond the scope of negative rights to encompass positive rights and benefits. Their conception of 'a world of human-animal relationships that takes seriously the idea that animals and humans can co-exist, interact, and even cooperate on the basis of justice and equality' (p. 24) is in essence trans-species spirituality expressed in political terms. It imagines pragmatically ways of being with other beings in which non-human animals are seen 'not solely as vulnerable and suffering individuals but also as neighbours, friends, co-citizens, and members of communities ours and theirs' (p. 24). For social workers concerned with strengthening the welfare and well-being of marginalized and oppressed groups of people, a trans-species spirituality supports applications in social work of human–animal bonds and other types of interactions, especially regarding vulnerable populations, that are just beginning to be recognized.

References

Arkow, P., 1997. The relationships between animal abuse and other forms of family violence. *Protecting Children*, 13(2), pp. 4–9.

Arkow, P., 2003. Breaking the cycles of violence: a guide to multi-disciplinary interventions: a handbook for child protection, domestic violence and animal protection agencies. Alameda: Latham Foundation.

Ascione, F. R., 2005. Children, animal abuse and family violence – the multiple intersections of animal abuse, child victimization, and domestic violence. In K. A. Kendall-Tackett and S. M. Giacomoni, eds., *Child victimization: maltreatment, bullying and dating violence: prevention and intervention*. Kingston: Civic Research Institute. Ch. 3.

Ascione, F. R., 2007a. Emerging research on animal abuse as a risk factor for intimate partner violence. In K. Kendall-Tackett and S. Giacomoni, eds., *Intimate partner violence*. Kingston: Civic Research Institute. Ch.3.

Ascione, F. R., 2007b. Men in prison who abused animals and who abused their wives and girlfriends: voices of perpetrators. 11th International Conference on Human–Animal Interactions, People and Animals: Partnership in Harmony, International Association of Human–Animal Interaction Organizations (IAHAIO). Tokyo, Japan, 5–8 October.

Bekoff, M., 2007. *The emotional lives of animals*. Novato: New World Library.

Best Friends Animal Society, 2007. *A religious proclamation for animal compassion*. Available at: http://onevoiceministry.com/Docs/AAR_PROC_HORIZ_FINAL_COLOR%20htm.pdf. [Accessed 4 December 2015.]

Bethel, J. C., 2004. Impact of social work spirituality courses on student attitudes, values, and spiritual wellness. *Journal of Religion & Spirituality in Social Work: Social Thought*, 23(4,) pp. 27–45.

Canda, E. R., 1988. Spirituality, religious diversity, and social work practice. *Social Casework*, 69(4), pp. 238–247.

Canda, E. R., 1999. Spiritually sensitive social work: key concepts and ideals. *Journal of Social Work Theory and Practice*, 1(1), pp. 1–32.

Canda, E. R., 2008. Spiritual connection in social work: boundary violations and transcendence. *Journal of Religion and Spirituality in Social Work: Social Thought*, 27(1–2), pp. 25–40.

Cascio, T., 1998. Incorporating spirituality into social work practice: a review of what to do. *Families in Society: The Journal of Contemporary Human Services*, 79(5), pp. 523–531.

Chandler, C., 2012. *Animal assisted therapy in counseling.* New York, NY: Routledge.

Crisp, B. R., 2010. *Social work and spirituality.* Surrey: Ashgate Publishing.

DeMello, M., ed., 2010. *Teaching the animal: human animal studies across the disciplines.* Brooklyn: Lantern Books.

Donaldson, S., and Kymlicka, W., 2011. *Zoopolis: a political theory of animal rights.* New York: Oxford University Press.

Faver, C., 2009. Seeking our place in the web of life: animals and human spirituality. *Journal of Religion & Spirituality in Social Work: Social Thought*, 28, pp. 362–378.

Faver, C., 2011. Seeing ourselves in all: a spiritual perspective on the unity of life. *Journal of Religion & Spirituality in Social Work: Social Thought*, 30(2), pp. 113–124.

Flynn, C. P., 2000. Why family professionals can no longer ignore violence toward animals. *Family Relations*, 49, pp. 87–95.

Flynn, C. P., 2008. Social creatures: an introduction. In C. P. Flynn, ed., *Social creatures: a human and animal studies reader.* Brooklyn: Lantern Books. Ch: Introduction.

Graham, J., Coates, J., Swartzentruber, B., and Ouellette, B., 2007. *Spirituality and social work: select Canadian readings.* Toronto: Canadian Scholars' Press.

Graham, J., Coholic, D., and Groen, J., 2012. *Spirituality in social work and education: theory, practice, and pedagogies.* Waterloo: Wilfred Laurier University Press.

Graybeal, C., 2001. Strengths-based social work assessment: transforming the dominant paradigm. *Families in Society: The Journal of Contemporary Human Services*, 82(3), pp. 233–242.

Hanrahan, C., 2011. Challenging anthropocentrism in social work through ethics and spirituality: lessons from studies in human–animal bonds. *Journal of Religion and Spirituality in Social Work: Social Thought, Special Edition*, 30(3), pp. 272–293.

Hanrahan, C., 2013. Social work and human animal bonds and benefits in health research: a provincial study. *Critical Social Work*, (14)1, 63–79. Available at: www1.uwindsor.ca/criticalsocialwork/SWhumananimalbonds. [Accessed 22 March 2016.]

Hanrahan, C., 2014. Integrative health thinking and the new *One Health* concept: All for 'one' or 'one' for all? In T. Ryan, ed., *Animals in social work: why and how they matter.* Basingstoke: Palgrave Macmillan. Ch. 3.

Holloway, M., and Moss, B., 2010. *Social work and spirituality.* Palgrave Macmillan: London, England.

Jacobs, C., 1997. On spirituality and social work. *Smith College Studies in Social Work*, 67(2), pp. 171–175.

Linzey, A., 2008. Animal rights as religious vision. In C. P. Flynn, ed., *Social creatures: a human and animal studies reader.* Brooklyn: Lantern Books. Part IV, Ch. 11.

Long, D., Long, J., and Kulkarni, S., 2007. Interpersonal violence and animals: mandated cross-sector reporting. *Journal of Sociology & Social Welfare*, 34(3), pp. 147–163.

Manes, C., 1997. *Other creations: rediscovering the spirituality of animals.* New York: Doubleday.

Marvin, J., n.d. The growing field of animal studies. *The Washington Post.* Available at: www.washingtonpost.com/lifestyle/magazine/the-growing-field-of-animal-studies/2012/04/10/gIQA9AvjCT_gallery.html. [Accessed 17 December 2015.]

Noske, B., 2008. Speciesism, anthropocentrism, and non-western cultures. In C. P. Flynn, ed., *Social creatures: a human and animal studies reader.* Brooklyn: Lantern Books. Part III, Ch. 7.

One Health Initiative, 2013. *About one health.* Available at: www.onehealthinitiative. com/about.php. [Accessed 16 November 2015.]

Pollard, K., and Miers, M., 2008. From students to professionals: results of a longitudinal study of attitudes to prequalifying collaborative learning and working in health and social care in the United Kingdom. *Journal of Interprofessional Care,* 22(4), pp. 399–416.

Randour, M. L., 2000. *Animal grace: entering a spiritual relationship with our fellow creatures.* Novato: New World Library.

Serpell, J. A., 2006. Animal-assisted interventions in historical perspective. In A. Fine, ed., *Handbook on animal-assisted therapy,* 2nd edn. San Diego: Academic Press, Part 1, Ch. 2.

Serpell , J. A., 2008. *In the company of animals: a study of human–animal relationships.* Cambridge: Cambridge University Press.

Shapiro, K., and DcMcllo, M., 2010. The state of human–animal studies. *Animals & Society Journal,* 18(3), pp. 1–16.

Shapiro, K., 2008. Human–animal studies: growing the field, applying the field. *Animals and Society Institute Policy Papers series.* Ann Arbor: Animals and Society Institute, pp. 1–14.

Shapiro, K., and Church, H., 2000. *It's academic: the growing field of animal studies.* April 15. Available at: www.animalsagenda.org/animal_studies.htm. [Accessed 26 November 2015.]

Shapiro, K., and DeMello, M., 2010. The state of human–animal studies. *Animals & Society Journal,* 18(3), pp. 1–16.

Sheridan, M., 2004. Predicting the use of spiritually-derived interventions in social work practice: a survey of practitioners. *Journal of Religion and Spirituality in Social Work,* 23(4), pp. 5–25.

Trans-species living: an interview with Gay Bradshaw, 17 September 2010. *Animal Visions.* Available at: https://animalvisions.wordpress.com/2010/09/17/trans-species-living-an-interview-with-gay-bradshaw/. [Accessed 15 December 2015.]

Walsh, F., 2009. Human–animal bonds: the relational significance of companion animals. *Family Process,* 48(4), pp. 462–480.

Watkins, S. A., 1990. The Mary Ellen myth: correcting child welfare history. *Social Work,* 35(6), pp. 500–503.

Witkin, S. L., 1998. Chronicity and invisibility [editorial]. *Social Work,* 43, pp. 293–295.

Wolf, D., 2000. Social work and speciesism. *Social Work,* 45(1), pp. 88–93.

Zilney, L. A., and Ziley, M., 2005. Reunification of child and animal welfare agencies: Cross-reporting of abuse in Wellington County, Ontario, Canada. *Child Welfare,* 84, pp. 47–66.

Notes

1 For an in-depth discussion of how my professional self and ethics within the context of social work practice and education have been shaped by what are termed 'environmental epiphanies and revelations' in my personal life, see Hanrahan (2011).

2 'Other species' refers to the companion animals, dogs and cats with whom I interact on a regular basis, as well as all other animals, including wildlife, those born into animal agribusiness and those used in experimentation who are daily impacted by my choices, actions and inaction regarding the foods, products and services I purchase, consume and endorse.

3 I use the terms 'other animals', 'non-human animals' and 'animals other than human' interchangeably throughout. Although this phrasing may at first appear cumbersome to readers unaccustomed to this language, it is important that the language used accurately reflects the reality that humans are animals too.

4 Growing popular interest reflects greater attention to and conversation in mainstream media about other animals and the environment. Topics include factory farming, climate change, environmental degradation and resource development versus environmental conservation, and species at risk, to name a few.

5 Within the discipline of social work, see Institute for Human–Animal Connection (IHAC), Graduate School of Social Work, University of Denver; and, the Veterinarian Social Work Program (VSW), Graduate School of Social Work, University of Tennessee in Knoxville, TN, which 'is an area of social work practice that attends to the human needs that arise in the intersection of veterinary medicine and social work practice' (in 'About Us, What is Veterinary Social Work?').

6 See, for example, *Animals & Society Institute*, 'the leader in translating research on human–animal interaction into practice, providing essential knowledge and tools, and promoting evidence-based approaches that get results' (www. animalsandsociety.org/about-asi/); Human–Animal Bond Research Initiative Foundation (HABRI), 'a non-profit research and education organization that is gathering, funding and sharing the scientific research that demonstrates the positive health impacts of animals on people' (www.habri.org); and the section on Human–Animal Interaction: Research & Practice, of Division 17 (Society of Counseling Psychology) of the American Psychological Association, dedicated to 'the role of the [HAB] in empathy development, the ability to form and express attachments, reaction to grief and loss, the challenges of aging, and other developmental passages throughout the lifespan; the ways in which human interaction with animals promotes health; the role of animal-assisted therapies in prevention and intervention programs in a variety of settings; violence prevention as it relates to the link between animal abuse and family, juvenile, and community violence; and training programs on topics such as pet grief counseling, assessment and treatment of animal abuse, as well as counseling programs to address the needs of veterinary students, animal shelter volunteers, and animal rescue workers' (www. div17.org/sections/human-animal-interaction/).

7   The Canadian Association for Social Work Education (CASWE) outlines the program content for curriculum in the standards for accreditation. Comparable American standards are listed with the Council on Social Work Education (CSWE).

8   The term 'speciesism' was coined by British clinical psychologist and animal rights activist Richard D. Ryder, who was an original member of the Oxford Group, in *Speciesism* (1970). For a concise introduction and overview of Ryder's legacy to animal welfare, see Tom Regan, 'The More Things Change', *Between the Species*, Spring 1991. Peter Singer, an Australian moral philosopher, popularized the term in *Animal Liberation* (1975), the foundational text of the animal liberation movement. For views on speciesism and anthropocentrism in non-Western cultures, see Noske (2008) and Serpell (2006; 2008).

9   For groundbreaking research on the links between speciesism and racism and sexism, respectively, as interconnected oppressions, see Marjorie Spiegel's book *The Dreaded Comparison: Human and Animal Slavery* (1996) [1988] and Carol Adam's book *The Sexual Politics of Meat* (1990).

10 For two excellent discussions on cross training and reporting between human and animal health and welfare agencies, see Long, Long and Kulkarni (2007) and Zilney and Ziley (2005).

11 Faver's (2011) phrase the 'connections in suffering' captures how 'one implication of interconnectedness is that harm inflicted on any part of life results in suffering for all' (p. 114).

12 According to the UK-based Centre for the Advancement of Interprofessional Education (CAIPE), an independent 'think tank', 'Interprofessional education occurs when two or more professions learn with, from and about each other to improve collaboration and the quality of care' (2002). See CAIPE website, 'Defining IPE', http://caipe.org.uk/about-us/defining-ipe/.

13 For a critical discussion of integrative health thinking in social work, and in particular within the larger context of One Health, see Hanrahan (2014).

14 See G. A. Bradshaw (2009) *Elephants on the Edge: What Animals Teach Us about Humanity* (New Haven: Yale University Press).

SECTION

III

Eastern Influences in
Spiritual Practices

7 A Cultivation Journey with the Falun Gong

Maria Cheung

I emigrated from Hong Kong to Canada in 1992. I submitted my application to the Canadian embassy the day after the 4 June 1989 massacre in Beijing which crushed the student democratic movement. Tanks moved into Beijing, rolling towards Tiananmen Square, where students had peacefully gathered for seven weeks, merely to ask for a more open and non-corrupt government. My family and I decided to give up a comfortable middle-class life in Hong Kong and ventured into an immigrant life in Canada. As resonated by many immigrants, there is much to learn but also to give up by moving to a new country. In my search to reconnect to my Chinese cultural roots in the Diaspora, I learned about Falun Dafa (commonly known as Falun Gong) at a time when the persecution against this meditative practice had just been launched in 1999.

Falun Gong is a body-mind-spiritual practice which upholds the principles of truthfulness, compassion and tolerance (in Chinese, *zhēn* 真, *shàn* 善 and *rěn* 忍). *Falun Gong* (translated as 'Practice of the Law Wheel') is also known as *Falun Dafa* (translated as 'Great Way of the Law Wheel'). The practice can be traced back to the Buddhist and Daoist philosophies in the Chinese tradition (see Falun Dafa Information Center: www.faluninfo. net/). Falun Gong practitioners practise a self-cultivation based on the moral teachings of *zhēn*, *shàn* and *rěn* to search their paths in order to 'return to their original, true selves' as 'human beings are actually lost in a maze' (Li, 2000, p. 5). Through a process of giving up human attachments such as greed, self-interest, jealousy, hatred, anger and so on, Falun Gong practitioners acquire a state of insight and spiritual transcendence to a purer realm (Li, 2000). The cultivation process also involves the cultivation of the body, which includes five sets of gentle exercises that consist of four standing exercises and a sitting meditation. By engaging in a mindful meditative practice, the body experiences transformation in parallel with the cultivation of the mind and heart in acquiring virtues or moral behaviours.

In this chapter, I reflect on my personal spiritual journey, drawing upon my life path with Falun Gong and research experiences with Falun Gong practitioners in Canada. I explore how my personal experiences have broadened my understanding about life, and I draw on the resilience of Falun Gong practitioners that inspired my personal and professional life. I conclude with a critical reflection on the connection of Falun Gong experience to social work professional practice.

My spiritual journey with the Falun Gong: an integration of mind, body, emotion and spirit

I started with a rational mind in deciphering the diverse and nearly paradoxical discourses during the early days of the persecution of Falun Gong practitioners. For myself, as for many Western scholars, Falun Gong was unheard of before the launch of the persecution by the Chinese Communist Party in 1999. Living in the West, I am required to grapple with the narratives of the Falun Gong practitioners versus the official version from Mainland China under the control of the Communist regime. James Tong (2009) captures aptly the official Chinese documentation and that of the Falun Gong communities as being nearly opposite each other. As with the Tiananmen Square massacre, the Chinese regime denied the killing of Falun Gong practitioners, whereas the Falun Gong communities documented thick descriptions of the killings and first-person witness stories by victims of the persecution on the Clearwisdom website (http://en.minghui.org).

As I investigate the reasons for the persecution of the Falun Gong, I find it is beyond what someone in a democratic country could think of as being possible, but makes perfect sense in a totalitarian regime. The popularity of the Falun Gong, widely represented by practitioners' inner search for spiritual meaning, was perceived as an ideological competition and loss of control by the Chinese Communist Party (CCP) leader despite the innate fact that Falun Gong teaches looking inside versus becoming involved in outside politics. With the decision of a few top party leaders at the time, Falun Gong, together with a few other qigong practices, was banned. The order to persecute Falun Gong was neither constitutional nor under the country's legal establishment. The CCP leader, then-President Jiang Zemin, personally ordered a persecution and launched a systematic campaign with the aim of eradicating the Falun Gong through extensive defamatory hate propaganda, mass imprisonment, torture and the more horrific organ harvesting of Falun Gong practitioners.

In my search for the truth of what has happened and why a widespread persecution was launched by the Chinese communist regime against a peaceful meditative group, I embarked on the practice of Falun Gong. I find healing for ailments in my body which were a result of the pressures from immigration, coping with my doctoral study, raising two young children and the family's disorientation in a new culture. After a few months of practising Falun Gong, I felt the lightness of my body without needing medication. My insomnia has gone since I started practice. I regained my energy level, which increases my work productivity. The practice of Falun Gong helps me to integrate my body, mind, emotion and spirit. I feel an emotional emancipation when I espouse the teachings of the Falun Gong and start ridding myself of many attachments, to temper, fame and wealth, for example. I attain a sense of inner peace to remain calm to ride through the few turbulent waves that are a result of the vicissitudes of an immigrant's life. Furthermore, the spiritual cultivation of Falun Gong enlightens me with a different angle to approach human rights issues, which is a core mission of my social work profession.

The context: an international human rights issue of the Falun Gong

'Genocide' is a loaded word. It is the worst form of large-scale violation of the most basic human rights regarding physical integrity (Rost, 2013). Rost articulates that 'authoritarian and in particular totalitarian and communist regimes are more likely to kill civilians – 'absolute power kills absolutely'. This is especially true for the killing of a country's own citizens [when political power is concentrated]' (p. 42). As I have been researching the persecution of Falun Gong over the last 16 years, it has become clear that it is an ongoing genocide, according to the definition by the United Nations Convention on the Prevention and Punishment of the Crime of Genocide (1948). The convention provides that genocide can be committed both in war and in peace times. The CCP, under the control of Jiang Zemin in the 1990s, targeted Falun Gong practitioners with an intention to destroy them. All arms of the party-state follow the policy of 'defame their reputations, bankrupt them financially and destroy them physically' to deal with the Falun Gong practitioners (Matas and Kilgour, 2009, p. 23). As a result, practitioners have been arbitrarily arrested and tortured when they refused to recant their belief. According to Ethan Gutmann's empirical research (2014) into the issue of forced organ harvesting, at least 65,000 Falun Gong practitioners in China have experienced the harvesting of their organs for economic profit by the China party-state, without their consent. Though other dissident groups like Uighurs, Tibetans and house Christians are also subjected to the forced organ pillaging, the Falun Gong prisoners of conscience have been particularly targeted, and they comprise the vast majority of victims of forced organ harvesting (Gutmann, 2014; Sharif et al., 2014). Readers are referred to my recent article (Cheung, 2016) for more detailed information on the reasons and extent of the persecution of Falun Gong.

China admits to performing about 10,000 transplants each year, which ranks them as second highest in the world (Sharif et al., 2014). Yet voluntary donation in China is abysmally low (Matas and Trey, 2012). Sharif and colleagues (2014) found that between 2003 and 2009, among the 1.3 billion population, there were only 130 freely donated organs in China. Matas and Kilgour (2009) also found that 41,500 organs transplanted in China from the same period were unaccounted for. Gutmann (2014) traced back the history of forced organ harvesting by the party-state of China to the Cultural Revolution, with executed prisoners such as Uighur dissidents, and found that live organ procurement from prisoners was in fact a 'routine procedure' (p. 228). The lucrative transplant business in China encourages organ transplant tourism in the globalized world, whereby desperate patients pay substantial amounts of money to go to China to receive a live 'donor' organ transplant within weeks; sometimes these are even prescheduled. From 1999 onwards, a large number of Falun Gong practitioners, being defined as 'enemies of the state', have been detained in all forms of confinement and imprisonment (Sharif et al., 2014; Gutmann, 2014). Because practitioners of Falun Gong are known to benefit from the health gains of their meditative practice, the Falun Gong group provides a ready healthy market for the state's exploitation (Matas and Kilgour, 2009). The evidence of forced organ harvesting is also linked to the Chinese bodies used for 'bodies exhibitions' (in particular, the *Bodies ... the Exhibition* that was popular in Western countries [Gutmann, 2014]).

When we practise a mindful meditation, we pause and take a deep breath to make sense of the vast amount of evidence that is available for us. What does this mean for a social work practitioner whose mission is to protect human rights and social justice? If society is built upon people living together, then killing people for their organs is undermining this foundation. What can we do to protect the good of a peaceful society from an evil disruption in the form of forced organ harvesting? When I worked in a social work project during the height of organ harvesting under the CCP in China and saw road signs leading to forced labour camps, imagine what came to my mind. Shall we learn from past human history to make a stand against the forced organ harvesting of innocent people? If we take a minute to feel how a Falun Gong practitioner would respond to such a human atrocity, what can we learn from it and what can be done?

Hate propaganda

Propaganda is always the number-one weapon in every genocide in history (Staub, 2011). It is used to eliminate public support for the victims by painting them as people who somehow deserve what is happening to them, thus allowing the persecution to continue. In order to gain international legitimacy, the Chinese regime denied the human rights violations by legitimizing their action via propaganda messages. It has been a common tactic of the CCP to take Falun Gong teachings out of context to discredit them in order to confuse the public's understanding of what Falun Gong is (Matas and Cheung, 2012). Falun Gong practitioners are being portrayed and objectified by the Communist-controlled media in derogative and demonized terms. The regime was successful in alienating the public from, and ensuring there was little or no support of, this outcast group. The hate incited by the Chinese propaganda was extended to countries outside China, such as Canada (Matas and Cheung, 2012). During the many years of being a Falun Gong practitioner, I have had to confront this propaganda almost on a daily basis. However, the spiritual practice helps me confront hate and marginalization not with anger, but in a compassionate manner which I learned from my research with Falun Gong practitioners in Canada.

The yin and yang of silence

Meditation brings us to a state of silence. A recent articulation of mindfulness is that it is an awareness of our inner self and a connection to our surroundings in a here-and-now manner. In the midst of ongoing persecution of the Falun Gong, the silence attained in meditation goes hand in hand with public protest to break the silence. They are the two sides of the coin in the peaceful resistance. Falun Gong practitioners launched 24-hour protests outside the Chinese consulates in major Canadian cities like Toronto, Vancouver, Montreal, and Calgary for ten years. All that practitioners did was sit in meditation, with banners at the backdrop to expose the persecution. Their silence conveys power: a peaceful force expressed in unison of silence to bring a stop to an ongoing persecution. It also brings a message to the perpetrators and the world that justice prevails; as well as to break the silence of the public majority.

In my research with Falun Gong practitioners in Diaspora Chinese communities in Canada, the respondents told me how important the breaking of silence is. When I interviewed a Falun Gong practitioner who had experienced torture in China due to his belief, he told me that he went on protest against the Chinese Communist regime not only because his family was being persecuted in China, but also because he wanted to promote the humanitarian value to all people. This is what he said:

We can't do nothing when we see Falun Gong practitioners in China are being sent to forced labour camps and some are tortured to death. We need to tell the truth to the international community to expose the violent act of the Chinese Communist Party and ask them to stop these brutal acts. It's not just to defend our rights, but also for rights of all humankind. When all people have a better human value, there'll be a better future.

He recalled that when the persecution first started in 1999, he was fully aware that practitioners who meditated with him were disappearing. He could not sit there and meditate without doing something within his reach to resist a brutal persecution. Speaking out against the ongoing oppression becomes an integral part of the identity of today's Falun Gong practitioners in living out the values and principles of justice. The teachings of compassion thus are not only limited to the Falun Gong practitioners themselves but expand and encompass society around them, expressed by the teachings' words about being considerate of others.

When we are in touch with our inner silence that is when we can tap into our inner awareness and resources, which forms the basis of empowerment. Kittel (2011) underscores the connection between one's inner self with the outer environment by linking the heart and the mind. On the other hand, Renita Wong articulates that contemplative practice is to 'bring different aspects of one's self into focus, restore wholeness, and awaken an appreciation of the interconnectedness of all life [...] and to turn the light of investigation inward' (Wong, 2013, p. 271).

I learn from the practice of Falun Gong that cultivation is about cultivating the self which comes from within. Meditation is about emptying the mind and achieving a state of no intention. Emptying the mind in a sitting meditation with silence, which grounds a person in composure, develops a deep connection with the self and surroundings. The spiritual practice of Falun Gong helps me to be in touch with my inner self and builds the bridge for my connection with the outer world through the practice of morality, as a human being and a social worker. In social justice and peace work, morality is a choice to make a stance between good and evil (Staub, 2011).

Peace within: looking inside by developing reflectivity and reflexivity

Authentic power is achieved by searching inward rather than looking outward. An outward search for power often results in dominance and oppression while an inward search of power empowers one's own strength and resilience. A central tenet of the Falun Gong teachings is to search within. Mr. Li Hongzhi, founder of Falun Gong, said in his classic book *Zhuan Falun*, 'In genuine cultivation practice one must cultivate one's own heart and inner self. One should search inside oneself rather than outside'

(Li, 2000, p. 358). Cultivation comes from one's heart. There is an ancient saying that 'the great Dao [way] has no formality' (Da Tao Wu Xian 大道无形). Mr. Li said in an earlier lecture that 'Dafa itself doesn't have a formality of any kind. We've taken a true "great way without form"'(Li, 1998). Falun Gong has no institutional hierarchy in any way comparable to that of any religion. During the years of my cultivation, I have followed my heart guided by the enlightenment I obtain from the teachings of Dafa.

I have confronted the hate propaganda against the Falun Gong for over 15 years since I began practising this meditative practice after the persecution had started. I have received unfriendly gazes from people that I know who have taken on the CCP's propaganda messages. I have had students from Mainland China, or other acquaintances influenced by the hate messages, who wanted to distance themselves from me after I raised the issue of the persecution of Falun Gong. I am not alone. In my research with Falun Gong practitioners, it has become clear that this gaze and marginalization have been nearly daily experiences for many Falun Gong practitioners in Diaspora Chinese communities. The disinformation exported from Mainland China has affected many Chinese people and therefore resulted in human rights violations as well as the marginalization and exclusion of this group in their respective communities. My research found that Falun Gong practitioners' experiences range from microaggression (Sue, 2010) to aggression. The microaggressive acts include intense gaze, having pictures taken without consent, being laughed at and about, and so on. The aggressive acts include practitioners being beaten up and spat upon in public. A number of severe discrimination cases have been brought before Canadian tribunals (Matas and Cheung, 2012).

What I have learned from Falun Gong practitioners is that they always use the principles of 'truth, compassion and tolerance' to deal with the aggressive and microaggressive acts, with dignity and integrity. The acts that violate the Canadian Charter of Human Rights, such as defamation and violent acts, have been brought to police attention, and some cases have proceeded to Canadian courts. For the microaggressive acts, practitioners usually have responded with a smile and have not fought back. The most powerful 'weapon' is to clarify the truth: let people know what has happened, what Falun Gong is, reasons for the persecution instigated by the CCP and so forth. These peaceful means have begun to bring about positive results in recent years. After many years of truth clarification, Falun Gong exhibition materials are no longer being torn apart. Many Chinese people in Chinatown respond with a smile and address female practitioners they meet often as 'Falun Gong sisters'. With the composure and integrity cultivated from the heart, a holistic approach to conflict resolution has begun to prove itself successful.

From a traditional Buddha teaching of the Falun Gong, cultivation is a constant strive for self-improvement. Falun Gong practitioners persistently look inside and are reflective of their daily behaviours in order to improve and elevate their *xinxing* (one's heart nature manifested in moral character) (Li, 2000, p. 28). The practitioners' compassionate acts are also accompanied by practitioners' daily mediation and readings on literature that guide their behaviours. The following poem is in my heart, and the meaning of cultivation helps me greatly to stay calm in interpersonal conflict situations. The constant self-reflection brings insight:

> Don't Argue
> Don't argue when people argue with you.
> Cultivation is looking within for the cause.
> Wanting to explain just feeds the attachment.
> Breadth of mind, unattached, brings true insight. (Li, 2005)

The inner search and cultivation has brought me great insight in life and taught me how to respond to challenging situations, no matter whether at the personal or structural levels. I reflect rather than react. I stay calm mostly and take a step back to reflect on why I have certain reactions and what I can respond to in a compassionate manner. I stay focused on doing critical structural analysis of the nature of the genocide issue. I previously suffered from insomnia in the earlier years of my professional life, particularly when working in the field of community development, where I witnessed a lot of injustices faced by new immigrants as a result of power imbalance in society. I took on vicarious trauma from the oppressed people with whom I worked. This resulted in debilitating my energy and passion so that I had to change jobs in order to preserve my mental health. Today, engaging in research on human atrocities such as the forced organ harvesting is heart-wrenching work. However, the practice of 'truth, compassion and tolerance' provides me with the time and space to contain frustration and challenges. I find it easier to see the subject issue as its own entity. I am less emotionally reactive to the nature of the issue than before. The inner strength gives me more vital energy to deal with the various demands in life and the challenges encountered in working with a difficult issue: an ongoing genocide which is not yet recognized by the public.

Compassion

In examining the frequency of the use of the word 'compassion' in social work literature, we find a higher rate of its use than two decades ago. A positive force behind this growth in its use and understanding is the revival of the discourse of spirituality in social work. The discussion of spirituality is much more present (Canda and Furman, 1999; Coates et al., 2007), and spirituality and religion are much more differentiated now, rather than being treated as interchangeable concepts.

In the practice of my spirituality, I search for the meaning of compassion from the teaching of Falun Gong to guide my practice of being compassionate. I find the following qualities:

1. Being selfless: In the teaching of 'What Is a Dafa Disciple? Fa Teaching Given at the 2011 New York Fa Conference', Mr. Li said, 'True compassion doesn't have any selfishness mixed in, and one will, when dealing with anyone, or sentient beings in general, look at things with righteous thoughts and loving kindness' (Li, 2011).
2. Compassion (shàn) is being unconditional: the act of compassion is for the sake of others and one does not expect return. After letting go of the endless quest to fight for one's advantages and goals, what remains is an inner peace that is self-satisfied and can give one's presence and personal affection without seeking returns. In his teaching at the Fa Teaching at the 2009 Washington, DC, International Fa Conference, Mr. Li said, 'True *shàn is what a cultivator attains in the process of cultivation and cultivating goodness [...]* It is offered unconditionally and has no thought of reward – it is fully for the sake of sentient beings. When this compassionate goodness emerges, its strength is without equal, and it will disintegrate any bad factors. The greater the compassion, the greater the power' (Li, 2009).

Compassion (shàn) is manifested through cultivation which flows from the heart. In the research I conducted with the Falun Gong community, practitioners stated they engage in truth-telling efforts because they believe that people who are convinced by the propaganda messages are also victims of an oppressive persecutory system and that they have the right to know about the truth of what happens. Out of their compassion, practitioners use various means to raise awareness to let people (in a Buddhist term, 'sentient beings') know about the unconstitutional treatment and killing of Falun Gong practitioners. What impressed me the most was the pure heart of Falun Gong practitioners who just wanted to save sentient beings – helping people to choose good rather than evil.

Like Eichmann, a perpetrator of the Holocaust under the Nazi regime portrayed by Arendt (1963) as 'simply doing his job' (p. 135), the medical professionals, many renowned professionals in the transplant field, most likely have no motivation to kill. However, their silence has made them complicit to a crime against humanity. In her book, *Eichmann in Jerusalem:*

A Report on the Banality of Evil, Hannah Arendt portrayed these perpetrators in the following manner:

> The trouble with Eichmann was precisely that so many were like him, and that the many were neither perverted nor sadistic, that they were, and still are, terribly and terrifyingly normal. From the viewpoint of our legal institutions and of our moral standards of judgment, this normality was much more terrifying than all the atrocities put together. (Arendt, 1963, p. 276)

Many medical professionals who have participated in the forced organ harvesting subscribe to the Communist regime, and willingly or unwillingly themselves commit this crime. In some ways, it is as if they are being held hostage by a totalitarian regime to extract organs from the unwilling victims for simple reasons of survival, such as personal and job security. A crime against humanity is a crime against all. Everyone needs to make a choice about where to stand in relation to good and evil. Practitioners forbear the humiliation and gaze of scepticism to help the silent majority to take a positive stance. They hold no grudges or hostility against those who participate in the persecution. The compassion I witness from Falun Gong practitioners is a sincere concern for others – those who have committed evil deeds and the silent majority – and not the practitioners themselves. They have used their own resources to call the transplant centres in China to talk to the doctors and nurses about the forced organ harvesting, and have asked them to save the captured live 'donors' in their hospitals. The virtue of being other-orientated and the selflessness cultivated in many Falun Gong practitioners' *shàn* is like a lotus flower, a flower which grows up from muddy water but turns to pureness. The endurance they have and the heart they give out to fellow Chinese, including the perpetrators and those who are mostly hostile to them, is not something anyone can do.

The majority of Falun Gong practitioners have come from Mainland China and have settled in Diaspora Chinese communities in Canada. Those who had been persecuted in China mostly came to Canada as refugees. They face multiple challenges adjusting to a new environment (Glick, 2010). In addition to the material loss due to downward career mobility, language barriers and the various challenges they face in the vicissitudes of life that many newcomers face, many Falun Gong newcomers have to face the additional marginalization and discrimination mostly by their own people, to some extent reliving the persecution they experienced in China. In an ongoing persecution that is happening in a country like China, the only way for affected victims to seek redress is by bringing the perpetrators to justice in foreign countries where there is an instrument of law to do so. The purity of heart cultivated in this form of spirituality to seek justice becomes a connecting point for Falun Gong practitioners which displays a collective resilience when they act as one body to combat the genocide that is ongoing.

A critical reflection on the connection of Falun Gong experience to social work professional practice

Walking the spiritual path of the Falun Gong not only helps me to (re) visit my cultural roots and integrate my body-mind-emotion-spirit, the struggle in the peaceful resistance brings me insight to further the social work profession in our role of promoting global justice and human rights. I reflect on the following three areas which I find are meaningful for our profession:

1. In recent decades, social work has embraced an anti-oppressive and structural approach which underscores a clear stance on walking the path with the oppressed. Dorothy Smith's (2005) standpoint theory informs us of the importance of making a stand on issues of injustice in the context of structural power relations. Social work is a profession which embraces actions against social injustice and the violation of human rights. However, many authors on human rights (Brooks, 2015; Healy, 2008) critique social work for not paying enough attention to global human rights issues. The Falun Gong issue challenges social work to rethink its role in the protection of global human rights and to make a stand.

2. The Falun Gong issue calls for reflexivity which is a prerequisite for anti-oppressive practice. Reflexivity within a model of critical reflection of practice is more than self-awareness. It involves self-reflection that questions how knowledge is generated and how relations of power operate in a historical, structural and political process. Though reflexivity calls for an introspective understanding of ourselves, it moves beyond a personal level to situate oneself and other in the web of oppression. Fook and Gardner (2007) emphasize that knowledge is not purely objective and is shaped by what is said and what is not said under a political influence. Being reflexive is an important aspect of being able to critically analyse the various discourses and to be open to alternative perspectives.

3. Indigenous knowledge has informed social work such that we must ensure we listen to the voices of the oppressed. There have been many lessons learned about how researchers from the dominant groups conducted research studies on the Indigenous population that were disrespectful (Schnarch, 2004). Those researchers imposed their own frame of mind on the interpretation of findings which grossly misrepresented

Indigenous people. Research regarding Indigenous knowledge urges re-searchers to listen to the voices of the oppressed and allow marginalized and victimized groups to define themselves. The situation confronting the Falun Gong reinforces this stance. In the early days of the perse-cution in 2000, most Western scholars adopted an 'objective' stance and 'balanced' approach, looking at both Chinese Communist Party (CCP) and Falun Gong materials, which creates further confusion in the discourses of the subject matter (Matas and Cheung, 2012). Despite researchers on Falun Gong finding that the Chinese government reports are mostly inconsistent and adversarial (Ownby, 2008; Tong, 2009), the Western 'balanced approach' discourses became dominant. This formed an oppressive force which marginalizes the Falun Gong practitioners in an all-powerful repressive regime and in the Diaspora Chinese commu-nities outside China (Cheung, 2012). The Falun Gong issue reminds us as researchers to be respectful of the voices of the populations we study.

A concluding remark

The persecution of Falun Gong practitioners is awful enough, but the perpetuation of the killing of Falun Gong practitioners is sustained by the silence of the majority. As Martin Luther King Jr. once said, 'The ulti-mate tragedy is not the oppression and cruelty by the bad people but the silence over that by the good people' (www.goodreads.com/quotes/18870-the-ultimate-tragedy-is-not-the-oppression-and-cruelty-by). Ervin Staub (2011) describes three parties in a global human rights atrocity: (i) the perpetrator, (ii) the victims and (iii) the bystanders. With the vast resources at hand, the CCP hate propaganda against the Falun Gong is spread through the consulates in different parts of the world and the media they support. The polarization of the CCP and Falun Gong discourses poses difficulties for the outsiders to comprehend the truth of the suppression of the Falun Gong. However, a critical analysis of the nature of CCP combined with listening to the detailed descriptions of the Falun Gong communities provides a starting point to confront the issue.

When I sat on the lawn of the Washington Monument at the candle vigil to commemorate Falun Gong practitioners who had died as a result of the persecution, I found hope and resilience. I recall the 'critical hope' that Regan (2010) describes regarding the struggle of freedom for Indigenous people. She quotes bell hooks as having said, 'Hopefulness empowers us to continue to work for justice even as the forces of injustice may gain great power for a time' (p. 23). The critical hope and collective resilience culti-vated out of compassion empower me to confront social justice and human rights issues and challenges brought by my immigrant identity.

The spiritual practice of the Falun Gong sustains my courage and effort when I am aware and conscious of my thoughts and actions in my contemplative practice. The cultivation journey connects my inner self with the outer environment linking my heart and mind in pursuit of global justice. Increased mindfulness through meditation results in an inner strength and peace which I find empowering for me to cultivate resilience in confronting social justice and human rights issues. The compassion I cultivate brings me deep connection to life and fellow human beings to build solidarity with people who are suffering from oppression and persecution in my social work profession. The inner transformation I and fellow practitioners experience through the spiritual practice of Falun Gong brings a new level of hope and energy in our struggle to stop an evil crime of harvesting innocent people's organs and the persecution of the Falun Gong.

References

Arendt, H., 1963. *Eichmann in Jerusalem: a report on the banality of evil.* New York: Viking Press.

Brooks, A., 2015. Torture and terror post-9/11: the role of social work in responding to torture. *International Social Work*, 58(2), pp. 320–331.

Canda, E. R., and Furman, L. D., 1999. *Spiritual diversity in social work practice: the heart of helping.* New York: The Free Press.

Cheung, M., 2012. 'Invisible minorities' of the Falun Gong community: challenge to social inclusion and integration in Canada. In M. Baffoe with M. Cheung, L. Asimeng-Boahene and B. Ogbuagu, eds., *Strangers in new homelands: the social deconstruction and reconstruction of 'home' among immigrants in the diaspora.* Cambridge: Cambridge Scholars Publishing. Ch. 17.

Cheung, M., 2016. The intersection between mindfulness and human rights: the case of Falun Gong and its implications for social work', *Special Issue of Journal of Religion and Spirituality in Social Work: Social Thought*, 35(1–2), pp. 57–75.

Coates, J., Graham, J. R., Swartzentruber, B., and Ouellette, B., eds., 2007. *Spirituality and social work: Selected Canadian readings.* Toronto: CSPI.

Fook, J., and Gardner, F., 2007. *Practising critical reflection: a resource handbook.* Maidenhead: Open University Press.

Glick, J. E., 2010. Connecting complex processes: a decade of research on immigrant families. *Journal of Marriage and Family*, 72, pp. 498–515.

Gutmann, E., 2014. *The slaughter: mass killings, organ harvesting, and China's secret solution to its dissident problem.* New York: Prometheus Books.

Healy, L. M., 2008. Exploring the history of social work as human rights profession. *International Social Work*, 51(6), pp. 735–748.

Hick, S. F., and Furlotte, C., 2009. Mindfulness and social justice approaches: bridging the mind and society in social work practice. *Canadian Social Work Review*, 26(1), pp. 5–24.

Kittel, L., 2011. Healing heart and mind: the pursuit of human rights in engaged Buddhism as exemplified by Aung San Suu Kyi and the Dalai Lama. *The International Journal of Human Rights*, 15(6), pp. 905–925.

Li, H. Z., 1998. *Lecture at the First Conference in North America*, 29–30 March 1998. Available at: en.falundafa.org/eng/lectures/19980329L.html. [Accessed 10 November 2014.]

Li, H. Z., 2000. *Zhuan falun*. New York: Tianti Books.

Li, H. Z., 2005. Don't argue. *Hong Yin*, III. Available at: www.falundafa.org/book/eng/hy3_010.htm. [Accessed 10 November 2014.]

Li, H. Z., 2009. *Washington, DC, International Fa Conference*. Available at: en.minghui.org/html/articles/2009/7/26/109522.html. [Accessed 10 November 2014.]

Li, H. Z., 2011. *What is a Dafa disciple? Fa teaching given at the 2011 New York Fa Conference*. Available at en.minghui.org/html/articles/2011/9/15/128106.html. [Accessed 10 November 2014.]

Lundy, C., and van Wormer, K., 2007. Social and economic justice, human rights and peace: the challenge for social work in Canada and the USA. *International Social Work*, 50(6), pp. 727–739.

Matas, D., and Cheung, M., 2012. Retrospects and prospects: Canadian tribunals, human rights, and Falun Gong. *Canadian Journal of Human Rights*, 1(1), pp. 62–91.

Matas, D., and Kilgour, D., 2009. *Bloody harvest: the killing of Falun Gong for their organs*. Niagra Falls: Seraphim Editions.

Matas, D., and Trey, T., 2012. State organs: transplant abuse in China. Niagra Falls: Seraphim Editions.

Ownby, D., 2008. *Falun Gong and the future of China*. New York: Oxford University Press.

Regan, P., 2010. *Unsettling the settler within: Indian residential schools, truth telling, and reconciliation in Canada*. Vancouver: UBC Press.

Rost, N., 2013. Will it happen again? On the possibility of forecasting the risk of genocide. *Journal of Genocide Research*, 15(1), pp. 41–67.

Schnarch, B., 2004. Ownership, control, access, and possession (OCAP) or self-determination applied to research: a critical analysis of contemporary First Nations research and some options for First Nations communities. *Journal of Aboriginal Health*, 1(1), pp. 80–94.

Sharif, A., Fiatarone Singh, M., Trey, T., and Lavee, J., 2014. Organ procurement from executed prisoners in China. *American Journal of Transplantation*, 20, pp. 1–7.

Smith, D. E., 2005. *Institutional ethnography: a sociology for people*. Toronto: Altamira Press.

Staub, E., 2011. *Overcoming evil: genocide, violent conflict and terrorism*. New York: Cambridge University Press.

Sue, D. W., 2010. *Microaggressions and marginality: manifestation, dynamics, and impact*. New Jersey: John Wiley & Sons.

Tong, J. W., 2009. *Revenge of the forbidden city: the suppression of the Falun Gong in China, 1999–2005*. New York: Oxford University Press.

United Nations, 1948. United Nations convention on the prevention and punishment of the crime of genocide (pdf). Available at: https://treaties.un.org/doc/Publication/UNTS/Volume%2078/volume-78-I-1021-English.pdf. [Accessed 10 November 2014.]

Wong, Y-L R., 2013. Returning to silence, connecting to wholeness: contemplative pedagogy for critical social work education. *Journal of Religion & Spirituality in Social Work: Social Thought*, 32(3), pp. 269–285.

8 Mindfulness for Practitioners: Bringing Attention and Awareness to Personal and Professional Experience

Lisa McCorquodale

Introduction

From an early age I can recall seeking moments of stillness and quiet. Growing up on a farm, where work naturally ebbs and flows with nature, may have leant me towards this disposition. Dedicating time for quiet is a relative rarity in modern professional life, whereas busyness and action tend to dominate (Wilkins, 2007). In fact, 'doing' is so important in many cultures that it is impossible to envision life without it:

> People spend their lives almost constantly engaged in purposeful 'doing' even when free of obligation or necessity. They 'do' daily tasks including things they feel they must do, and others that they want to. Human evolution has been filled with ongoing and progressive 'doings', which, apart from enabling the species to survive, has stimulated, entertained and excited some people and bored, stressed, alienated or depressed others according to what was done. (Wilcock, 2006, p. 64)

Doing makes up the bulk of our lives: a pleasurable leisure pursuit, a stimulating job or the intimacy of caring for young children. Many people fail to notice that life can, and perhaps should, be more than this constant activity (Kabat-Zinn, 2005a). In this chapter, I argue that perpetual *doing*, to the point where other ways of living in the world are subjugated, may be particularly problematic for professionals who work in health and social care. *Being*, as another mode of life, is introduced as a potential corrective. I discuss the inherently spiritual nature of the being mode and offer *mindfulness*, a contemplative and reflective way of engaging in the world, as one way to tap into being. I conclude by using examples from my own life as a working mother in both academia and clinical practice as an occupational therapist to exemplify how mindfulness, as a spiritual practice, has helped me live a more authentic and purposeful life.

Doing and being

Doing is an essential part of human existence. Action and activity have the potential to build and maintain physical and mental capacities, are tied to health and wellness, and are necessary for (wo)man's very survival (Wilcock, 1998). However, in modern society, doing has become so heavily linked with economics and neoliberal culture that its connection to health and wellness is increasingly tenuous (Wilcock, 2006). In fact, perpetual doing, without the time for repose, may have the exact opposite effect. Busyness can also artificially blur what philosopher Damon Young (2008) convincingly describes in his book *Distraction* as existential angst. Stopping to notice habitual thoughts, distractions or obsessions can be uncomfortable and is often replaced with a reach for a glass of wine or the remote control to calm the unsettled feeling (Webster-Wright, 2013). This may be especially true for those who work in health and social care settings, where there are seemingly constant demands on time (Frasner et al., 2009). Further, *being* tends to be further subsumed in these settings because of an ever-increasing shift to rationalized and standardized practices (Kinsella, 2012). Slipping out of autopilot can be a difficult task, particularly because many habits and patterns are taken for granted and assumed to be natural (Greene, 1973). This may be particularly true for those who work in health and social care settings where work can be stressful, and burnout and compassion fatigue are common (Wilkins, 2007).

When professionals relinquish the dominant compulsion to *do*, and slip into a more contemplative way of *being*, the meaning and purpose they derive from their life may shift. Maslow (1968) says that *being* is the contemplation and enjoyment of the inner world and is the opposite of action. To *be* allows the opportunity to discover, think, reflect and simply exist. Being honours (wo)man's quest for meaning, contributes to quality of life and creativity, and is linked with consciousness (made up of attention, memory and awareness) (Wilcock, 2006).

Because of being's intimate connection with meaning, purpose and creativity, it is often described as a spiritual way of living. How to slip into the *being* mode, and further what spirituality is, are equally elusive: they mean different things to different people (Tisdell, 2008). As an occupational therapist, spirituality has always figured centrally within my profession's discourse, though in practice it is poorly understood and executed (McColl, 2003). In one of the first scholarly papers on the topic in the field of occupational therapy, Muldoon and King are quoted as stating that spirituality:

> [...] is the way that person leads his or her life. In this sense, every human being has a spirituality. The direction given to one's life, the story one

tells with one's life, is itself rooted in and embodies a certain way of looking at life. This lived-out vision of life relies on certain individual or group activities and practices in order to be sustained and expressed. These may be forms of reflection, prayer, conversation, ritual, social involvement, or even the assimilation of attitudes fostered by the mass media. (Muldoon and King in Egan and Delaat, 1994, pp. 100–1)

More recently, spirituality was the focus of a comprehensive literature review of all articles published in occupational therapy over a 20-year period from 1991–2011 (Humbet, Sedlak and Rossi, 2014). The authors describe spirituality as a personal practice comprised of roles which afford life meaning and bring value to daily activities and contexts, and contribute to connections with others (Humbet et al., 2014). While many people find a connection to their spirituality through religion and other doctrinal practices, it can also be found through relating to nonphysical aspects of who we are, independent of religious interpretations. Taking time to disengage from action (doing) and to engage with nonphysical aspects of who we are (being) can be a profoundly spiritual act (Wilcock, 2006).

As Maslow (1968) asserts, spirituality can become lost in the blur of daily life: 'This inner nature [being] is not strong and overpowering and unmistakable like the instincts of animals. It is weak and delicate and subtle and easily overcome by habit, cultural pressure and wrong attitudes toward it' (p. 4). Kinsella and Whiteford (2009) note that the dominant tendency to privilege rational thought in health and social care may contribute to the subjugation of being and spirituality for professionals. This subjugation may have unacknowledged consequences when professionals minimize the role of *being* and spirituality in their lives. I personally manage the demands of two young children, and work academically and clinically. My mindfulness practice helps remind me, as Sartre (1956) offered, that while I may not be able to change the circumstances of my life, I can change the way I respond and react. Existentialists argue for living intentionally and authentically (Morris, 1998). This can be deceptively challenging:

[...] standing back from daily habits to develop clarity, as we do consciously in mindfulness, we can be aware of an inner call to authenticity and stand up for what matters in life. Our everyday choices and actions form the contours of the ground on which we take such a stand in our lives. (Webster-Wright, 2013, p. 560)

In the remainder of this chapter, I discuss how mindfulness, a practice focused on 'being', has the potential to support the daily 'doings' of those who work in health and social care. I first introduce mindfulness and then use Noffke's (2009) framework for professional practice to explore three ways mindfulness may contribute to spiritual life, using examples from my own life to highlight the unique contributions the being mode can offer.

Mindfulness: provisional definitions

I began a mindfulness practice over a decade ago after being introduced to the concept while recovering from a car accident. Mindfulness, while ripe with misunderstanding, is a basic human quality, though many do not have the language to consciously label moments as 'mindful'. People can be more or less mindful, depending on how well developed the quality is (Dyche and Epstein, 2011). To be mindful is to be aware and attuned to the constant stream of lived experience (Varela, Thompson and Rosch, 1992). It is the opposite of mindlessness or autopilot, which is often the default for the 'doing' mode. In the doing mode, people typically rely on habitual patterns. These taken-for-granted ways of engaging with the world become the basis for all interactions in the world and can either contribute to, or work against, meaning, purpose and quality of life (Cutchin et al., 2008). Mindfulness enables practitioners to slip out of autopilot and bring full attention to the present moment, and allows for a clearer understanding of how thoughts, feelings and emotions influence health and quality of life.

Mindfulness is cultivated formally through meditation and may also be cultivated informally (e.g. through aesthetic work, yoga, tai chi, walking, body scans and mindful eating) (Kabat-Zinn, 2005b). During mindfulness meditation, practitioners initially stabilize their attention by focusing on their breath, without trying to change or alter it, and refocus when the mind wanders. Once attention is stabilized, practitioners can focus on whatever arises in the field of awareness and attend to those processes (e.g. thoughts, feelings, sensations) with curiosity, openness, acceptance and kind regard (Epstein, Siegel and Silberman, 2008).

Mindfulness can be traced back over 2500 years to Buddhist psychology and has a varied and intimate connection to many world religions and philosophies (Miller and Nozawa, 2002). Mindfulness, as a quality, has been referred to as many things. Among them, reflection and reflective practice (Johns and Freshwater, 1998), metacognition (Fogerty, 1994), prereflectivity (Greene, 1995; Kinsella, 2012; Merleau-Ponty, 1962/2012), mindfulness meditation (Germer, Siegel and Fulton, 2005), receptivity (Willis, 1999) and contemplation (Miller, 1994). Not surprisingly, a definitive definition remains elusive. Jon Kabat-Zinn's (2005b) definition is one of the most commonly cited: 'The awareness that emerges through paying attention, on purpose, in the present moment, and non-judgmentally to the unfolding of experience moment by moment (p. 145). While mindfulness has roots in many religious traditions, it can be both a secular and non-dogmatic spiritual practice. Mindfulness at its core is a way of being in the world that honours the spirituality and existential elements of life.

Mindfulness is increasingly secularized, and researchers are keen to demonstrate scientifically proven outcomes. Some intriguing findings from researchers include positive structural and functional changes in the body, including increased telomerase length and enhanced immune system functioning (Carlson et al., 2014; Davidson et al., 2003; Holzel et al., 2011). Siegel (2007) also reports stronger integrative fibres connecting the left and right frontal cortical hemispheres, resulting in more emotional balance and overall well-being, leading to what he calls 'integration'. Empirical research with clinical populations, though suffering from various methodical flaws, has proven the practice effective at alleviating suffering from a variety of illnesses and improving well-being (Baer, 2003). There are many conceptual and theoretical papers and books on the role of mindfulness in professional life (Epstein, 1999; Reid, 2009; Turner, 2009). Generally, mindfulness appears to play a powerful role in self-efficacy of practice, patient safety, ethical practice and self-care (Gura, 2010; Tusaie and Edds, 2009).

All of these potential benefits stem from the basic human capacity for awareness and attention (Stern, 2004). Consciousness, the human capacity for *awareness* and *attention,* is easily overlooked with respect to its importance in human well-being because almost everyone has some level of awareness and attention (Brown and Ryan, 2003). However, when time is dedicated to slow down and notice, more meaning, purpose and joy may arise. For example, a professional may notice a look of gratitude from a person he or she is caring for, or tension in the posture of a family member who may need additional support. Maslow (1968) writes with enthusiasm about what he calls the basic inner state (being) of humans as being either positive or neutral, and rejects the idea that humans are inherently pathological. He argues that destructive outer behaviours (doing) are reactions against unexamined inner states. For this reason, he suggests that attention to being is essential. In the remaining section of this chapter, I use moments from my own life to exemplify how attention and awareness to being can fruitfully contribute to daily life.

Mindfulness: contributions to the life of a professional

Drawing from my own personal experiences, I use Noffke's (1997, 2009) seminal work regarding professional practice to demonstrate how my own personal mindfulness practice contributes to my own personal and professional life. Noffke offers three dimensions of professional action or 'doing': the professional, the personal and the political (see Table 8.1). These

Table 8.1 Dimensions of Professional Action. Adapted from Noffke (1997, 2009)

Dimension	Related actions
Professional	Professional development, including the production of a knowledge base, which may enhance professional quality and professional status
Personal	'Self-studies', seeking answers to questions about individual problems in professional practice
Political	Enhanced democracy and social equality

dimensions represent the different actions professionals may undertake in practice, and each is discussed in the following sections.

Professional

Noffke (1997, 2009) notes that the professional dimension of practice is about growing and developing knowledge, enhancing quality practice and attaining a level of professional status that affords respect and under-standing. Intuition or tacit knowledge can contribute to this professional dimension of practice. In practice, expert practitioners, drawing on tacit and intuitive knowledge, simply know or sense the best course of action (Benner, Tanner and Chesla, 1996). McNeill (2013) notes that what 'feels like' intuition is more often the fine attention to environmental cues that, when added to the professional's acquired knowledge and own experience, results in the best course of action. Mindfulness, in particular, may help practitioners tap tacit and intuitive knowledge. Intuition helps people act, even when they are not consciously aware of the mental events leading to a particular course of action. Tacit knowledge represents that which is hard to put into words, suggesting we know more than we can say (Polanyi, 1983).

Due to this form of knowledge being hard to put into words, it is often overlooked. Intuitive knowledge, found primarily in the subcortical regions of the brain, comes from internal data typically left at the non-conscious level (Epstein et al., 2008). The intuitive act is passive; all one can do is create the conditions to allow the knowledge to surface (Depraz, Varela and Vermersch, 2003). The assumption is, with mindfulness training, practitioners can access and use this information (Epstein, 1999). An interesting study by Xerri (2014) looked at how accessing intuition contributed to quality of life for nurses. He found that nurses who felt engaged and connected to their work accessed their intuition more frequently than those who were disengaged or dissatisfied with their role. Further, Chin, Ananthoraman and Kim Tong (2011) suggest that to tap into intuition enhances daily functioning, encourages people to better themselves and their work, and brings a sense of contribution and engagement.

My own intuition feels like a deep sense of knowing without having, at least initially, facts to back up my knowing. For instance, in previous roles I was partly responsible for hiring new professionals into the organization. On one particular occasion, we had a 'tie' between two individuals, both having impressed us with their answers. I had a sense that one candidate in particular would be a better fit for the team, but could not really articulate why. For the second round of interviews, I wanted to focus on questions that looked at character rather than clinical skills. The other members of the panel felt a highly skilled clinician was what the organization needed, but agreed that clinicians who live the values of an organization make good employees as well. During the second round of interviews, it became abundantly clear to us that one clinician had a depth of character that the other did not. Without my sense of needing to know more about values and attitudes, we may have missed this crucial information in our decision making. In this example, I was able to rely on intuitive judgements to seek out a colleague who later proved to be an excellent team member.

Personal

Noffke's (1997, 2009) second dimension focuses on self-study and finding solutions to individual challenges. One of the most pressing challenges for those in the helping professions is developing effective self-care habits (Irving, Dobkin and Jeeson, 2009). When a professional's inner state is stressed, anxious and overwhelmed, quality of life for both service recipient and professional can suffer. Almost 50 per cent of those who work in health and social care identify themselves as stressed or very stressed at work (Wilkins, 2007). Further, cynicism and burnout often accompany stress (Gupta et al., 2012). Broadly speaking, mindfulness can work against this burn-out, professional apathy and disconnection (Frasner et al., 2009). Although the purpose of mindfulness is not to induce relaxation or have a 'better' life, the practice has been shown to circumvent stress reactions by lowering blood pressure and stress hormone levels, and fosters the adoption of healthy lifestyle choices (Hibel, Mercado and Trumbell, 2012; McCabe Ruff and MacKenzie, 2009). In fact, Jon Kabat-Zinn (2005b) built his entire program around the notion that mindfulness can reduce stress.

I offer a vignette from my life to exemplify the ways mindfulness may assist in de-stressing, and how life affirming it can be to notice the present moment. In the early part of my career, my home was immaculate, and I was impeccably organized. As the years and responsibilities have grown, I have had to make concessions. My home is often what my younger self might have called a 'disaster'. However, mindfulness has helped me find what truly matters in my life. For example, my six-year-old son is a sweet and precocious little boy who is typically eager to help my equally precocious three-year-old daughter. When we arrive home at the end of each workday, my son often holds her hand as they climb the steps into our home, and he will usually get her a snack out of the cupboard, without her asking. I am grateful that mindfulness has helped me notice this simple ritual. Without it, the remnants of breakfast strewn around the room and the chaos that ensues when my kids arrive home might be all that captures my attention. I find myself noticing many seemingly mundane, but nevertheless life-affirming events; small things like birds chirping when I head out the door, or a beam of sunlight hitting my desk, connect me to my life in ways for which I am grateful.

Political

Noffke's (1997, 2009) final dimension, the political, is about enhancing social justice. Spiritual practices can be used to pursue social justice issues, though this may not be explicitly stated or even cognitively acknowledged (Tisdell, 2008). Stanley (2013) encourages practitioners to reinterpret mindfulness as not only an inner state of mind but also an outward social practice. He furthers that with mindfulness, practitioners can ask a central important question: 'What forms of life or being are we to create?' (p. 64). Stanley also suggests a life worth living must include care and ethical engagement with others.

The former Czech president, Vaclav Havel (1992), who steadfastly believed that the political must be moral, wrote, '[A] huge potential of goodwill is slumbering within our society. It's just that it's incoherent, suppressed, confused, crippled and perplexed – as though it does not know what to rely on, where to begin, where or how to find meaningful outlets' (p. 4). Mindfulness may help in rousing this slumber. While mindfulness heightens a practitioner's ability to be open and non-judgemental to experience, this does not necessarily result in complacency. Substantive insights about the type of life we want to live and the systemic barriers impeding a life worth living may be revealed.

I have always been interested in making a difference, and wanted a career that was rewarding, challenging and exciting. When I was younger I was hesitant to have children as I was unsure whether these two ambitions could merge. During meditations I would notice that when thoughts of children arose, I would simultaneously experience a feeling in my gut I can now see as being mixed with anxiety. Over time, I began to see that my hesitation to have children was rooted in my unease with society's 'ideal' mother. I cerebrally knew a 'good' mother is someone who models ambition, love for life, and is caring. But I had also begun to internalize the belief that a good mother is typically a stay-at-home mom who spent inordinate amounts of time entertaining and generally giving her life over to her children. I had unwittingly bought into the widely circulated 'intensive' parenting model (Liss et al., 2013). In meditation I could feel how this socially constructed ideal was living in tension with what I felt I could offer a child. Thankfully, my husband and I had the courage to parent and work out of the home on our terms. I am eternally grateful that mindfulness helped me notice this contradiction, and my two beautiful children are here as a result. I see this new insight as political in that it resists conventional and normative ways of being that can be harmful to myself and presumably other women. These simple acts of resistance, made on a personal level, are crucial for change to arise (Stanley, 2013). I was so taken with this insight that this became the focus of my doctoral work. I undertook a study with other working mothers to better understand how mindfulness supports them in light of tensions created by sociopolitical realities. These include a lack of publicly funded child-care, limited support from employers for meeting family obligations and long full-time hours as the norm (Buchanan, 2013).

Conclusion

Ignancy Jan Paderewski, a concert pianist, said: 'If I do not practice one day, I notice it. If I do not practice a second day, the orchestra notices it. If I do not practice a third day, the world notices it' (Paderewski in Dillon and Brown, 2011, p. 4). His words have always resonated with me. I believe that mindfulness, as a practice focused on being, can profoundly impact outer actions in the world. Professional life is often fraught with challenges, but, as I have offered in this chapter, mindfulness can lead practitioners to more spiritual pursuits including greater purpose, meaning and quality of life. Mindfulness is not about finding eternal happiness or eliminating the challenges of professional life. As I have suggested, taking the time to slow down and pay attention to the present moment can have surprisingly life-affirming consequences in professional, personal and political ways. John Ralston Saul (1995) notes that a life worth living is only possible through self-knowledge. Self-knowledge is difficult when caught in incessant action and activity. Mindfulness has offered me the chance to live a life worth living. My hope is that I have similarly inspired others who work in health and social care to consider mindfulness and how it might contribute to their spiritual life, both personally and professionally.

References

Baer, R. A., 2003. Mindfulness training as a clinical intervention: a conceptual and empirical review. *American Psychological Association*, 10(2), pp. 125–143.

Benner, P., Tanner, C., and Chesla, C., 1996. *Expertise in nursing practice: caring, clinical judgment, and ethics*. New York: Springer Publishing.

Brown, K. W., and Ryan, R. M., 2003. The benefits of being present: mindfulness and its role in psychological well-being. *Journal of Personality and Social Psychology*, 84(4), pp. 822–848.

Buchanan, L., 2013. *Rhetorics of motherhood*. Chicago: Southern Illinois University Press.

Carlson, L., Beattie, T., Giese-Davis, J., Faris, P., Tamagawa, R., Fick, L., and Speca, M., 2014. Mindfulness-based cancer recovery and supportive-expressive therapy maintain telomere length relative to controls in distressed breast cancer survivors. *Cancer*, 43(1), pp. 1–9.

Chin, S., Anantharaman, R., and Kin Tong, D., 2011. The roles of emotional intelligence and spiritual intelligence at the workplace. *Journal of Human Resources Management Research*, 2011, 1 (1), pp. 1–9.

Cutchin, M. P., Aldrich, R. M., Bailliard, A. L., and Coppola, S., 2008. Action theories for occupational science: the contributions of Dewey and Bourdieu. *Journal of Occupational Science*, 15(3), pp. 157–165.

Davidson, R., Zinn-Kabat, J., Schumacher, J., Rosenkranz, R., Muller, D., Santorelli, S., Urbanowski, K., Harrington, A., Bonus, K., and Sheridan, J. 2003. Alterations in brain and immune function produced by mindfulness meditation. *Psychosomatic Medicine*, 65(4), pp. 564–570.

Depraz, N., Varela, F. J., and Vermersch, P., 2003. *On becoming aware: a pragmatics of experiencing*. Philadelphia: John Benjamins.

Dillon, S. C., and Brown, A. R., 2011. *Sound thinking: tips and tools for understanding popular music*. Brisbane: National Library of Australia.

Dyche, L., and Epstein, R., 2011. Curiosity and medical education. *Medical Education*, 45(7), pp. 633–668.

Egan, M., and Delaat, M., 1994. No title. *Canadian Journal of Occupational Therapy*, 61(2), pp. 95–101.

Epstein, R., 1999. Mindful practice. *Journal of the American Medical Association*, 282(9), pp. 833–839.

Epstein, R., Siegel, D., and Silberman, J., 2008. Self-monitoring in clinical practice: a challenge for medical educators. *Journal of Continuing Education*, 28(1), pp. 5–13.

Fogerty, R., 1994. *How to teach for metacognitive reflection*. Thousand Oaks: Sage Publications.

Frasner, M., Epstein, R., Beckman, H., Suchman, A., Chapman, B., Mooney, C., and Quill, T., 2009. Association of an educational program in mindful communication with burnout, empathy, and attitudes among primary care physicians. *Journal of the American Medical Association*, 302(12), pp. 1284–1293.

Germer, C. K., Siegel, R. D., and Fulton, P. R., 2005. *Mindfulness and psychotherapy*. New York: The Guilford Press.

Greene, M., 1973. *Teacher as stranger: educational philosophy for the modern age*. Belmont: Wadsworth.

Greene, M., 1995. Social vision and dance of life. *Releasing the imagination: essays on education, the arts, and social change*. San Francisco: Jossey-Bass. Ch 5.

Gupta, S., Paterson, M. L., Lysaght, M., and von Zweck, C. M., 2012. Experiences of burnout and coping strategies utilized by occupational therapists. *Canadian Journal of Occupational Therapy*, 79(2), pp. 86–95.

Gura, S. T., 2010. Mindfulness in occupational therapy education. *Occupational Therapy in Health Care*, 24(3), pp. 266–273.

Havel, V., 1992. *Summer meditations*. New York: A.A. Knopf.

Hibel, L. C., Mercado, E., and Trumbell, J. M., 2012. Parenting stressors and morning cortisol in a sample of working mothers. *Journal of Family Psychology*, 26(5), pp. 738–747.

Holzel, B. K., Carmody, J., Vangel, M., Congleton, C., Yerramsetti, S. M., Gard, T., and Lazar, S., 2011. Mindfulness practice leads to increase in regional brain grey matter density. *Psychiatry Research Neuroimaging*, 191(1), pp. 36–43.

Humbet, T., Sedlak, A., and Rossi, L., 2014. *A conceptual model of spirituality and occupational therapy: constructs from a comprehensive literature review*. Paper presented at the American Occupational Therapy Association Annual Conference: boldly navigating a challenging world. Baltimore, 3–6 April.

Irving, J. A., Dobkin, P. L., and Jeeson, P., 2009. Cultivating mindfulness in health care professionals: a review of empirical studies of mindfulness-based stress reduction (MBSR). *Complementary Therapies in Clinical Practice*, 15(2), pp. 61–66.

Johns, C., and Freshwater, D., 1998. *Transforming nursing through reflective practice*. Toronto: Blackwell Science.

Kabat-Zinn, J., 2005a. *Coming to our senses: healing ourselves and the world through mindfulness*. New York: Hyperion.

Kabat-Zinn, J., 2005b. *Full catastrophe living: using the wisdom of your body and mind to face stress, pain, and illness*. New York: Random House.

Kinsella, E. A., 2012. Practitioner reflection and judgement as phronesis: a continuum of reflection and considerations for phronetic judgement. In E. A. Kinsella and A. Pitman, eds., *Phronesis as professional knowledge: practical wisdom in the professions*. Rotterdam: Sense Publishing. Ch. 2.

Kinsella, E. A., and Whiteford, G., 2009. Knowledge generation and utilization in occupational therapy: towards epistemic reflexivity. *Australian Occupational Therapy Journal*, 56(4), pp. 249–258.

Liss, M., Schiffrin, H., Mackinstoch, V., Miles-McLean, H., and Erchull, M., 2013. Development and validation of a quantitative measure of intensive parenting attitudes. *Journal of Child and Family Studies*, 22(5), pp. 621–636.

Maslow, A., 1968. *Toward a psychology of being*. Princeton: Van Nostrand.

McCabe Ruff, K., and MacKenzie, E. R., 2009. The role of mindfulness in healthcare reform: a policy paper. *Explore*, 5(6), pp. 313–323.

McColl, M. A., 2003. *Spirituality and occupational therapy*. Ottawa: CAOT Publications ASCE.

McNeill, W., 2013. Accessing intuition in massage and bodywork therapies using mindfulness, knowledge, empathy and flow. *Journal of Bodywork & Movement Therapies*, 17(1), pp. 116–120. Available at: http://resolver.scholarsportal. info/resolve/13608592/v17i0001/116_aiimabumkeaf.xml. [Accessed 23 June 2015.]

Merleau-Ponty, M., 1962/2012. *Phenomenology of perception.* London: Routledge and K. Paul.

Miller, J., 1994. *The contemplative practitioner: meditation in education and the professions.* Westport: Bergin and Garvey.

Miller, J., and Nozawa, A., 2002. Meditation teachers: a qualitative study. *Journal of In-Service Education*, 28(1), pp. 179–192.

Morris, D. B., 1998. *Illness and culture in the postmodern age.* Berkeley: University of California Press.

Muldoon, M. H., and King, J. N., 1991. A spirituality for the long haul: response to chronic illness. *Journal of Religion and Health*, 30(2), pp. 99–108.

Noffke, S. E., 1997. Professional, personal and political dimensions of action research. *Review of Research in Education*, 22(1), pp. 305–343.

Noffke, S. E., 2009. Revisiting the professional, personal, and political dimensions of action research. In S. E. Noffke and B. Somekh, eds., *The SAGE handbook of educational action research.* Washington: Sage. Ch.1.

Polanyi, M., 1983. *The tacit dimension.* Glouchester: Doubleday and Company.

Ralston Saul, J., 1995. *The unconscious civilization.* Concord: House of Anansi Press.

Reid, D., 2009. Capturing presense moments: the art of mindful practice in occupational therapy. *Canadian Journal of Occupational Therapy*, 76(3), pp. 180–188.

Sartre, J., 1956. *Being and nothingness: an essay on phenomenological ontology.* New York: Philosophical Library.

Siegel, D., 2007. *The mindful brain.* New York: W.W. Norton.

Stanley, S., 2013. From discourse to awareness: rhetoric, mindfulness, and a psychology without foundations. *Theory & Psychology*, 23(1), pp. 60–80. Available at: http://resolver.scholarsportal.info/resolve/09593543/v23i0001/60_fdtarmaapwf. xml. [Accessed 23 June 2015.]

Stern, D. M., 2004. *The present moment in psychotherapy and everyday life.* New York: W.W. Norton and Company.

Tisdell, E. J., 2008. Spirituality and adult learning. *New Directions for Adult and Continuing Education*, 119, pp. 27–36. Available at: http://resolver.scholarsportal. info/resolve/10522891/v2008i0119/27_saal.xml. [Accessed 17 June 2015.]

Turner, B., 2009. Mindfulness: the present moment in clinical social work. *Clinical Social Work Journal*, 37(2), pp. 95–103.

Tusaie, K., and Edds, K., 2009. Understanding and integrating mindfulness into psychiatric mental health nursing practice. *Archives of Psychiatric Nursing*, 23(5), pp. 359–365.

Varela, F. J., Thompson, E., and Rosch, E., 1992. *The embodied mind: cognitive science and human experience.* Cambridge: The MIT Press.

Webster-Wright, A., 2013. The eye of the storm: a mindful inquiry into reflective practices in higher education. *Reflective Practice*, 14(4), pp. 556–567.

Wilcock, A., 1998. Reflection on doing, being and becoming. *Australian Occupational Therapy Journal*, 46(1), pp. 1–11.

Wilcock, A., 2006. *An occupational perspective of health*. Thorofare: Slack.

Wilkins, K., 2007. Work stress among health care providers. *Health Reports*, 18(4), pp. 33–36.

Willis, P., 1999. Looking for what it's really like: phenomenology in reflective practice. *Studies in Continuing Education*, 21(1), pp. 91–112.

Xerri, M. J., 2014. Antecedents and outcomes relating to public and private nurses' use of intuition in England, 34(6), pp. 389–396. Available at: http://resolver. scholarsportal.info/resolve/09540962/v34i0006/389_aaortpnuoiie.xml. [Accessed 25 June 2015.]

Young, D., 2008. *Distraction: a philosopher's guide to being free*. Carlton: Melbourne University Press.

SECTION

IV

Celtic Spirituality and Monastic Influences

9 The Rule of Saint Benedict: Considering Hospitality, and Welcoming Spaces in Contemporary Therapeutic Practice

Laura Béres

Introduction

When I first took up my current position as a social work academic at a Roman Catholic liberal arts university in Canada, I would from time to time meet with the Roman Catholic campus minister to discuss any questions I had about the role of Catholicism in the university and to chat about issues related to spirituality more generally. During one of these chats, in relation to having mentioned a recent pleasant evening when a colleague had popped in for a visit, he suggested that one of my gifts seemed to be hospitality. I have the distinct feeling that at the time I was not particularly impressed with this thought; I think it just seemed too mundane, ordinary or perhaps too much of a mainstream expectation for a female. It is therefore somewhat ironic that since that time I have become more and more interested in the concept of hospitality and what it might offer as a skill for health and social service care providers.

Since then I also have become interested in Celtic spirituality, or Celtic Christianity, and have visited communities in Iona, in the Hebrides off the west coast of Scotland, and Holy Island Lindisfarne off the north east coast of England. This has involved learning about the role of monasteries in the development of Celtic spirituality's beliefs and practices.[1] So, perhaps it is not all that surprising really to realize these two interests have come together in my current interest in the concept of hospitality in the Benedictine monastic tradition.

There has, indeed, been growing interest in the concept of hospitality and what it suggests as an ethical manner of engagement in contemporary society (Cotter, 1996; Derrida and Dufourmantelle, 2000; Homan and Collins Pratt, 2007; Kramer, 2011; Pearson, 2011). As someone who enjoys entertaining guests in my home, and as a university professor and therapist[2] who attempts to create safe spaces for students and service users to engage in critical reflection, learning and the sometimes difficult work of change, I am also interested in what might be gained by examining the concept of hospitality more thoroughly. I have written about the idea of hospitality in therapeutic settings previously (Béres, 2014), but in a limited manner. In this chapter, I build upon those initial ideas and explore in detail what *The Rule of Saint Benedict (RB)* offers in the way of considerations regarding hospitality, and how these ideas written in the sixth century c.e. are relevant to therapeutic practitioners in the contemporary world.[3] These considerations also touch on the issue of space and place[4]. Developing skills of hospitality and the nurturing of welcoming and safe spaces, although discussed from the point of view of Christian spirituality/monasticism of the sixth century, are skills that can be usefully developed by any professional practitioner regardless of religious orientation or lack of experience with the topic of spirituality.

Although much of the commentary about the *RB* and Benedict's descriptions of hospitality focuses on the need to be hospitable to the stranger, because in doing so we welcome Christ (Chittister, 1992/2004; de Waal, 1995; Homan and Collins Pratt, 2007), what interests me more is what Swan (2005) and de Waal (1995) describe as the need to hold two commitments in tension. De Waal comments that Benedict recommends providing a generous reception to guests but then also suggests withdrawing and stepping back in order to ensure the needs of the monastic community are also being met. She goes on to explain, 'It is precisely the sense that its own way of life has an integrity which must be respected, that the silence and the prayer is preserved, which ensures that it has something of value to give to the passing guest' (de Waal, 1995, p. 156).

I first spent a weekend silent retreat in the guest wing of a convent (The Sisters of St John the Divine's Convent in Toronto) when I was in the final stages of writing my doctoral dissertation and needed quiet time away from work and family commitments. I have returned for several more weekend retreats since then and have found, just as de Wall describes it, that there is something about the silence and contemplative nature of the nuns' lifestyle that protects the space and provides time for rejuvenation. They invite guests to attend all their prayer and worship services during the day if they wish to attend them, but this is not a requirement or even an expectation. Meals are eaten in contemplative silence, and I experience the quietness as a wonderful gift.

de Waal links the above recommendations to what she has discovered in her own experience, explaining that if she does not ensure the protection of enough space and time to look after her own inner life, then she becomes too exhausted to be fully available to anyone else who might approach her. 'Benedict is establishing boundaries [...] and as any good psychologist would tell us, this is one of the most essential lessons that we all need to learn' (de Waal, 1995, p. 156).

Swan (2005) also points out that Benedict's guidelines are to protect the communal monastic lifestyle aimed at preserving the interior spiritual quest:

> He wanted guests to be received *as Christ* without serious disruption to the community. Ritual prayers and blessings are said in order to discern the heart of the guest. In this way the Living Word within the guest is received by the monastic but any influence of the Evil One is exposed. (Swan, 2005, p. 125)

Directions to hold these two needs in tension may partly be a result of Benedict's focus on developing and maintaining a balanced life. Beginning by considering the context in which Benedict wrote his Rule provides one framework for further exploring his recommendations.

Background

Stewart (1998) points out that monastic life had already become well established by the time Benedict became a monk in the early sixth century: '[I]nformal ascetical communities, often home-based, had long been part of the Christian landscape in places as far apart as Rome, Asia Minor and Syria' (p. 17). What we might currently call 'monasticism' became more developed and institutionalized in the fourth century, and as monasteries committed to an ascetical life continued to be developed throughout Italy, Gaul and North Africa, bishops from outside of the monasteries began to pressure them for greater regulation and structure of their life (Stewart, 1998). Sheldrake (2013) indicates that the development of monastic Rules shifted the focus of obedience from a particular spiritual mother or father to a Rule instead. The superior in any monastery would then act as the spiritual interpreter of that Rule, which was not intended to be a '*legislative* document but a medium for the communication of a spiritual ethos' (p. 56).

Sheldrake indicates that Pachomius in the fourth century has been credited as writing the first Rule, which influenced then the 'Rules of St. Basil in the East and St. Benedict in the West' (Sheldrake, 2013, p. 56). He also points out the importance of the *Rule of St Augustine*, which was the earliest of the Western Rules, having been written in the late fourth century, and suggests all these Rules had an influence on Benedict when he was writing the *RB*.

Stewart (1998) explains that prior to Benedict's writing of the *RB*, an Italian monk in the early sixth century, who is now only known as The Master, wrote the *Rule of the Master* (*RM*) (p. 19). The *RB*, although original and about a third the length of the *RM*, was influenced by the *RM* in addition to the Bible and more general monastic literature.

Drawing upon Gregory the Great's stories of Benedict in *Dialogues*, Stewart (1998) says that after Benedict had spent time as a hermit in a cave near modern-day Subiaco in Italy, he was recognized for his holiness by nearby monks and asked to become their spiritual leader. This was not a smooth transition, and Stewart quotes Gregory as saying 'they found it hard to let go of what they had thought about with their old minds in order to ponder new things' (Stewart, 1998, p. 23), and so they decided to poison Benedict. However, as soon as Benedict made the sign of the cross to bless the carafe that was passed to him, which contained the poison, it shattered. He then got up to leave, telling them they should find a leader more compatible to their tastes. His return to solitude did not last long; he set up 12 monasteries nearby and then, in approximately 530, he went to the mountain of Casinum, where he razed the temple of Apollo and built two oratories for preaching (Stewart, 1998, p. 25).

I find this anecdote about Benedict's near poisoning interesting as it may have highlighted for him the importance of discerning people's/guests' intentions and the need to ascertain whether they are in fact congruent with the needs of those living in community within the monastery, which I will describe in more detail later in this chapter.

Taylor (1989) particularly comments on the effects of the time and context in which Benedict would have written the *RB* and Benedict's resulting focus regarding the need for balance and moderation. He argues that many monks in Benedict's day would have looked to the examples of the early Egyptian desert monks as a type of monastic hero. Taylor says:

And heroes they were, accomplishing extraordinary feats, athletic in their intensity. If one monk knew of a neighboring brother who fasted for three months, he would do six, and on top of a pillar at that! As romantic as all this sounds, the European monks failed to live up to the tradition of the desert monks. Instead they went to the opposite extreme, living lives of undisciplined license. Into this atmosphere, Benedict introduced his humane approach of zealous moderation, ordinariness, and balance. (Taylor, 1989, p. 32)

This context and the resulting approach in the *RB* towards moderation, ordinariness (I particularly like this) and balance are helpful to keep in mind when considering in more detail what Benedict says about hospitality. In fact, Taylor points out that although there are no formal vows expected of a monk following the *RB*, Chapter 58 of the *RB* simply asks a monk 'to promise stability, *conversatio*,[5] and obedience' (Taylor, 1989. p. 15). By describing these commitments, Taylor underscores the manner in which together they can provide balance. He says, 'Without change and growth, stability is a prison. Without stability, change is chaos. Without a mutual commitment, obedience is slavery. And without obedience to a higher authority, change is capricious. [...] this provide[s] a way of living life in a balanced tension' (p. 16).

Hospitality in the Benedictine tradition

An English translation of Chapter 53 of the *RB* states the following:

> All guests who present themselves are to be welcomed as Christ, for he himself will say: *I was a stranger and you welcomed me* (Matt 25:35). Proper honor must be shown *to all. Especially to those who share our faith* (Gal 6:10) and to pilgrims.
>
> Once a guest has been announced, the superior and the brothers are to meet him with all courtesy of love. First of all, they are to pray together and thus be united in peace, but prayer must always precede the kiss of peace because of the delusions of the devil.
>
> All humility should be shown in addressing a guest on arrival or departure. By a bow of the head or by a complete prostration of the body, Christ is to be adored because he is indeed welcomed in them. After the guests have been received, they should be invited to pray; then the superior or an appointed brother will sit with them. The divine law is read to the guest for his instruction, and after that every kindness is shown to him. The superior may break his fast for the sake of a guest, unless it is a day of special fast which cannot be broken. The brothers, however, observe the usual fast. The abbot shall pour water on the hands of the guests, and the abbot with the entire community shall wash their feet. After the washing they will recite this verse: *God, we have received your mercy in the midst of your temple* (Ps 47[48]: 10).
>
> [...]
>
> The kitchen for the abbot and guests ought to be separate, so that guests – and monasteries are never without them – need not disturb the brothers when they present themselves at unpredictable hours. Each year, two brothers who can do the work competently are to be assigned to this kitchen. [...]
>
> The guest quarters are to be entrusted to a God-fearing brother. Adequate bedding should be available there. The house of God should be in the care of wise men who will manage it wisely.
>
> No one is to speak or associate with guests unless he is bidden; however, if a brother meets or sees a guest, he is to greet him humbly, as we have said. He asks for a blessing and continues on his way, explaining that he is not allowed to speak with a guest. (Fry, 1981, pp. 255–259)

de Waal (1995) reflects further upon what Benedict is challenging us to do when we meet a stranger. She suggests it sounds easier said than done, and also could too easily remain only theoretical, so Benedict makes it practical by describing the steps by which a guest is to be welcomed. She says, 'The balance is kept nicely between the spiritual and the material and the guests are invited to share in the holistic way of life of the community' (p. 157). She highlights the tension that Benedict is setting out as he describes the ways in which particular members of the monastic community are to welcome guests while at the same time other monks should continue on in their monastic commitments and limit interaction with the guests. Although she acknowledges it might initially seem as though Benedict's warmth for guests is lost as he tells the monks not to mix with guests unnecessarily, she sees this more as Benedict telling her to do two things at once and to hold them in tension:

> This is true and responsible care for my own self. It is part of Benedict's total approach to life which all the time tells me about the handling of everything human and non-human, with respect and reverence. This is caught once again when he says so delicately and beautifully towards the end of the chapter [...] that 'the house of God', where the guests will be housed (the name is in itself significant), is to be in the care of wise men who will manage it wisely even down to the details of adequate bedding. Everyone and everything matters in the eyes of God. (de Waal, 1995, p. 156)

I agree with de Waal's (1995) reflections on Benedict's directions about hospitality, and the manner in which he is suggesting balance and boundaries. These are not only matters that 'any good psychologist would tell us [are] essential lessons that we all need to learn' (de Waal, 1995, p. 156) but are also useful for therapists to keep in mind in their own professional practice. I suggest that therapists may not only learn about balance and boundaries[6] but will also be encouraged to consider issues of physical space and appropriate fit between client needs, therapist skills and workplace mandates when examining Benedict's hospitality in the *RB*.

Contemporary applications for therapeutic practices

I began reflecting upon the concept of hospitality when writing about working within the area of spirituality in *The Narrative Practitioner* (Béres, 2014). My interest in hospitality and what it offers therapists as a model of engaging ethically with service users was further sparked by comments made by Epston (2012), who pointed out that 'hospitality' derives from the same root word as 'hospice' and 'hospital' and was an important tradition in some monastic traditions.[7] His main argument was that therapists should consider how to be welcoming and hospitable to those requesting therapeutic services and should also remind themselves to be respectful guests when meeting with clients in their home environments. However, his comments regarding the link to monastic traditions reminded me of a former clinical supervisor, Denis Costello, who actively used Chittister's (1992/2004) insights on *The Rule of St Benedict* as a guide for how to manage the counselling office of which he was director and how to provide clinical and administrative supervision to those of us working in the agency. I distinctly remember the sudden change of furniture in his office as he brought in much more comfortable seating from his home to ensure a more welcoming and hospitable set up in his office for clients and staff. This rekindled curiosity about hospitality took me in search of articles about its use in therapeutic settings.

The importance of space in professional practice

Aman (2006), who was also inspired by comments Epston made about 'therapist as host' in a workshop she attended, has written about hospitality in her narrative practice. She builds upon Epston's ideas by reflecting upon what she witnessed in her grandmother's welcoming care of others. She does not link these reflections to any analysis of monastic Rules but rather focuses on how mainstream ideas of hospitality have assisted her in ensuring that her private practice office is set up as a warm and inviting space and that she markets her practice in a welcoming manner. Although not directly linked to *Benedictine* considerations, these are not insignificant reminders as the physical and psychological space created in therapeutic settings will affect the types of interactions that occur in that space. A welcoming and hospitable space can encourage egalitarian therapeutic relationships and natural flowing conversations. Whereas some spaces might encourage more hierarchical interactions and pathology-focused interviews, a hospitable environment and exchange may be more apt to integrate curiosity about the strengths, resilience and knowledge service users already possess.[8]

Aristarkhova (2012) presents a more complex analysis of hospitality, presenting Levinas's and Derrida's descriptions of it and suggesting that feminists should take up the concept and show the link between hospitality and the maternal. Although she presents a clear review of how Levinas and Derrida were influenced by Jewish and Christian accounts of hospitality, and how they struggled with how people could welcome the 'Other'/stranger against the backdrop of the Holocaust, I am not convinced by her arguments that femininity and the maternal are natural forms of hospitality[9].

What is interesting is how she points out that for Derrida hospitality is a 'radical concept that tries to open up other possibilities for treating others and therefore as a movement beyond tolerance' (p. 167). Thinking of the definition of hospitality as 'the friendly and generous reception of guests, visitors or strangers (www.oxforddictionaries.com/definition/english/hospitality) and the element of welcoming the stranger that is part of hospitality, I am reminded of Derrida and Dufourmantelle's *Of Hospitality* (2000), in which Derrida reflects upon both the 'Foreigner Question' and then the 'Step of Hospitality/No Hospitality'. The translator comments that she primarily translates *étranger* in the text as 'foreigner', although it also could just as easily be translated as 'stranger'. She points out the word is similar to the Greek word *xenos* which also contains both meanings. In considering 'xenophobia' as it is currently and frequently being expressed in 2016 (more Islamophobia perhaps) as the fear of terrorists who could be disguised as refugees or immigrants, Derrida's comments appear relevant and timely. Derrida, in fact, discusses hospitality as involving a transgressive (radical?) step of crossing a threshold or border, and he moves on to both encourage and also problematize absolute hospitality, which he suggests should not come from a sense of duty, but which should allow for a welcoming of the stranger without question or expectation. A thorough analysis of how these ideas might be relevant to the current refugee crisis would take far more space than is available in this chapter. Since social workers often work with refugees and immigrants, these ideas would be relevant for social work practitioners engaged in settlement work, but this is somewhat of a digression from the focus of this paper, which is regarding therapeutic and counselling work or clinical social work.

Homan and Collins Pratt (2007) also describe hospitality as a radical act. They describe Benedict as having lived in a time of chaos as the Roman Empire was falling. His context could be described as sharing similarities with the chaos many people are experiencing in 2016. In this context, many people become fearful of strangers and even more fearful of welcoming them into their communities. It is also possible for therapists to sometimes become fearful of people with whom they work, as service users can present in a wide range of manners, from despairing and suicidal to angry and hostile. Homan and Collins Pratt (2007) say, 'When we speak of the depth of hospitality, we are proposing something scary and radical. But it's worth the risk. Unless we find and practice ways of hospitality we will grow increasingly hostile' (p. xxii). Reflecting upon the *RB*, they point out, 'Monastic hospitality creates sacred space where the guest is free to be alone, to enter silence, to pray and rest. No one is compelled to fill up the guest's spare time or set an agenda for him or her' (p. xvii). At a later point, they use the image of preparing a table as an overall metaphor for hospitality, saying this is more than merely providing comfort for a few days, but rather is a type of hospitality that 'seeps into your soul and shapes your identity. We can give this kind of hospitality to each other only if we take the time to prepare sheltering places around us' (p. 114). They point out the following:

> The table, for the teacher or social worker, is her or his desk. Whatever the specific physical structures of your work might be, you give something to others from them. You create a space for others because work is always for the service of others. (Homan and Collins Pratt, 2007, p. 115)

Contemporary therapeutic practitioners create space to work with others and so may also learn from reflecting upon Benedictine hospitality. Benedict describes a method of hospitality which includes instructions about how to bow to welcome guests; read, pray and eat with them; and provide adequate space for quiet and bedding for comfortable sleep. I am not suggesting that contemporary therapists should be praying with people who come to consult them, but this list certainly reminds therapists of the need to attend holistically to service users, responding not only to the emotional aspects of their lives but also to the physical, social, intellectual and spiritual (Swinton, 2001).

Balance

As Patrick Moore described in classroom lectures and private discussion (6 October 2015), one of Benedict's greatest discoveries was the benefits of balance and order (rhythm) for a healthy life. This balance ensures space and time for labour, sleep and study as well as for leisure and contemplation, which professionals can too easily discount in the busyness of contemporary society (Pieper, 1952/2009). This balance partly comes about from reflecting upon the tensions inherent with providing space for hospitality and also needing to step back and nurture that space.

Beginning professional practitioners (social workers, nurse practitioners, counsellors, etc.) often need to develop methods of setting limits with work expectations and service users' needs so that they leave unfinished tasks and worries at work, and maintain the space and time for leisure and the nurturing of their own spiritual, personal and social lives. In the work world of caring professionals, where wanting to care for and help people motivated their career choices, therapists need to commit to the type of balance and boundaries that Benedict suggests. When at work, they can improve their interactions with people if they consider them guests looking for hospitality and the space for contemplation and rejuvenation, but then they protect themselves from burnout by maintaining a healthy balance and retreating back to their own private spaces. Guests are drawn to the monastery for the space and time it has to offer, which is only possible because of the monks' commitment to that lifestyle, so the monks withdraw and maintain that lifestyle which will then benefit themselves and the guests. So, too, a service user is drawn to a therapeutic practice and a particular therapist, due to what that therapist is able to offer. The therapist needs to take care of her- or himself in order to be healthy enough to take care of others. The directive to welcome everyone as if welcoming Christ within each person can lead to problems if the host has not ensured a healthy life balance involving contemplation and the time with guests to discern their intention.

This directive to be discerning at the same time as we are to welcome all guests provides a form of balance which again can offer a reflection for contemporary therapists. Although therapists might wish to be able to help everyone who requests assistance, this might not be possible if they do not have the specific skills or experience required or if the services requested do not fall within the mandate of the agency in which the therapist works. Although wanting to help people often motivates the choice to become a therapist, it is important for therapists to realize they cannot help everyone. Welcoming everyone without discernment can lead to difficulties.

As I completed the first draft of this chapter, I contacted my former clinical supervisor, Denis Costello, who first introduced me to the *RB* as he reflected on it each day in his role as branch manager and supervisor. I was interested in his thoughts on what I had written, especially because he is now executive director of that same social work counselling agency and continues to be committed to nurturing the development of effective and ethical social work professionals. In personal communication (2 December 2015), he pointed out that he particularly liked the image of the ability of the monastic community to welcome hospitably the stranger as being based on a healthy tension: the guest master welcomes and hosts the visitor, but this hospitality is founded on the contemplative life of the community, and particularly the contemplative life of the rest of the monks. He reflected on the number of times he has gone to monasteries for retreat and refreshment, and so recognizes this as true. As visitors, we need both the guest master and the background context/space of the praying community, as they work in tandem.

He then moved on to suggest that by transferring this image to therapy, he would suggest the wise therapist is both host and contemplative community at the same time in the office with the client. He agreed that we need the balance of work and personal time outside of the office, but he very helpfully pointed out that we need to provide that balance also within the session. He said he worries about staff who work so hard in sessions that they are then in desperate need for much rest and recreation outside of work. He proposed that the secret is to make work refreshing: make it both contemplative and active. Although he pointed out that beginning therapists tend to work too hard, he appreciated the idea that they can improve their interactions with people if they consider them guests looking for hospitality and the space for contemplation and rejuvenation.

His final thought was that it might help to consider hospitality as a virtue or to use a virtue framework to consider hospitality. If, for instance, virtue can be defined as being an acquired human characteristic, therapists do not need to have been born naturally hospitable; rather, they can gain this characteristic with practice. Also, if virtues exist on a continuum, too little means a therapist may be closed off from the 'Other'; too much means a therapist will have no boundaries. He suggested prudence and reflection/contemplation may then be needed to find the right balance between those two ends of the continuum.

Conclusion

I have primarily focused this chapter on an examination of what the *RB*, although written in the sixth century C.E., offers contemporary practitioners, whether they would describe themselves as spiritual or not. I believe it continues to present a thoughtful and pragmatic method for developing an attitude of hospitality in contemporary society. Benedict's specific advice about how to balance the directive to welcome everyone as if we are welcoming Christ, with the need to ensure the ongoing commitments to 'stability, *conversatio,* and obedience' (Taylor, 1989, p. 15) is particularly helpful for contemporary therapeutic practitioners. This balanced approach to developing a welcoming therapeutic space and interaction ensures that radical hospitality does not endanger the ongoing well-being of the therapist and is a good reminder of the importance of self-care prior to care of the 'Other'. Benedict and his monks could not be all things to all people and were required to set limits. Professional therapeutic practitioners also need to be encouraged not to be swept along by the pressures of the 'culture of now', as Brueggemann (2014) describes it, and by the expectations of some service users to always be available, as it is beneficial to both service users and therapists if we also step back at times, ensuring a commitment to contemplation, study, sleep and recreation as well as a commitment to work.

My hope is that readers of this chapter will have found that these descriptions of hospitality have provided useful concepts for further consideration regarding how they might also integrate these elements into their own personal and professional contexts. We can all develop a sense of a safe space and hospitality, whether in traditional counselling offices, out in the community, in medical settings or even as visitors ourselves to service users' homes, as being a respectful and caring guest is just as important.

To return to my opening thoughts within this chapter, my examination of the concept of hospitality has certainly made me appreciate it as a skill in others and no longer feel dismissive of being complimented on my own ability to be hospitable. I am now able to more consciously decide how to integrate this not only in my personal life but also in classrooms and counselling settings.

References

Aman, J., 2006. Therapist as host: making my guests feel welcome. *International Journal of Narrative Therapy and Community Work*, 3, pp. 3–10.

Aristarkhova, I., 2012. Hospitality and the maternal. *Hypatia*, 27(1), pp. 163–181.

Béres, L., 2012. A thin place: narratives of space and place, Celtic spirituality and meaning. *The Journal of Religion and Spirituality in Social Work: Social Thought*, 31(4), pp. 394–413.

Béres, L., 2013. Celtic spirituality and postmodern geography: narratives of engagement with place. *Journal for the Study of Spirituality*, 2(2), pp. 170–185.

Béres, L., 2014. *The narrative practitioner*. Basingstoke: Palgrave Macmillan.

Béres, L., forthcoming. Celtic spiritualty: exploring the fascination across time and place. In B. R. Crisp, ed., *The Routledge handbook of religion, spirituality and social work*. New York: Routledge. Ch. 15.

Brueggemann, W., 2014. *Sabbath as resistance: saying no to the culture of now*. Louisville: Westminster John Knox Press.

Chittister OSB, J., 2004, 1992. *The rule of Benedict: insights for the ages*. New York: Crossroad.

Cotter, J., 1996. *Love rekindled: practising hospitality*. Sheffield: Cairns Publications in association with Evesham: Arthur James.

Derrida, J., and Dufourmantelle, A., 2000. *Of hospitality: Anne Dufourmantelle invites Jacques Derrida to respond*. Translated by R. Bowlby. Stanford: Stanford University Press.

de Waal, E., 1995. *A life-giving way: a commentary on the Rule of St. Benedict*. Collegeville: The Liturgical Press.

Epston, D., 2012. Master Class Conference sponsored by Re-authoring Teaching: creating a collaboratory, Waltham, VT. 9–11 October.

Fry, T., ed., Baker, I., Horner, T., Raaba, A., and Sheridan M., assoc. eds., 1981. *RB 1980. The Rule of St. Benedict. In Latin and English with notes*. Collegeville: The Liturgical Press.

Homan OSB, D., and Collins Pratt, L., 2007. *Radical hospitality: Benedict's way of love*. Glasgow: Wild Goose Publications.

Kramer, K. T., 2011. Radical hospitality. *America*, 2004 (6), p. 9.

Moffat, K., 1999. Surveillance and government of the welfare recipient. In A. Chambon, A. Irving and L. Epstein, eds., *Reading Foucault for social work*. New York: Columbia Press. Ch. 9.

Moore, P., 2015. Classroom discussion in Core Module 1 of MA in *Christian Spirituality* at Sarum College, Salisbury, Wiltshire, UK. 6 October.

Pearson, P. M., 2011. Hospitality to the stranger: Thomas Merton and St. Benedict's exhortation to welcome the stranger as Christ. *American Benedictine Review*, 62(1), pp. 27–41.

Pieper, J., 2009, 1952. *Leisure: the basis of culture.* San Francisco: Ignatius Press.

Sheldrake, P., 2013. *Spirituality: a brief history*, 2nd edn. Chichester: John Wiley and Sons.

Stewart OSB, C., 1998. *Prayer and community: the Benedictine tradition.* London: Darton, Longman and Todd.

Swan, L., 2005. *Engaging Benedict: what the Rule can teach us today.* Notre Dame: Ave Maria Press.

Swinton, J., 2001. *Spirituality and mental health care: rediscovering a 'forgotten' dimension.* London: Jessica Kingsley.

Taylor, B. C., 1989. *Spirituality for everyday living: an adaptation of the rule of St. Benedict.* Collegeville: The Liturgical Press.

Notes

1   See Beres (forthcoming) in *The Routledge Handbook of Religion, Spirituality and Social Work* for a full description of Celtic spirituality.

2   I teach in the School of Social Work in King's University College at Western University in Ontario, Canada. I am a registered social worker in Ontario and practice as a clinical social worker. In Canada the scope of practice for social work is broader than in the United Kingdom. The type of clinical social work I practice is what would more likely be described as counselling or therapy in the United Kingdom.

3   I believe the *RB* also offers insights for the contemporary lay person and university professor as regards hospitality and, in fact, much more generally provides a method of working towards balance in life for anyone attempting to lead a healthy life.

4   See Beres (2012, 2013) for full descriptions of Celtic spirituality, thin places, space and place and how these ideas are relevant for social work practice.

5   Taylor (1989) explains that *conversatio* is generally not translated because of the debates about its proper meaning. He says it is generally agreed that it means a monk is to live fervently as a monk, following Christ's example, committed to a life that will involve changing and becoming more like Christ over the course of life, and acknowledging that the monk may sin but needs to commit to the process of always turning back to Christ (pp. 20–21).

6   As a registered social worker in the Ontario College of Certified Social Workers and Social Service Workers, I am bound by the College's Code of Ethics and Values. Most professions are bound by Codes of Ethics which stipulate what constitutes unethical behaviour; much of the unethical behaviour could be described as not maintaining appropriate boundaries between client and professional.

7　www.oxforddictionaries.com/definition/english/hospitality defines hospitality as 'the friendly and generous reception and entertainment of guests, visitors or strangers', and its origins as coming from the Old French *hospitalite*, and from the Latin *hospitalitas*, and *hospitalis* 'hospitable' and then suggests seeing the definition of 'hospital'. The definition of hospital then is linked to 'hospice' and the Knights Hospitaller, or Knights of the Order of the Hospital of St John of Jerusalem in the eleventh century.

8　In *Reading Foucault for Social Work* (1999), Moffat describes the impact of the physical space of an interview room on the dynamics of the interaction between social worker and service user. Drawing upon Jeremy Bentham's 'panopticon' and Foucault's 'technologies of power', he says, 'The design of the office assumes that the worker will take on the role of supervisor and interrogator' (p. 225).

9　She makes the argument that women, since we have wombs and provide a form of hospitality when pregnant, which also involves a form of giving up of control over one's body, naturally experience a form of radical hospitality that problematizes ownership.

Utilizing Availability and Vulnerability to Operationalize Spirituality

Melanie Rogers

Introduction

In this chapter I introduce the concepts of 'availability and vulnerability' (A&V) and offer a rationale for adapting these concepts and using them as a framework for operationalizing spirituality in practice. I reflect on the concepts of A&V, describe how they have come to have personal significance for me, provide findings from a recent research study and suggest how they are helpful for integrating spirituality in nursing, social and psychological care.

The Northumbria Community is a dispersed Celtic Christian monastic community with a 'mother house' based in Northumberland, United Kingdom. (Readers who are unfamiliar with the language of 'monasteries', 'monastic communities', and 'monastic "Rules"' may find it useful to read Chapter 9, in which Laura Béres gives a background to these ideas prior to describing the concept of 'hospitality' in the *'Rule of St Benedict'* and implications for practice.) I became a companion, or member, of this community 17 years ago, and have chosen to integrate their 'Rule of Life' and embrace the concepts of 'availability and vulnerability' into my own life and work as an advanced nurse practitioner in primary care. Similar to other monastic communities, the Northumbria Community has a 'Rule of Life', which is like a structure of suggestions companions attempt to follow and which often incorporate vows. The two vows taken by companions of the Northumbria Community are in regards to 'availability' (to God and others) and intentional, deliberate 'vulnerability' (before God and others).

My journey

My interest in spirituality stemmed from an early age, although at that time I would not have labelled it as such. I grew up in a family affected by severe depression which had a significant impact on my childhood. I learnt at an early age that my inner journey held a way to understanding some of the inconsistency and challenges that faced me in my outer journey. Although there was no Christian influence in my family, I became involved in my local church through the Girl Guide movement, where I was an active participant. I am not sure I thought a great deal about 'God' or even listened that much at the church services, but something about the liturgy gave me solace and opened up many of the ontological and existential questions of life.

Throughout my teens, I spent much of my time seeking meaning and purpose in my life through achievements. I became a young leader for the Guides; I worked as a shop assistant and waitress from the age of 14; attained my Duke of Edinburgh Awards; was selected to represent Yorkshire on Sail Training expeditions; and also represented my school on an expedition to the Himalayas. As a teen, I was sociable and keen to find out about others' lives through the experiences and adventures I had. I always had a nurturing, caring and compassionate personality, and naturally followed my vocation as a nurse to St Bartholomew's Hospital in London. On completing my nursing studies, I went on to work in Africa for a charity on a hospital ship before commencing my nursing career in London, followed by time in Canada, and then finally returned to Leeds in the United Kingdom.

These teenage experiences and varied work experiences led me to see the world in a different light; I saw poverty, affliction and struggle as well as the human determination to face trials and live in a way that cultivates the human spirit. I developed a vision to care for others and walk alongside them in their suffering. This vision later became a source of deep reflection as I started my nurse training and worked with many patients and their loved ones facing illness, adversity and death.

Throughout my formative years, significant people mentored and inspired me to consider my inner journey. They helped me see the way my life, work and developing spirituality could make a difference to those around me. These people radiated an altruistic view of the world. They lived their spirituality by their caring, compassionate understanding of struggle in humanity and the pain associated with being human. They helped to nurture me in a way that cultivated my deepest compassion for others and led me to fulfil my vocation as a nurse, which has been the focus of my working life for over 25 years.

These formative relationships, my childhood experiences and the expeditions to differing cultures contributed to my considerations regarding 'the meaning of life.' This led to my exploration of Christianity. and I made a commitment to become a Christian at 19 years of age. In many ways, my faith journey created more questions than answers. The belief I had when I was younger was that 'God' and 'spirituality' were synonymous. This has been challenged and refined to a completely different stance in my forties, where I now see that for some faith and spirituality are synonymous, but for many spirituality comes from other avenues, for example from relationships, work, hobbies, their pets or nature. As a young woman, I found a level of safety in what seemed to be the 'black and white' Christian values that were taught to me through different courses and groups I attended. As life in my early years had seemed inconsistent and at times chaotic, I clung to the structure of this 'Christian box' in which I kept myself safe. The values of Christianity, then as now, deeply influence my view on life and my care for others. However, I have moved to a way of living which could be described as having a deeper spirituality rather than a religious way of living in that my faith is very much an inner journey rather than expressed through outer aspects of church attendance and following doctrine. The 'black and white' values I held onto are now very much 'grey', which has created many more challenges in my life but has led to much more richness.

My journey through faith to what I now describe as spirituality has been the hardest 'adventure' of my life. It has challenged my core beliefs, values and moral compass. I have seen how within church settings people can become disillusioned. Some individuals within a church setting seem to feel they need to put on a mask of 'Christian living' whilst they struggle with the challenges we all face which make us human: love, fear, pain, selfishness, jealousy, lust, betrayal, loss, sexuality and morality, for example. Often, I witnessed those involved in a church setting feel as though they couldn't be real for fear others might think they did not have enough faith. Some of my work in church settings involved supporting and counselling those who attended a course I ran about relationships, sexuality and trauma. Through this I helped to foster a place where people could be vulnerable and real in safety. I found many people had felt trapped by their belief that they had to be a certain way which seemed to stem from church politics. I became passionate about being authentic in my life and faith, which led me to explore how this was expressed in my own day-to-day living.

Part of this journey led me out of 'church' and towards other faith communities who were struggling with what it means to have a faith and live authentically. This journey has been a roller coaster, with times of major activity within church settings and other times of disillusionment and frustration about the chasm that often existed between people's day-to-day life and their appearance and attitudes on Sunday at church. I had been seeking something external to bring me to a place of authenticity in my faith, rather than considering my inner journey.

The Northumbria Community

I came across the Northumbria Community through a chance conversation with an acquaintance. Having just finished facilitating a year-long course on the deeper issues of life, and feeling burnt out, I went to the community for a week-long retreat, not knowing what to expect. I was surprised to find a diverse group of people who were all struggling with organized church and were seeking companions with whom to be authentic in their questioning of organized religion. What I found there was an embracement of others irrespective of their life journey. During the first ten years of being a companion of the community, I was never asked about my occupation; people were interested in me for me – a revelation as nursing formed part of my sense of self. Part of the values of the Northumbria Community is 'the conviction that who a person is counts far more than what a person does' (Miller, 2003, p. 34). I also found an acceptance for my faith journey which was reinforced on my first visit by one of the house team members, who said, 'You are where you are on your journey, and that's okay.' What struck me was that this community of people was wrestling with how to live authentically as Christians. When I first attended, it was embryonic; there was little written guidance for the people who visited or became companions. Individuals focused on reflecting on their own journeys, experiences and challenges, following a rhythm each day which included time to read, pray, work, reflect, eat and live together.

The Northumbria Community's 'mother house' was initially a house deep within the beautiful countryside of the Cheviots straddling the England/Scotland border, where people could go to retreat. There is a rhythm of the day based on monastic practices of prayer, work, rest and community, with specific influences of a rich Northumbrian Celtic Christian heritage in order to integrate faith into daily life. These influences come from the heart of Celtic Christianity, including living simply and following Jesus and the journey of life in its everyday ordinariness. Miller (2016) suggests that reflecting on the deep heritage of Celtic Christianity and the journeys of Celtic Saints like Cuthbert, Bede, Aidan and Hilde, for example, reminds us of their simple lives, service and care of others and faithful witness. Many stories of these saints are reflected in the daily readings of the community and continue to encourage and inspire companions of the community (Northumbria Community, 2002). The Celtic tradition was monastic in nature, committed to God and others, with hospitality at its heart, reflecting the community call to availability and vulnerability.

As the community grew, it formed a dispersed community of people with a similar vision and ethos, with most companions living across the country and only a few based at the mother house, which was a place for companions to come together to meet, retreat and take time out of their busy lives for contemplation. (The Iona Community, based on Iona in the Scottish Hebrides, and The Community of Aidan and Hilda, on Holy Island off the north-east coast of England, are two other dispersed Celtic Christian communities.) I often would go for retreat to the Northumbria

Community to give myself time to reflect on my own life and explore questions I had about my spirituality with people who would listen and could relate to some of my questioning. What often struck me were the advantages of living as a dispersed community (part of their vision for a 'church without walls'), where relationship, rather than denomination or place, was the priority.

The Northumbria Community has steadily grown from when I joined, when there were approximately 50 companions, into a larger community with 375 companions worldwide, 1700 friends and around 1000 visitors (Askew, 2014). Many people visit the community's new mother house, which is now in Felton, Northumberland, where retreats are held, giving time to study specific areas, including spiritual formation, living authentically and being available and vulnerable. Individual retreats are offered weekly, where companions, friends and visitors can come for a time to seek God and find space for reflection and inner refreshment. When I joined the community, it was 'organic': there was a freedom to explore the community's ideas, with no set guidance. There is now a formal process involved in becoming a companion, where a number of core modules are followed, with a mentor, to discern the vocation as a companion and understand the ethos and vision of the Northumbria Community. Additionally, a number of texts have been published, the most well-known being *Celtic Daily Prayer*, to guide readers through the rhythm of daily life (Northumbria Community, 2002). I think this is inevitable when a community grows, but the community tries to ensure that the guidelines offer individuals creativity and flexibility in following the modules and that they are treated just as a 'guide' rather than as regulations.

The Northumbria Community describes itself as an ecumenical 'new monastic' community: 'new monastic' in terms of a fresh expression and authentic living out of the Christian faith within a community setting and also in the sense of drawing from the traditional monastic lifestyle of living within a 'Rule of Life' (Northumbria Community, n.d.). As indicated earlier, a traditional 'Rule' is discussed in Chapter 9, where Béres describes the sixth-century *Rule of St Benedict*, which provided guidelines for Benedictine monasteries. The Northumbria Community's 'Rule of Life' was developed for companions to follow, integrating the concepts of 'availability and vulnerability' into their daily lives wherever they lived (Northumbria Community, n.d.). The 'Rule' was, and still is, the fundamental backbone of the Northumbria Community, which companions choose to embrace within their own lives. I felt drawn to this as it is not set to be prescriptive, but rather provocative: a challenge as to how to live one's day-to-day life with the flexibility and adaptability needed for individuals' varied journeys. The Northumbria Community suggests the 'Rule' 'serves as a framework for freedom – not as a set of rules that restrict or deny life (Northumbria Community, 2004, p. 5).

For me, the simplicity of the 'Rule of Life' is a framework for a way of living authentically which resonates with many of my personal inner struggles. To be part of a community that welcomes questions and indeed encourages them is freeing. A community where all are valued and status is not sought, where a real spirituality is reflected in daily life and where the value of being authentic is nurtured enabled me to reach a place where the dissonance between my faith and my way of living was no longer so great. Spirituality for companions of the community is grounded in the 'Rule' and comes out of each individual's difficult and challenging life journey; it comes out of deep questioning, including, 'How do I live with myself? How do I live with others? How do I relate to the world around me? How do I find time and space for God?' (Northumbria Community, 2004, p. 10). This naturally affects my professional life as well.

Availability and vulnerability

Trevor Miller, one of the founders of the community, suggested that A&V are the keys to authentic living (Miller, 2014). Being available is defined as being accessible, at the disposal of another and serving others (Northumbria Community, 2004). Miller takes this further, embracing hospitality as an outworking of 'availability' in the Christian context. His descriptions of 'availability' resonate for me as they call companions to be hospitable by welcoming others: in doing so, he suggests, we welcome Jesus into our own lives. This concept of 'hospitality', and its resulting implications for practice, is described fully in Chapter 9. 'Hospitality', as described by St Benedict in the sixth century, was also about welcoming the stranger as if we were welcoming Jesus, but, in addition, included the need to discern whether it was safe to welcome the stranger, ensuring that the way of life of the monastery could continue to be protected. 'Availability' is extended into care and concern for others through action, prayer and intercession, being hospitable to others and following Jesus in our own 'vocation' (Miller, 2014). This definition of 'availability', if taken literally, has far-reaching consequences for one's life and work. Companions are encouraged to work this out in their own way within the context of their own lives.

Choosing 'availability' as a bedrock for their approach to others evoked a significant question for the community, which continues to be a place of exploration for companions. The question that follows from the principle of availability is 'How then shall we live?' It is all very well choosing 'availability', but if one is to be authentic, this decrees 'vulnerability' and not just an embracing, but a living out of these vows. This is something I continue to reflect upon as I have values and beliefs that are fundamental to my life, and I want to live authentically by these. What I often struggle with, though, is my own selfishness that means sometimes I do not want to be available and vulnerable. However, the 'Rule' recognizes that we are 'human' and that this is a journey, not a destination. This gives me hope that as I continue to mature and reflect, my ethos can be evolving. Additionally, it would not be possible to live in a way that is consistently available and vulnerable all the time. Perhaps this acknowledges some of what is described in Chapter 9 about the need for balance, including boundaries, as described in the *Rule of St Benedict.*

The marrying of A&V significantly brings with it a desire and willingness to fully connect with others and God. Vulnerability for many is seen as weakness and a place of potentially being hurt (Herrick and Mann, 1998). On the other hand, the community suggests a position of choosing to be '*intentionally* vulnerable', thus exposing oneself to or being willing to risk being harmed and wounded. Counter-intuitive though this may seem, the community asserts that embracing 'vulnerability' in this way can lead to extraordinary freedom and connection with others. Herrick and Mann (1998) suggest that it takes courage to risk being vulnerable, but by doing so we engender hope in others. Rolheiser (2004) talks about not becoming a 'doormat' by becoming vulnerable and going to the extreme of letting every aspect of our lives 'hang out'. He suggests true vulnerability is held within the strength of being able to be present oneself to another without the 'false props' we often use to bolster our egos. Vanier (1982) talks about how our choice of vulnerability over ego can transform those in our care by creating the safety for them to feel loved and accepted: able to lift their masks and risk being vulnerable themselves. These viewpoints speak significantly to me and have helped me to understand more about vulnerability and the power of embracing this attitude and stance in my own life. Many times, through illness and difficulties, patients who are already vulnerable come to see me; it is part of my job to acknowledge this and create a context of safety for them to feel 'held'.

The community is attentive to how embracing A&V can impact companions positively and adversely. They encourage accountability through connection with 'soul friends'. O'Donohue (1997) suggests soul friends walk alongside one another, sharing intimately about their journey with God and life. In this relationship, companions can be authentic and accountable, and share the ups and downs of the journey with someone who sees, accepts and supports them for the beauty of who they really are. The Northumbria Community describes a soul friend as 'someone you choose to be there for you on that inner journey; to be there for you in the good and bad times. The soul friend sees the best and the worst in you and is committed to supporting you' (Northumbria Community, 2005, p. 10).

Choosing a life of embracing A&V is risky, and yet I have also found it profoundly helpful to be able to talk through the implications and experiences of living this way and to be seen as who I am. Reflection and discussion with a soul friend have often helped me to discern how to live out the values of the community in a healthy way at home and at work. Herrick and Mann (1998) caution that it is not possible to be vulnerable with every person in every situation and that discernment must come into play to be able to be vulnerable in a healthy life-giving way. Within this, boundaries need to be established, not to prevent relationships developing, but to actually give them more freedom within the limits individually set. An example for me has been in my support offered to friends struggling with addiction. I have supported friends through alcoholism, sex addiction and eating disorders, and have been there with and for them over long periods of time. It would not have been helpful for me at every point of need to drop everything and come to their physical aid. There was a need to establish some boundaries in order to attempt to empower them to address their issues; however, consistently affirming acceptance and care was profoundly helpful for them in their journey. The boundaries laid, and the discernment of when to be there physically and when to support from afar, was what enabled me to truly offer care and support within the context of A&V, without becoming bitter or burnt out. Nouwen (1998) suggests that without boundaries the needs of others can become overwhelming; in order to remain in a place of mutuality, people must hold onto their own identity and not try to be everything to everyone. A&V involve a measure of control in order to relate in a healthy way (Herrick and Mann, 1998). The intention of holding to A&V as one's ethos and then working to put that ethos into practice is actually strengthened through healthy boundaries, rather than diminished by them.

For the community, being 'vulnerable' also includes being willing to be teachable, being willing to learn and willing to change. This often comes about through listening to God in the context of prayer and the study of scriptures, but also through dialogue with others and by being willing to reflect upon and challenge one's values, attitudes and behaviours. Faith in God is seen as an absolute; however, understanding other people and being accepting and open to differences encourages companions to allow their convictions to be challenged and sometimes changed. Life as a companion to the community includes being open to change whilst remaining in the context of the stability of relationship with God. Being open and willing to be teachable, and also willing to consider changing or refining my views, has been important in my own journey, which, as mentioned above, began in the 'black and white' context of an evangelical church. The move to uncertainty in many aspects of my life, whilst holding onto the certainty of my faith in God, has been freeing and has enabled me to continually reflect upon and review my own experiences and conceptions of life. Vulnerability and willingness to learn and adapt stem from companions being asked to embrace the 'Heretical Imperative' for self and others (Northumbria Community, 2002). This is practised through 'challenging the assumed truth, being receptive to criticism, affirming that relationship matters more than reputation' (Miller, 2014). Accepting to live in this way, making a choice to challenge rather than just accept the status quo at times, can be a very vulnerable position to take.

Context for using availability and vulnerability as a way of operationalizing spirituality

I have chosen to work in a way which is available and vulnerable in my professional practice, and I have seen how this has impacted my connection with patients and how it has enabled me to integrate spirituality into my practice. My view of spirituality is that it is a way of finding hope, meaning and purpose: it is innately human. This is foundational to my practice where I daily work with patients who are struggling to find hope, meaning and purpose in their own lives. As I relate to them 'human to human', I can support them in these struggles.

Personal reflection, observation of clinical practice, empirical research and study of the spirituality literature has highlighted the difficulty many practitioners have operationalizing spirituality. Holistic practice is well recognized and includes spirituality, yet many clinicians struggle to know what spiritual care actually means and often feel unequipped to address these issues in practice (Coyle, 2002; Agrimson and Toft, 2008; Cook, 2011). A research project I conducted offered advanced nurse practitioners an opportunity to reflect on A&V and whether these concepts could be used as a framework to integrate spirituality into their work. Eight participants were interviewed face-to-face during two in-depth interviews spaced 18 months apart. The dialogue that occurred between the participants and me allowed for the development of a thick description of the phenomenon of spirituality in their practice.

Although participants indicated having struggled with how to conceptualize and integrate spirituality into their practice, having had the concepts of A&V introduced to them, and after thorough exploration, they recognized and identified that A&V were concepts which could be a useful lens for integrating spirituality in ANP (Advanced Nurse Practitioner) consultations. This framework can be transported to settings where faith, religion and the spiritual beliefs of those concerned cannot be assumed, offering structure and direction in practice. There is a precedent for this in the example of how mindfulness has been adapted from Buddhism and integrated into health care as a recognized treatment option (Williams and Penman, 2011). Lisa McCorquodale discusses mindfulness and its use in occupational therapy in Chapter 8.

Translating A&V into life and work means giving not just time to patients and those in our personal lives but also being truly present through listening, care and compassion (Helming, 2009; Carron and Crumbie, 2011). It involves being intentional in our work and life relationships to try to be present, to understand and give of ourselves unconditionally within the boundaries of context. It necessitates standing up when we have seen injustice and standing alongside others as they struggle to be heard. It leads to saying 'yes' to being 'human' especially in the context of our work, allowing our patients to see us as people and not just clinicians. This requires, at times, appropriate sharing of self within the boundaries of our regulatory bodies. For example, I was meeting with a patient who I thought had bowel cancer who had been referred for investigations. I saw him regularly and spent time talking through his feelings and concerns about the diagnosis, treatment and his prognosis; I shared with him that my dad had been through a similar situation and that I understood some of how he might be feeling. This helped this particular patient to feel 'held' and cared for by someone who could empathize rather than merely sympathize. What was important for me in my sharing was that my emotional distress about my dad was not present; he had had bowel cancer ten years previously. It would not be appropriate to share something which could lead to the consultation becoming about my distress; the aim in my sharing was to be supportive and to empathize appropriately. Other times I have tried to offer patients hope when they are going through significant illness by sharing learning from other patients' experiences (anonymously) that I have witnessed and what helped others in similar situations. Occasionally, my sharing may be something seemingly small and incidental, like talking about a recent trip to somewhere the patient too may have been, or a connection with a hobby the patient may also have. The times I share something of myself are often spontaneous, though within me there is a strong sense of boundaries and the need to not confuse the professional relationship. This means that the aspects shared are often incidents from the past where the emotions for me have been worked through and I feel contained in my sharing, or they may involve something which is not at a depth where it would have an adverse impact on me. It would not benefit my patients if I became distressed about aspects of my life whilst trying to support them or if the consultation lost focus from them. However, the sharing of my experiences and myself has repeatedly shown me that patients appreciate this and feel more understood and able to trust me when they recognize my 'humanity' within my professional role.

In these choices and ways of practicing with my patients, I have chosen A&V to integrate spirituality into practice.

In this next section, I integrate my own experiences with my research findings to propose a framework for practice.

Availability and vulnerability: A framework for operationalizing spirituality

Availability

Availability to 'ourselves'

In order to integrate 'availability' into practice, awareness of our inner life and the places from which our values and beliefs emanate is important. This is certainly consistent with critical reflection of practice and the findings of Jan Fook's work presented in Chapter 2. Many of the participants in my study viewed their work as vocational and consistently gave of themselves, sometimes unfortunately to the point of 'burnout'. Burnout is not uncommon amongst health professionals who often put their 'heart' into caring (Wright, 2005). Being conscious of our 'inner journey' personally and professionally enables us to be able to practise holistically whilst also being aware of our own needs. Self-reflection, self-acceptance, self-care and supervision are vital for healthy relationships that are needed in the helping professions. Self-acceptance is important before we can truly accept others as they are (Vanier, 2004). Being comfortable with self, being at home in one's skin, is a foundational starting point for authentically working with patients. Vanier states, 'People reach maturity as they find the freedom to be themselves, and to claim, accept and love their own personal story, with all its brokenness and beauty' (Vanier, 2004, p. 23). By consistently reflecting on our journey, the authentic self becomes an agent for increased compassion and honest relationships through true self-acceptance.

The first aspect of availability, therefore, involves being available to ourselves in our inner lives, continuing as clinicians to be self-reflective and self-accepting, embracing spirituality (broadly defined as understanding of one's meaning, purpose and direction in life) as key to our inner journey.

Availability to others through welcome

How we welcome our patients often impacts the whole interaction. Simply introducing ourselves to patients and offering them time to talk about their presentation and anxieties is akin to offering hospitality and welcome. Hospitality here can be defined as simply providing a friendly and open reception (Thompson, 1995) (see also Chapter 9 for a full discussion of the complexity of, and limits to, hospitality). By consciously welcoming patients and by being open and willing to be available to them and to truly listen to them, the ground is laid for a mutual exchange based on equality and acceptance. There is no need to justify attendance when one feels welcomed, heard and accepted. The key to welcoming a patient is to truly listen. Nouwen (1996) links listening to welcoming and acceptance. He suggests that true listening is not about just letting people speak, but rather is about paying full attention to what they are saying, what they are not saying and who they are. Expanding upon this, he says, 'The beauty of listening is that those who are listened to start feeling accepted, start taking their words more seriously and discovering their true selves. Listening is a form of spiritual hospitality' (Nouwen, 1996, p. 85).

The second aspect of 'availability' involves being welcoming to patients: offering time, acceptance and understanding whilst being truly present and listening attentively.

Availability to others through caring

Care and concern are the primary focus of our work. To care for another is to commit to give of self and in doing so welcome a patient's story, creating a safe place where patients, free to be themselves, can 'tell it like it is'. This is, in Nouwen's words, 'the highest form of hospitality' (Nouwen, 1973, p. 95). To be able to do this, we need to have an understanding of our own inner journey and also our areas of experience and expertise. Many beginning clinicians seeing patients may rigidly hold onto taught models of practice which may include specific questions and approaches. As clinicians mature, they are often aware of how interactions become more meaningful for patients when they simply feel listened to (Balint, 1964), and they no longer rely so rigidly on the taught practice models. In order for this to happen, clinicians need to open themselves up to letting the patient lead the interactions and give time to hear the patient's story.

The third aspect of availability involves offering care and concern for patients through active participation, creating a safe place for patients to tell their story as it is.

Availability in response to the needs of patients and the community

For many clinicians, our work is dynamic and aims to respond to the needs of those in our care. Over time many of us may have developed specialist areas of practice where we see the needs of patients beyond what is normally offered in our practice. By responding to the needs of our patients and by being aware of ongoing needs within the community in which we practise, we can develop and be flexible in our work. (For example, in Chapters 11 and 12, Rumbold and Béres, respectively, both comment on the need to develop compassionate cities and communities that will better respond to the needs of people within the community.)

Therefore, the final aspect of 'availability' is being available and willing to develop practice in response to the needs of communities and to the needs of patients in communities.

Vulnerability

Vulnerability may need further exploration and a change of emphasis to be understood as a helpful way to operationalize spirituality. It necessitates moving away from seeing it as 'weakness' or as 'defencelessness' and towards seeing it as intentional. Several aspects of vulnerability will resonate for many, especially the idea of embracing vulnerability by being teachable. The wide varieties of interactions we face each day constantly challenge us to ensure we are kept up to date about the issues impacting our practice. Additionally, being willing to learn from our patients and seeing working with them as a privilege often reframes our practice. Being willing to learn from our relationships, our interactions and the responses of our patients can be incredibly powerful. Duvall and Béres (2011) discuss the vulnerability and tentativeness of language in their chapter regarding 'Circulation of Language.' They also describe vulnerability as incorporating tentativeness that suggests moving away from rigidity and towards greater flexibility and openness to new learning.

Embracing vulnerability by being teachable

Being teachable includes being willing to learn, adapt and gain new knowledge. None of us will ever have 'arrived' in terms of knowing all that could ever be needed for our work. Using our knowledge, experience, skills and discernment aids practice. Equally, choosing to work collaboratively with our patients develops trust and may be key to recovery or working together to solve problems and anxieties. Within the many complex and challenging situations we face, we will not have all of the necessary knowledge; referring to other colleagues for support and advice may be needed at times and can be considered through supervision and reflection, helping us to recognize our learning needs. In order to do this, we must be willing to accept our ongoing need for education, training, supervision and reflection in order to provide a service where patients feel safe, supported and able to know they will be listened to and treated with understanding and respect.

The first aspect of vulnerability therefore involves developing an openness to be teachable; accepting the vulnerability of our clinical role and the reality that within our work we will never 'know all'.

Willingness to be accountable to others

Accountability is fundamental to practice as a clinician. The Nursing and Midwifery Code of Professional Conduct (Nursing Midwifery Council, 2015) suggests this is a way of ensuring practice is safe and transparent. Patients need to feel safe and to trust us. In light of the reality of us not knowing everything, patients often value our honesty about our limitations. Statements of honesty can actually improve the clinician–patient relationship. For example, 'I'm not sure what is going on here, but let's try this and see how things go', 'I'm going to ask a colleague to see you as I don't have much experience of …', or 'What do you think is going on here?' can all add to the sense of honesty and transparency in the working relationship. These sorts of admissions make the clinician accountable to the patient and often engender healthy relationships. Additionally, admitting mistakes as a clinician helps us to recognize our own limitations and recognize the need for further training and education as well as support from other colleagues. Miller, paraphrasing the theologian Thomas Merton, reminds us that the only mistake is one you don't learn from (Miller, 2014).

The second aspect of vulnerability involves being willing to embrace accountability, engaging in supervision, reflection and admission of mistakes, and being receptive to constructive criticism. It requires being willing to share uncertainty with patients and act in a way that is open, honest and transparent, working within our limitations.

Willingness to be vulnerable by advocating for patients

Embracing the 'heretical imperative' as part of vulnerability may come to the fore in terms of us being willing to speak up for those who may not have a voice (to be an advocate); to speak the truth, even if it means challenging colleagues or the systems within which we work. We strongly desire to meet our patients' needs, and through advocacy patients can see that they are valued and listened to, which can lead to a stronger sense of meaning. In order to advocate, not only do we need to consider challenging colleagues but also the wider systems, including the political arena and the culture of 'individualism'.

The third aspect of vulnerability involves being willing to be an advocate for patients. If necessary, it may require questioning authority, being honest and truthful with the best interests of the patient at heart.

Vulnerability and authenticity

Another aspect of vulnerability includes being willing to receive constructive criticism to develop personally and professionally, which necessitates maturity and resilience so as not to lose confidence. The goal with this aspect of vulnerability is to put building relationship with the patient before reputation. Though professionally, of course, reputation is of importance, the goal here is not to put value as a professional above the relationship with the patient. Relationship based upon care for patients is another mainstay of all clinical practice.

The final aspects of vulnerability involve a willingness to be authentic in the approach to care of patients and a willingness to be challenged and questioned without defensiveness.

Perspectives on implications for practice

Seeing A&V as a framework for operationalizing spirituality could have a major impact on us and our patients and lead us towards fully integrating holistic care. A&V supports practice in a way which is freeing and adaptable, recognizing the patients' and our own spirituality. It certainly promotes a tangible and pragmatic method for operationalizing patient-centred care.

Aspects of being available and vulnerable have also been explored in a number of nursing, psychology and sociology texts (Rogers, 1959, 1961, 1962, 1997; Schmid, 2001; Van Deurzen and Arnold-Baker, 2005; Martinsen, 2006; Brown, 2010, 2012; Thorup et al., 2012; Alvsvåg, 2014; Lindström, Nyström and Zetterlund, 2014).

From a Christian perspective, Martinsen (2006) and Eriksson (2007), both Nordic nurse theorists, suggest that nursing is founded on giving of oneself to care for others and offering neighbourly love (agape) and charity (caritas) as reflected in Jesus's commandment. Within the concepts of agape and caritas, prescencing (being available) is paramount (Lindström et al., 2014). Alvsvåg (2014) suggests that the agape love and caritas offered are coupled with discernment which is moral, practical and professional. This enables healthy relationships to occur whilst maintaining professional boundaries. Discernment necessitates balancing the emotional involvement with patients with the mutual vulnerability which must be present partly due to the caring role, but also because of shared humanity (Martinsen, 2006; Heaslip and Ryden, 2013).

Rogers (1997), writing about vulnerability in health care, identified that all are vulnerable to differing extents and that this can have negative consequences leading to harm, hurt and neglect. She recognizes the mutual vulnerability of caring which can be positive or negative depending on the situation, because of the emotional investment needed to care for others. Like the Northumbria Community, Rogers (1997) also recognizes that a truly therapeutic relationship requires commitment and emotional investment. She acknowledges that emotionally distancing from patients is unhelpful and suggests that feeling vulnerable may be a facet of good-quality care (Rogers, 1997). Denying emotional engagement with patients to reduce personal vulnerability may unintentionally increase vulnerability in patients as it can limit therapeutic connection.

The psychotherapist and researcher Carl Rogers detailed and explored the well-recognized core conditions needed in therapeutic practice; empathy, congruence and unconditional positive regard (Rogers, 1959). Schmid (2001) and Van Deurzen and Arnold-Baker (2005) consider these core conditions as necessary to connect with another as human to recognize their uniqueness and their inherent worth, and to love and respond to them with understanding and solidarity. Schmid (2001) recognizes Rogers' concepts of prescencing, authenticity and empathy as fundamental to building a relationship with another where the other can feel truly accepted. The unconditional positive regard Rogers describes must be free from 'buts' and 'ifs' in order to allow the other to experience acceptance in a way he or she may not have experienced before. Rogers reminds therapists that the offer of emotional warmth does not lead to 'emotional over-involvement', but to the other being able to 'actualise' (1961, p. 4). Schmid (2001), like the nursing theorists, values the individual as a fellow human being of inherent worth who deserves to be loved and accepted as he or she is. The fundamental acknowledgment of a shared humanity and a call to love, care and accept others echoes A&V.

Pollard (2005) and Brown (2012a) suggest that authenticity is what makes meaningful relationships. Authenticity is the key to wholehearted living and is evident in A&V. It involves being willing to be seen, being available to others, and being real; it necessitates vulnerability. Schmid (2001) proposes that being authentic comes out of prescencing and is the place where the other recognizes congruence, unconditional positive regard and empathy; it is being fully human and fully open. In being authentic, one learns to encounter the other as fully human. He suggests that a person is created to be authentic, to be open, to be transparent, in order to enter into dialogue with others and acknowledge their need (Schmid, 2001). Herrick and Mann (1998), Nouwen (1998) and Rolheiser (2004) recognize that boundaries are needed in order to maintain one's own identity and not to become overwhelmed and fully enmeshed in another's suffering.

Brown (2012a), from a sociological perspective, discovered the importance of vulnerability. This reflects the work previously cited of Carl Rogers and Martinsen. In her work on vulnerability, Brown (2012a) asserts that humans are 'hardwired' for connection and stresses that empathy fuels connection, whereas sympathy drives disconnection. Her research identifies vulnerability as the precursor to wholehearted living. Human-to-human connection is present when we meet with all our vulnerabilities. Brown's (2010) extensive research on vulnerability suggests that those willing to be connected, authentic, available and vulnerable live a more wholehearted and connected life than those who see vulnerability as a weakness. She suggests that blocking authenticity and vulnerability occurs by striving for perfection (not allowing others to see our weaknesses) and numbing emotions through alcohol, drugs, overeating or obsessive shopping, for example. In her research, the participants who chose to be authentic about their own vulnerabilities and who connected with others with the willingness to not have any guarantees were more joyful, more hopeful and more secure (Brown, 2010). Being willing to be authentic and courageous is, from her perspective, the most vulnerable but freeing and wholehearted way to live (Brown, 2012b). She suggests that true belonging only happens when presenting our authentic imperfect selves to the world; our sense of belonging can never be greater than our level of self-acceptance (Brown, 2010).

Van Deurzen and Arnold-Baker (2005) have written widely on existential therapy, and again, aspects of A&V can be seen which are fundamental to the therapist–client relationship. They suggest that the spiritual dimension is the most controversial of all human experiences, yet it is the dimension which allows the fullness of individual uniqueness, values and experiences to be explored with a therapist who listens fully, respects the individual, is authentic and values humanness (Van Deurzen and Arnold-Baker, 2005). Gilson (2014), offering a feminist critique, focuses on the ethics of vulnerability and reiterates that to be human is to be vulnerable. She states that this cannot be avoided; it is fundamental to being human and something we share. She also recognizes the dangers of vulnerability in that it can be unpredictable and uncontrollable, leading to many actively avoiding it. However, she asserts that, depending upon the viewpoint held about vulnerability, it can be an ethical imperative for human connection (Gilson, 2014). If the view of vulnerability is that it denotes weakness, powerlessness and harm, it will be actively avoided; if it is seen as part of the human condition, it will lead to ethical and moral action and a shared humanity.

All of these perspectives suggest that A&V are paramount to building professional and therapeutic relationships. They are also important considerations if choosing to truly integrate spirituality within health and social care practice.

Conclusion

The aim of this chapter has been to offer a description and an understanding of my own spiritual journey through becoming and living as a companion of the Northumbria Community. I have also described the concepts of A&V within the Northumbria Community 'Rule of Life' and provided a declaration of my personal position and influences in order to ensure transparency.

Finally, I have proposed a framework of A&V for operationalizing spirituality which can be simply used in clinical practice, and offered examples of availability and vulnerability from nursing, sociological and psychological perspectives. Practitioners do not need to be spiritual or religious in order to integrate A&V into their practice. The aspects of the framework are not widely different from professional codes of conduct, but they offer further ways in which we can understand how to authentically connect with others 'human to human' in direct practice. Additionally, they are methods of supporting our own development both as individuals and practitioners. I suggest that spirituality is innately human but sometimes difficult to conceptualize and apply to practice. A&V is one simple way of practically operationalizing spirituality.

References

Agrimson, L., and Toft, L., 2008. Spiritual crisis – a concept analysis. *Journal of Advanced Nursing,* 65(2), pp. 454–461.

Alvsvåg, H., 2014. Philosophy of caring. In M. Alligood, ed., *Nursing theorists and their work,* 8th edn. Grand Rapids: Elsevier. Ch. 10.

Balint, M., 1964. *The doctor, his patient and the illness,* 2nd edn. London: Pitman Medical.

Brown, B., 2010. *The gifts of imperfection.* Center City: Hazelden.

Brown, B., 2012a. *Daring greatly: how the courage to be vulnerable transforms the way we live, love, parent, and lead.* New York: Gotham.

Brown, B., 2012b. *The power of vulnerability: teachings on authenticity, connection, and courage* (audio course). Boulder: Sounds True Learning.

Carron, R., and Cumbie, S., 2011. Development of a conceptual nursing model for the implementation of spiritual care in adult primary health care settings by nurse practitioners. *Journal of the American Academy of Nurse Practitioners,* 23(10), pp. 552–560.

Cook, C., 2011. *Recommendations for psychiatrists on spirituality and religion.* London: Royal College of Psychiatrists.

Coyle, J., 2002. Spirituality and health: towards a framework for exploring the relationship between spirituality and health. *Journal of Advanced Nursing,* 37(6), pp. 589–597.

Duvall, J., and Béres, L., 2011. *Innovations in narrative therapy: connecting practice, training, and research.* New York: W.W. Norton.

Eriksson, K., 2007. The theory of caritative caring: a vision. *Nursing Science,* 20(3), pp. 201–202.

Gilson, E., 2014. *The ethics of vulnerability: a feminist analysis of social life and practice.* New York: Routledge.

Heaslip, V., and Ryden, J., 2013. *Understanding vulnerability: a nursing and healthcare approach.* Chichester: Wiley Blackwell.

Helming, M. A., 2009. Integrating spirituality into nurse practitioner practice: the importance of finding the time. *Journal for Nurse Practitioners,* 5(8), pp. 598–605.

Herrick, V., 1997. *Limits of vulnerability: exploring a kenotic model for pastoral ministry.* Cambridge: Grove Books.

Herrick, V., and Mann, I., 1998. *Jesus wept: reflections on vulnerability in leadership.* London: Darton, Longman and Todd.

Lindström, U., Nyström, L, and Zetterlund, J., 2014. Theory of caritative caring. In M. Alligood, ed., *Nursing theorists and their work*, 8th edn. Grand Rapids: Elsevier. Ch. 11.

Martinsen, K., 2006. *Care and vulnerability.* Oslo: Akribe.

Miller, T., 2003. *The heretical imperative.* Northumberland: Cloisters.

Miller, T., 2014. *Principles of retreat.* Available at: www.northumbriacommunity.org/articles/principles-of-retreat/. [Accessed 3 August 2015.]

Miller T., 2016. *Celtic spirituality: a beginner's guide.* Available at: www.northumbriacommunity.org/. [Accessed 7 March 2016.]

Northumbria Community, 2002. *Celtic daily prayer: prayers and readings from the Northumbria Community.* San Francisco: Harper Collins.

Northumbria Community, 2004. *A way for living: introducing the rule of the Northumbria Community.* Northumberland: Cloisters.

Northumbria Community, 2005. *Soul friendship.* Northumberland: Cloisters.

Northumbria Community, 2014. *Availability and hospitality: module 5 novitiate process.* Felton: Northumbria Community.

Northumbia Community, n.d. *The rule of life.* Available at: www.northumbriacommunity.org/. [Accessed 3 August 2015.]

Northumbria Community, n.d. *Who are we?* Available at: www.northumbriacommunity.org/. [Accessed 3 August 2015.]

Nouwen, H., 1973. *Reaching out.* London: Fontana.

Nouwen, H., 1996. *Bread for the journey: reflections for every day of the year.* London: Darton, Longman and Todd.

Nouwen. H., 1998. *The inner voice of love: a journey through anguish to freedom.* London: Darton, Longman and Todd.

Nursing Midwifery Council, 2015. *The code of professional standards of practice and behaviour for nurses and midwives.* London: Nursing Midwifery Council. Available at: www.nmc.org.uk/standards/code. [Accessed 10 February 2015.]

O'Donahue, J., 1997. *Anam Cara: spiritual wisdom from the Celtic world.* London: Bantam Books.

Pollard, J., 2005. Authenticity and inauthenticity. In E. Van Deurzen and C. Arnold Baker, eds., *Existential perspectives on human issues: a handbook for therapeutic practice.* New York: Palgrave. Ch. 19.

Rogers, C., 1959. A theory of therapy, personality and interpersonal relationships as developed in the client-centred framework. In S. Koch, ed., *Psychology: a study of a science: formulations of the person and the social context.* Columbus: McGraw-Hill. Ch. 2.

Rogers, C., 1961. *On becoming a person: a therapist's view of psychotherapy.* London: Constable and Robinson.

Rogers, C., 1962. The interpersonal relationship: the core of guidance. *Harvard Educational Review*, 32(4), pp. 416–429.

Rogers, A., 1997. Vulnerability, health and healthcare. *Journal of Advanced Nursing*, 26(1), pp. 65–72.

Rolheiser, R., 2004. *The restless heart: finding our spiritual home in times of loneliness*. New York: Double Day.

Schmid, P., 2001. Authenticity: the person as his or her own author. Dialogical and ethical perspectives on therapy as an encounter relationship. And Beyond. In G. Wyatt, ed., *Congruence*. Llangarron, Ross-on-Wye: PCCS Books. Ch. 15.

Thompson, D., ed., 1995. *The concise Oxford dictionary of current English*. Oxford: Clarendon Press.

Thorup, C., Rundqvis, E., Roberts, C., and Delmar, C., 2012. Care as a matter of courage: vulnerability, suffering, and ethical formation in nursing care. *Scandinavian Journal of Caring*, 26, pp. 427–435.

Van Deurzen, E., and Arnold Baker, C., 2005. Introduction to the spiritual dimension. In E. Van Deurzen and C. Arnold Baker, eds., *Existential perspectives on human issues: a handbook for therapeutic practice*. New York: Palgrave Macmillan. Ch. 24.

Vanier, J., 1982. *Community and growth*. London: Darton, Longman and Todd.

Vanier, J., 2004. *Drawn into the mystery of Jesus through the gospel of John*. Ottawa: Novalis.

Wright, S., 2005. *Reflections on spirituality and health*. London: Whurr.

SECTION
V

Looking Back to Move
Forward

11 Spirituality in Palliative Care

Bruce Rumbold

Introduction

This chapter is an exercise in reflective enquiry that spans most of my working life. For the past 40 years, I've been involved, in one way or another, with spirituality and palliative care. These twin themes have shaped my professional practice, first as a research student, then as a minister of religion, a professor of practical theology and now a public health palliative care academic. What I hope to do here is outline how the experiences of working in these fields can identify some core developmental themes and key practice issues that may assist others involved in spirituality, palliative care, and health and social services more generally. I am certainly not claiming that my experience typifies those who practise and write in this area. Rather, I offer these reflections to invite others to reflect in a similar way upon their own life projects.

Many of my ideas have changed over the years, as have my allegiances and practices. But one thing that has remained constant is my view that spirituality describes our experience of and stance toward the world. Spirituality is expressed through relationships with places and things, with aspects of our selves, with other people, with communities of practice and interest, and with ideas or beliefs that transcend us (Lartey, 1997). Because it emerges within and is expressed through these various aspects of our existence, spirituality weaves them together. It is an integrative, not a separable, aspect of our lives. But because it is integrative, it can also deconstruct our analyses: spirituality transcends and confronts our attempts to capture it in one dimension or in the confines of a single discipline. My challenge, then, is to discuss what seems to be central without unnecessarily imposing boundaries.

Background

My interest in the field that became palliative care began in 1967 as a young physics postgraduate in Melbourne, Australia, reading John Hinton's (1967) *Dying*. This was the year St Christopher's Hospice, the prototype modern

Figure 11.1 Practical theological reflection.

hospice, opened in London. My interest continued to develop when, now a theology student taking honours in pastoral theology, I read Elisabeth Kübler-Ross's (1969) *On Death and Dying*, and some of the material that was spun off from this landmark publication. This in turn led to doctoral studies in Manchester, UK, in the mid-1970s, which gave me an opportunity to focus in some depth on the care of people dying in institutions. One product of this doctoral project was a method for reflective enquiry that continues to shape my work today (see Figure 11.1).

This is, of course, a hermeneutic circle, commonplace now, but less evident or available in the mid-1970s. For me it began as a way of describing how I found myself doing practical theology. Received traditions, expressed in doctrinal theologies, tend to be clear about the way the world ought to be but frequently struggle to deal with the way the world actually is. Practical theology, in contrast, begins with questions raised through experience within a community of practice, considers the various ways these experiences might be understood by the best available contemporary thought, asks how these various contemporary understandings or interpretations might be critically correlated with traditions that place them in historical, philosophical or religious contexts, then devises strategies that address the experiences, and the community, from which enquiry began. The aim of these strategies is to search for, enact, preserve or enhance particular values in that experience: to explore ways in which people undergoing that experience and engaged in that community might begin, or continue, to flourish (to use language of the 1990s more than the 1970s). Implementing these strategies, of course, results in fresh experiences, leading to enhanced or amended interpretations, renewed correlations and strategies revised to enhance community practice. And so the cycle continues.

First community of practice: the hospice

The key experiences informing my doctoral project came from a hospice community in northern England, where I undertook fieldwork. Here, as a researcher, I participated in efforts made to provide care at the end of lives that had been lived in various interesting, mundane or complicated ways. These experiences were juxtaposed with an emerging literature about achieving 'death with dignity' through emotional expressiveness and self-transcendence. This new literature about exemplary dying sat rather oddly with the ordinariness of dying and death in the hospice, where people were not expressive or romantic about dying, but nevertheless clearly brought to their dying – for better or for worse – the resources they had drawn upon in living. I tried to understand these diverse experiences through the lens of pastoral care – holistic care that mirrored the hospice ideal of caring for body, mind, relationships and spirit. The resources I gathered seemed impossible to integrate, comprising as they did personal accounts, clinical studies, social surveys, psychological and religious theories, and aspirational tales of a new day dawning for end-of-life care. Searching for an interpretive theme, I finally fell back on a paradoxical experience of my own; sometimes when I had felt the most helpless I had actually been helpful to others. I could identify times when my felt helplessness had somehow been trans-formative: as duty chaplain called out in the middle of the night to take over care of family members of a man who had just died in Coronary Care; sitting hour upon hour at the bedside of a dying indigenous man on the first anniversary of his mother's death; called into the room of a man in a full facial frame because he'd been through the windscreen of a car ...

I began to explore ways in which dying and death expose all concerned to the risk or possibility or inevitability of helplessness. Martin Seligman's (1975) book on helplessness had just been published, and I used this resource descriptively to understand how both the risk and the reality of helplessness were being managed by institutions and how this manage-ment might shape the responses of dying people, their family and friends, and professional caregivers. Institutional care, it seemed, established an economy of control that reduced the risk of helplessness for caregivers but correspondingly increased it for patients and families. Exploring this theme of helplessness, and its association with hope, took me into dialogue with existential philosophy, psychoanalysis, learning theory and Christian tradi-tions. From these conversations came a helping model that focused on the importance of seeking mutuality in care and negotiating care around those things that matter to both recipients and providers of care. The model stressed the need to be clear about what caregivers can and cannot offer, and drew attention to the way hope can emerge from caring relationships that are both realistic and open to possibility. Rather like the hospice vision itself, it was a vision of the possibilities inherent in caring about people as well as caring for them, reconnecting who caregivers are with what they do. It identified an economy of control in institutional care and asked how equity might be realized within institutional structures. (It was after all in the days before managerialism took over our health systems.)

Second community of practice: the local congregation

This approach to care developed within health care and academic settings in Manchester, but when I returned to Australia I moved into a community setting. I spent ten years as minister of a local congregation in Box Hill, a suburb of Melbourne. Here I found a community of people already committed to engagement with their neighbourhood, and over the following years I worked with them to develop youth support, housing, refugee resettlement and aged care drop-in programs. Intersecting this community development work was the pastoral work associated with a congregation in a neighbourhood that was in transition. Dying continued to be a significant focus, in part because I was regularly asked to provide pastoral care training to some of the emerging palliative care programs around Melbourne, but more particularly because a significant number of members of our congregation died during this period. At times these losses challenged our sense of purpose: the out-of-time deaths of some key leaders seemed to undermine new possibilities that struggled to emerge. We learned to consider the legacy of those who died, the ways in which they demonstrated faithfulness, how we might best remember and learn from their lives. We built reflection into weekly services, church meetings and annual reports. Somehow, out of uncertainty we found the resources to continue looking outward into the local community. While some members of the congregation lost heart and left, others responded to fill gaps, and some new people joined us.

Much of this story remains untold. However, some prayers I wrote for individuals' funeral services were later published (Falla, 1981, 1994), and during this time I finally wrote up the work I had undertaken in the United Kingdom, modified now by the palliative care encounters and congregational experience in Box Hill (Rumbold, 1986). In a number of respects, ideas formed in Manchester had proved transferable to the community setting of Box Hill – collaboration and sharing control are after all basic to community development work. But further themes emerged: the importance of working with the assets of the congregation to find directions in our life together, addressing the issues that emerged from the shared concerns of the community, finding courage and patience to wait for new possibilities as old structures gave way. The new experiences shared with this local community also confronted me with the limits of my helping model that had emphasized relinquishing control. Although in some circumstances this 'holding' approach that created space for people to seek their own meaning was appropriate, in others I found that I needed to use professional power constructively to persuade and direct whilst remaining aware that such power can also be abused in various ways. As a minister, I needed to provide leadership and support members of the congregation to deal with the effects on their lives of power exercised by a variety of professional caregivers, and this experience began to turn my attention to the place of power in helping relationships.

Third community of practice: the theological school

In mid-1986, I took up a position as professor of pastoral studies in Whitley College, Melbourne, a theological school where I'd been a sessional teacher during my years as a congregational minister. This new learning community extended questions about professional roles in a variety of ways. I was, of course, involved in the formation of people who would become congregational ministers. But the largest proportion of classes was made up of women and men whose interest in theological study was its capacity to develop their practice in education or health care or organizational leadership. Their questions were about how to embed their values in their professional practice. They wanted to act with integrity in workplaces that were changing as neo-liberal ideology began to shape institutional policy. Questions about the abuse of power became sharply focused with media stories about clergy abuse, and the extent of this abuse. Doing practical theology with my students began to involve grappling with psychological, sociological and political understandings of power, and correlating these with the analyses of power in biblical traditions. My understanding of pastoral care became organized around the appropriate use of power in leadership and in helping relationships. Not much of this reflection was published (although see Rumbold, 1989, 1993), but it set the stage for two further developments in reflective practice for me.

The first of these came through an invitation to write a chapter on spiritual care for a handbook being produced by a local palliative care service (Rumbold, 1989). This consolidated for me a shift in thinking about spirituality in palliative care. To this point, the framework in which I'd been working was pastoral care, a holistic model where spiritual care is an integral part of care overall. Pastoral care understood in this way expands the horizons of care, and most of the training I'd been offering in academic pastoral care courses and training events with health care and community organizations encouraged practitioners to see their work in a broader context. I was inviting students and practitioners to reflect on the way spiritual issues emerge within physical, psychological and social care, and how the practitioners' capacity to respond is shaped by their own values, experiences and beliefs. Now, as hospice programs began actively to seek access to health care funding, underlying concepts in the field began to shift. The holistic model of care that had informed local community-based programs gave way to the biopsychosocial framework that characterized the health care system. Spiritual care, which was a distinctive feature of hospice care, became an activity to be added to existing health system requirements, a strand in a biopsychosocial-spiritual model of care. Seeking to develop spiritual care as a discipline within the ahistorical context of health care practice has had a number of implications to which I'll return a little later in this narrative.

The second development came from my growing awareness of the structural dimensions of the issues with which I was working. I'd always resisted the conflation of pastoral care with (individual) pastoral counselling that had characterized the 1970s and 1980s, but nevertheless my starting point for pastoral reflection still tended to be individual experience. I was increasingly aware, however, that the quality of helping relationships, even the possibility of forming helpful relationships, was subject to the constraints of institutional structures. The very existence, let alone the exercise, of professional power is a social concern. And so I enrolled in a postgraduate health studies program that equipped me as a health sociologist. The systemic perspective I'd developed first as a physicist, then as a practical theologian, transferred nicely to this new community of scholarship and practice. The ideas I encountered provided fresh possibilities for integration of the experiences and understandings I brought, while the study program itself became a vehicle for exploring some of these possibilities, among them ways to understand the development of palliative care as a social movement (Rumbold, 1998).

Fourth community of practice: end-of-life care

Both these developments, participation in an emerging conversation about spiritual care and explicit access to sociological imagination, shaped my teaching and writing in the 1990s (see for example Rumbold, 1994, 1996, 1998). A new phase of reflection began unexpectedly when I was appointed to a half-time position in an innovative palliative care program commencing in the La Trobe University School of Public Health. The model from which this Palliative Care Unit operated, health-promoting palliative care (Kellehear, 1999), resonated with the pastoral care perspective I'd formed over the past couple of decades. Allan Kellehear and other colleagues opened up new strands of dialogue, particularly around an emerging sociological literature on death, dying and grief. When in 2002 a full-time position became available, I moved from working in dual theological school and university appointments and began to develop and frame ideas and experiences within a public health approach. I realized, for example, that much of my ten years of parish ministry resonated with public health community development approaches. I reflected on the ways in which pastoral care and public health might inform each other in strategy and social vision (Rumbold, 2009). I looked at social transformations of spiritual care at the end of life (Rumbold, 2002), and I began to focus more upon the practice of spiritual care as a health care discipline (Rumbold, 2003, 2007, 2010). I was able to establish a graduate program in pastoral care, now recast as a spiritual care major within the Master of Health Sciences program.

Reflecting on these developments in my own thought helps me to see the evolution of spiritual care first within palliative care, then more widely in health care systems. Spiritual care was, from the beginning, an aspect of hospice care, with spiritual need seen as a component of total pain, and spiritual engagement (meaning-making that places this imminent event in relation to the rest of life) acknowledged as a key component of dying well. Spirituality was embedded in this holistic approach. It was what enabled hospice workers to offer care that gave 'each individual the freedom to make their own journey towards their ultimate goals' (Saunders, 1996, p. 319). Hospice care in these early years had the characteristics of a social movement (James and Field, 1992). Not all who worked in the pioneering hospice care programs were conventionally religious, but their engagement was like that of a religious. To work in palliative care was seen as a vocation, and training was as much a matter of personal formation as it was the acquisition of specific skills. To be a hospice worker carried with it an aura of being 'special', someone who was comfortable in settings that most people avoided.

In the hospice, spiritual care as a component of holistic care was expressed through a 'watch with me vulnerability', as Walter put it (1997). It was not so much a discipline area as an aspect of everyone's work, although often a chaplain or pastoral care worker would lead this aspect of the work. Mainstreaming hospice programs into the health system as palliative care services, and the consequent formation of a distinctive practice community, narrowed the scope of discussion and critical reflection. Spirituality as an ethos that guided staff selection and directed the activities of the caring team was not acceptable to a health services management framework. If spiritual care was to continue as a component of palliative care, it had to be provided in measurable ways. This was addressed initially by framing spiritual care as a (professional) service provided by a designated appointee (pastoral care worker, chaplain), then as specific activities carried out and reported upon by a range of team members (Holloway et al., 2011).

Mainstreaming was thus both a routinizing and a secularizing process (James and Field, 1992; Rumbold, 1998). The embedded, often implicit spirituality of hospice's holistic approach was replaced by approaches to spiritual care consistent with a health services framework. The basis for these changes was pragmatic, and probably insufficiently scrutinized. Managers of health services assumed that spiritual care could be delivered in the same way as other professional services. Spiritual care providers accepted that, to access health services, spiritual care needed to be organized according to health service delivery models. The understanding of spirituality that results is generic (Swinton, 2010), conceptualized to accommodate a broad range of beliefs and practices. There are of course many ways in which this move to generic spirituality has been important, not least the fact that it has maintained the presence of spiritual care within palliative care and promoted its acceptance more widely within the health system. But there are costs as well.

One cost is that spirituality, as with other health care practice, loses its history. Typically health services define today's best practice, seldom indicating how, let alone why, today's best practice differs from yesterday's best practice. Consequently, the majority of contemporary health care spiritual care writings give no hint that there might be millennia-old traditions that are relevant to the concepts currently being produced as key components of spiritual care. Another cost, related to this, is the absence of a critical approach to spirituality. The literature by and large assumes that spirituality is a good thing; but religious traditions remind us that discernment is vital to spiritual life. There are spiritualities that lead to life, and spiritualities that lead to destruction; spiritual paths that can make people whole, and spiritual paths that can result in fragmentation, disillusion and despair. Traditions remind us that individual spirituality, and indeed the practice of spiritual care, is shaped (and may be distorted) by social, cultural and institutional structures. But the risk of spiritual care is almost entirely absent from health care discussions.

A further cost of developing a generic spirituality may be the way that, as a distinctive spiritual health care literature forms, practitioners look mainly, or only, to this literature, which in turn is developed around their immediate concerns. Protocols are developed to mesh with existing health service strategies, so that aspects of spiritual care can be added to existing disciplinary responsibilities. The focus of attention is upon problems, spiritual need and spiritual distress, not upon what might constitute spiritual health. Even if spiritual care practice continues to be reflexive, the scope of critical reflection may be grievously narrowed, reflecting Walter's concern that organized spirituality could become little more than pop psychology (Walter, 1997).

My concern here is that although spiritual care might need for pragmatic reasons to adapt itself to a health services framework, it is essential that spiritual care providers develop and maintain a broader, multidisciplinary, integrative perspective (Rumbold, 2012a). This broader perspective is needed to ensure effective critical reflection on health care spiritual care concepts and practices. One strategy for broadening health care discussions of spiritual care (and health care in general) is to place them within a public health framework. This framework is concerned with creating and preserving health, and understands that health is constructed within everyday communities. Although illness is the principal business of the so-called health system, health actually involves all aspects of social life. The health of a society is promoted when people have decent shelter, nutrition and work; are included in their communities; and have a say in the decisions that affect their lives (WHO, 2008). A public health perspective reminds us of the foundational importance of healthy settings: not just clean water and effective sewerage, but settings that promote equity and social inclusion.

Compassionate communities

Public health is now a major conceptual frame for my current reflections on spirituality and palliative care. The community shaping these reflections is made up of health care students and health care practitioners I teach in the university and collaborate with in community development projects. Public health perspectives remind us of the vital contribution to care made by families, friends, neighbours and other members of local communities (Salau, Rumbold and Young, 2007; Rumbold, Gardner and Nolan, 2011; Rumbold and Aoun, 2014). Public health perspectives also draw attention to disadvantaged dying (Grindrod and Rumbold, 2015) and the inability of our services to care adequately for marginalized people – thus reinforcing the link between spirituality and justice (Rumbold, 2006). While I continue to be interested in developments in health care spirituality (Cobb, Puchalski and Rumbold, 2012; Rumbold, 2013), a public health perspective pushes me to reflect upon the structures within which we attempt to provide spiritual care. Thus a further paradox of contemporary health care spiritual care, it seems to me, is the way the health care system is expected to demonstrate values the rest of society will not. We expect health care to be provided equitably to all, but elsewhere we endorse competition as the way to achieve efficiencies. We expect health care practitioners to be compassionate, but as a society we reward self-interest and greed. What social function can spiritual care perform within such a health system? What function should it perform? The language promoting spiritual care provision is altruistic, but the risk is that the introduction of spiritual care within the current health system could further compromise people's privacy and autonomy as yet another aspect of their lives is brought under health care surveillance.

Public health approaches to end-of-life care today are asking about the sort of community that is needed to provide and support good end-of-life care. A consensus is emerging around the concept of compassionate communities (Kellehear, 2005; Abel et al., 2013; Wegleitner, Heimerl and Kellehear, 2015). Compassion is the organizing principle, or embedded value, of communities which continue to include people nearing the end of their lives. Clearly compassion is central to spirituality, but it is also a fundamental human quality (the primary social emotion, Nussbaum [1996] suggests) and can be expressed through a myriad of caring activities, small and large (Rumbold, 2012b). The compassionate communities' model for end-of-life care reclaims an approach where spiritual perspectives are embedded, much as they had been in the earlier years of the hospice movement. Because public health has at its core the recurring philosophical questions 'What is a good life?' and 'What is a good society?', it challenges every attempt we make to narrow the scope of enquiry. Fundamentally, public health reminds us that health is created in communities and arises from all aspects of their life together, not something delivered by experts to the community.

Looking back and looking forward

Overall, my lifetime project seems to be about what makes for good care or, better, what makes care good. My principal avenues of enquiry have never strayed far from the linked themes of spirituality and palliative care. This is because spirituality as an integrative perspective crosses the boundaries that various caring disciplines use to contain their particular aspect of caring activity, while palliative care raises questions of ultimate meaning and purpose. Even when I have made excursions into other areas – for example exploring power in the 1980s and 1990s – the insights and experiences generated there have been applied to the ongoing conversation between spirituality and palliative care. Power is fundamental to understanding how policy is formed and implemented, how organizational change takes place and how professionalization affects the autonomy and shapes the experience of those who receive care.

Conclusion

In looking back over what I now see as the cycles of reflective learning I've described here, one thing that strikes me in particular is the importance of communities of practice in generating collaborative learning. Community provides content, method and organization – that is, rules for the conversation, clarity about the things that must be taken into account if the practitioner is to be credible to that community (the Bible to a Christian congregation; evidence to a health care audience; experience to arts-based practitioners [Rumbold, 2014]). Learning communities should promote diversity – either by engaging with different communities while bringing the resources of the past into the new discourse, or by ensuring that fresh perspectives and experiences are invited into continuing communities of practice. New communities bring about new experiences, fresh analyses, renewed strategy – and they also open up opportunity to reflect upon past experiences and understandings. (It also makes me rather uncomfortably aware of the extent to which knowledge and insight are co-produced while the academic who writes it up claims the credit.)

Reflective enquiry that uses experience as a source does not permit an easy separation of the personal from the professional. To state the obvious, as this reflective process outlined above has been unfolding, I've been growing older. In addition to expanding professional experience, I bring different capacities and interests to the enquiry. The hospice model of care took this blending of the professional and personal into account: emotional labour is involved because if you are to care for a person, you also need to care about that person. Personal formation goes hand in hand with professional development. One of the statements I recall from my early days in palliative care is that 'you need to come to terms with your own mortality if you're going to work in this field'. (I can't readily find written references, but I recall reiterated statements of this idea.) It puzzled me at the time and continues to puzzle me now. Have I, through detailed reflection upon my life and my experience in end-of-life care over 40 years 'come to terms with my mortality'? The answer is probably not: I understand that death is inevitable, but I don't necessarily welcome the idea. What I have learned from others, however, has the potential to be a resource I can take into my own ageing and dying. But I cannot predict how these linked processes will take shape or how well I'll be able to use what I've accumulated.

Our communities of practice include the dead as well as the living – in old age the former may begin to outnumber the latter. Increasingly, my reflections take place within a developmental community of family and friends – some recently arrived, others who've been part of my life for a long time. Increasingly, death is an active presence in this community. One member of my community who has been with me whilst writing this chapter is a long-time friend, Warwick Ashley, who died a few weeks ago. He was a psychiatrist in Hobart, Tasmania, and his last illness began just as he ended full-time work and entered active retirement. Recently I was to address a psycho-oncology conference in New Zealand, and I asked him what I should say to conference participants about what it might be like to receive their care.

In his reply, written only days before his death, Warwick reflected on his development as a clinician, the shift that takes place over the years, from getting useful information but being experience-distant to becoming experience-near, able to create and hold a space in which transformation can occur. He reflected on the journey he had been taking from the role of expert to that of patient, how he was now a recipient of others' care, having his ability to organize and understand his life profoundly tested, yet being held by 'good-enough' care from colleagues, and by the love of family and friends.

He talked about losses, including valuable time spent getting affairs in order, about questioning the value of what he had contributed to life, the experiential discovery that in this transition to death's domain he had no control at all. He noted that Erikson's integrity versus despair and Vaillant's transcendence versus nothingness were useful metaphors for what he was experiencing.

He talked about how different the actual experience of dying was to anything that might be anticipated or imagined: no matter how often we might have accompanied someone else, our own journey – its pitfalls and possibilities – is ours alone. It is mystery. It's fresh, frightening, awe-ful, yet also a place where hope can flourish. Transcendence was a word he used a lot in the last months of his life – but it was notable, I think, how much of what he said and did was a deeper apprehension of the ideas and commitments and places and people that had given meaning to his life to that point. His dying was a clarification and affirmation of what had supported him in life.

So how do we come to terms with mortality? Embrace it as a mystery, was Warwick's advice. His practical example was to bring to it the resources upon which he had based his life. In the last weeks or years of life, our life project comes to the fore. We may find ourselves completing the unfinished business of life, or focusing upon particular forms of resolution. We may strive to articulate one last time what our particular contribution has been, as Sacks has done in *Gratitude* (2015) or Hitchens in *Mortality* (2012) or Clive James in *Latest Readings* (2015). Attending to spirituality, to our webs of connection, meaning and transcendence, should ensure that conversation around dying is more than technical, that our death is placed in the context of our life. And it seems worth noting that effective spirituality is connected with or into a project – it's not merely a matter of abstract belief. Better to realize what this project is early rather than late so that it can be a resource whilst dying, not a quest begun in dying.

References

Abel, J., Walter, T., Carey, L., Rosenberg, J., Noonan, K., Horsfall, D., Leonard, R., Rumbold, B., and Morris, D., 2013. Circles of care: should community development redefine the practice of palliative care? *BMJ Supportive & Palliative Care*, 3(4), pp. 383–388.

Cobb, M., Puchalski, C., and Rumbold, B., eds., 2012. *The Oxford textbook of spirituality in healthcare*. Oxford: Oxford University Press.

Falla, T., ed., 1994, 1981. *Be our freedom, Lord: responsive prayers and readings for contemporary worship*. Adelaide: Open Book.

Grindrod A., and Rumbold B., 2015. OA49 disadvantaged dying: a compassionate communities approach for people with intellectual disability. *BMJ Support Palliative Care*. 5 (Suppl 1), A15.

Hinton, J., 1967. *Dying*. Harmondsworth: Penguin.

Hitchens, C., 2012. *Mortality*. London: Atlantic Books.

Holloway, M., Adamson, S., McSherry, W., and Swinton, J., 2011. *Spiritual care at the End of Life: a systematic review of the literature*. Available at: www.dh.gov.uk/publications. [Accessed 10 January 2016.]

James, C., 2015. *Latest readings*. New Haven: Yale University Press.

James, N., and Field, D., 1992. The routinization of hospice: charisma and bureaucratization. *Social Science and Medicine*, 34(12), pp. 1363–1375.

Kellehear, A., 1999. *Health promoting palliative care*. Melbourne: Oxford University Press.

Kellehear, A., 2005. *Compassionate cities: public health approaches to end of life care*. London: Routledge.

Kübler-Ross, E., 1969. *On death and dying*. New York: Macmillan.

Lartey, E., 1997. *In living colour: an intercultural approach to pastoral care and counselling*. London: Cassell.

Nussbaum M., 1996. Compassion: the basic social emotion. *Social Philosophy and Policy*, 13(1), pp. 27–58.

Rumbold, B., 1986. *Helplessness and hope: pastoral care in terminal illness*. London: SCM Press.

Rumbold, B., 1989. Spiritual dimensions in palliative care. In P. Hodder and A. Turley, eds., *The creative option of palliative care: a manual for health professionals*. North Fitzroy: Melbourne City mission. No chapter numbers.

Rumbold, B., 1993. Some reflections on clergy abuse and power. *Ministry, Society, Theology*, 7(2), pp. 45–54.

Rumbold, B., 1994. Pastoral care and spiritual care. *Ministry, Society, Theology*, 8(2), pp. 43–45.

Rumbold, B., 1996. Revisioning care. *Ministry, Society & Theology*, 10(2), pp. 33–48.

Rumbold, B., 1998. Implications of mainstreaming hospice into palliative care services. In J. Parker and S. Aranda, eds., *Palliative care: Explorations and challenges*. Sydney: MacLennan & Petty. Ch. 1.

Rumbold, B., 2003. Caring for the spirit: lessons from working with the dying. *Medical Journal of Australia*, 179(6), pp. S11–13.

Rumbold, B., 2006. The spirituality of compassion: a public health response to ageing and end-of-life care. *Journal of Religion, Spirituality & Aging*, 18(2/3), pp. 31–44.

Rumbold, B., 2007. A review of spiritual assessment in health care practice. *Medical Journal of Australia*, 186(10), pp. S60–62.

Rumbold, B., 2009. Building resilience: the local congregation as a health promoting community. In C. Hunter, M. Kelly and R. Prior, eds., *Together in ministry: essays to honour John Paver*. Melbourne: Uniting Academic Press. Ch. 3.

Rumbold, B., 2010. Spiritual and existential issues at the end of life. In M. Robotin, I. Olver and A. Girgis, eds., *When cancer crosses disciplines: a physician's handbook*. London: Imperial College Press. Ch. 48.

Rumbold, B., 2012a. Models of spiritual care. In M. Cobb, C. Puchalski and B. Rumbold, eds., *The Oxford textbook of spirituality in healthcare*. Oxford: Oxford University Press. Ch. 26.

Rumbold, B., 2012b. Compassionate care: engaging the spirit in care. *Progress in Palliative Care*, 20(2), pp. 106–113.

Rumbold, B., 2013. Spiritual assessment and healthcare chaplaincy. *Christian Bioethics*, 19(3), pp. 251–269.

Rumbold, B., 2014. Evidence in practice: nurturing aesthetic reflexivity. *Journal of Applied Arts and Health*, 5(2), pp. 263–271.

Rumbold, B., and Aoun, S., 2014. Bereavement and palliative care: a public health perspective. *Progress in Palliative Care*, 22(3), pp. 131–135.

Rumbold, B., Gardner, F., and Nolan, I., 2011. Spirituality and community practice in S. Conway, ed., *Governing death and loss: empowerment, involvement and participation*. Oxford: Oxford University Press. Ch. 14.

Sacks, O., 2015. *Gratitude*. New York: Picador.

Salau, S., Rumbold, B., and Young, B., 2007. From concept to care: enabling community care through a health promoting palliative care approach. *Contemporary Nurse*, 27(1), pp. 132–140.

Saunders, C., 1996. Hospice. *Mortality*, 1(3), pp. 317–322.

Seligman, M., 1975. *Helplessness: on depression, development and death*. San Francisco: Freeman-Scribners.

Swinton, J., 2010. The meanings of spirituality: a multi-perspective approach to 'the spiritual'. In W. McSherry and L. Ross, eds., *Spiritual assessment in healthcare practice*. Keswick: M&K Publishing. Ch. 2.

Walter, T., 1997. The ideology and organization of spiritual care: three approaches. *Palliative Medicine*, 11, pp. 21–30.

Wegleitner, K., Heimerl, K., and Kellehear, A., eds., 2015. *Compassionate communities: case studies from Britain and Europe*. London: Routledge.

World Health Organization (WHO) Commission on the Social Determinants of Health, 2008. *Closing the gap in a generation*. Available at: www.who.int/social_determinants/final_report/en/index.html. [Accessed 12 January 2016.]

12 A Few Concluding Thoughts

Laura Béres

Introduction

I have found the process of writing for, and editing, this collection of chapters an enriching and interesting experience. I hope readers will have found it just as engaging. Having asked people to contribute to a book titled *Practising Spirituality: Reflecting on Meaning-Making in Personal and Professional Contexts*, and then having only tentatively suggested what each author might like to write about, has allowed us all the freedom to follow our interests as they unfolded in the reflecting and writing process. This has meant the whole process for me was a little like setting out on an adventure where my path crossed with the authors' paths from time to time as we engaged with ideas presented in their chapters. We had a rough idea of where we were headed, but we could not have known ahead of time what we might learn on the way.

Although I have grouped chapters in certain sections that highlight some of the communalities between those chapters, I also believe there are other themes which cut across the majority of chapters; I highlight these broader themes in this concluding chapter.

In Chapter 11, Bruce Rumbold comments that personal formation goes hand in hand with professional development, and indeed each of us in our respective chapters has reflected on the links between our personal and professional lives. In particular, we have examined how spirituality has inextricably woven these two areas together, regardless of whether the professional practice is teaching, counselling, community development or advocacy for social justice.

In Chapter 2, Jan Fook, by reflecting upon the development of her approach to critical reflection of practice and spirituality, provides readers with a framework for approaching the following chapters since we have all integrated critical reflection of our personal and professional practices to a certain degree. She has also touched on themes in her chapter which have also arisen in other chapters; in fact, I have found it interesting to note many underlying similarities between the chapters collected here, despite the seemingly diverse range of spiritual and professional practices represented. Although the range has by no means been exhaustive, I hope readers have found it broad enough to have taken them out of their known and familiar experiences, and thus able to learn something new from different points of view.

Underlying themes

Maintaining an undogmatic stance

I have recently been reading Gadamer's (2000) *Truth and Method* and have found his approach to hermeneutical philosophy has added further breadth to my understanding of the benefits of examining various types of experiences, or incidents, in critical reflection of practice (Fook and Gardner, 2007). I was particularly stuck by his thoughts and descriptions of an 'experienced person'. He suggests a person is experienced not only due to having gone through a certain number of experiences, but also due to being open to new experience. He describes 'being experienced' as not consisting of knowing everything or knowing more than anyone else. He says that 'the experienced person proves to be, on the contrary, someone who is radically undogmatic' (Gadamer, 2000, p. 355). Being undogmatic is important as it allows for holding knowledge tentatively, being willing to be surprised by new ways of thinking and therefore able to develop new practices, which can all come about through the process of critical reflection of experiences in practice. Melanie Rogers' description of 'vulnerability' in Chapter 10, in fact, in which she stresses the importance of being teachable, shares something in common with this idea.

I have appreciated how all the authors who have contributed to this book have represented this undogmatic stance in their reflecting and writing, alongside their passion for, and focus on, their particular area of interest. I hope that this will have allayed any fears that accounting for, and integrating, spirituality into professional practice involves any dogmatic imposition of the practitioner's belief systems.

I hope it has also been clear that professional practitioners do not need to define themselves as spiritual in order to be able to develop comfort in speaking with others about what gives them a sense of hope, meaning or purpose, which for many people means being able to talk about their spirituality and/or faith. It may be necessary at times to refer some service users to spiritual directors or leaders within specific religious organizations and faith traditions, if they want to discuss specific religious details of which the professional practitioner is unfamiliar. However, for the most part people will just want to know that their service providers care enough to talk with openness and respect about what is important to them. On the other hand, it has also been evident in these chapters that spirituality not only has a place in clinical and direct practice but also has a place in social action, community development and teaching.

Spirituality defined as that which provides meaning and purpose as well as a recognition of the transcendent

As I discussed in Chapter 1 when presenting definitions of spirituality, it is not necessary to be religious in order to be spiritual, although some people would describe themselves as both. This has been demonstrated again throughout the chapters as authors have described how they understand spirituality and as some have described their own spiritual practices. Each author has provided examples or definitions that suggest spirituality is that which provides a sense of meaning and purpose in life. That which gives meaning and purpose provides answers to questions like 'Why am I here?' 'How does this event (like impending death) fit into my life?' and 'What is, or has been, my purpose while alive?'

Due to the very nature of those questions, some authors have commented on the transcendent in their understanding of spirituality. 'The Transcendent' is sometimes used interchangeably with 'The Divine' or 'God', yet a simple dictionary definition of 'transcendent' indicates it means that which is beyond the limits of ordinary experience or beyond rational comprehension. An interesting example is provided in the sentence 'The antislavery movement recognized the transcendent importance of liberty' (www. meriam-webster.com/dictionary/transcendent). With this in mind, some authors have highlighted the manner in which the spiritual aspects of lives have to do with that which is not necessarily understood by rational thought or able to be examined scientifically in cause-and-effect studies. It is rather understood as the part of life which is better experienced through intuition and artistic senses. Not surprisingly, this has resulted in some authors (Fiona Gardner, Rose Pulliam and Bruce Rumbold) also pointing out the dangers of positivism and an overreliance on scientific rational approaches to understanding and knowledge production, since these approaches ignore and minimize the importance of the transcendent, and spiritual, aspects of peoples' lives.

Balancing self-cultivation with an awareness of interconnectedness, authenticity and integrity

Michael White (2000) has noted three different methods of considering spirituality. The first he describes as the 'ascendant', which he suggests involves looking up and out towards an external higher power for guidance and meaning in life. He describes the second as 'immanent' and involving looking inside to our deeper selves for guidance and understanding. He suggests this second approach holds much in common with psychological approaches to understanding the self and thereby attempting to live an authentic life by being true to one's self. Finally, he suggests the third approach could be described as the 'ascendant/immanent' and involves looking inward in order to engage with a higher power/The Divine.

As I reviewed the chapters that are included in this collection, I thought of White's three categories and certainly saw the 'ascendant/immanent' approach to spirituality demonstrated in Fiona Gardner's description of Quaker spirituality, in the three chapters within the Indigenous spiritualities section, and also touched upon in relation to Celtic spirituality. All these spiritualities suggest there is a spark of The Divine in everything, including ourselves. Throughout many of the chapters was the suggestion that spirituality is woven into the fabric of daily life and certainly not something separate and only practised on certain days. In fact, Karlo Mila, in Chapter 5, asks, 'What is not spiritual?'

Mindfulness, authenticity and integrity

Interestingly, mindfulness was not only described by Lisa McCorquodale in her chapter specifically written about mindfulness, but was also touched upon by Jan Fook, Fiona Gardner and Maria Cheung. Although mindfulness is about slowing down to ensure 'being' as well as 'doing', it also has the potential for allowing for the process of recognizing how it might be possible to live authentically as well as connect with the 'ascendant' or 'transcendent' through what is experienced in the 'immanent' or the 'self'.

Although almost every author and every chapter touches on the way in which spirituality is integrated into daily life, both Lisa McCorquodale and Melanie Rogers discuss this in terms of spirituality (or mindfulness) assisting people to live authentic lives. In Chapter 11, Bruce Rumbold uses the term 'integrity', which shares something in common with this idea of authenticity. Integrating spirituality into daily life, being authentic and congruent across various aspects of life, can also assist with practising with integrity and acknowledging interconnectedness.

As Jan Fook mentions in Chapter 2, I have previously written about critical reflection of practice as a form of mindfulness, which can assist in being present to the 'Other' in therapeutic situations (Béres, 2009). In that chapter, I quote one of my favourite passages from Thomas Merton. He writes, 'I wind experiences around myself and cover myself with pleasures and glory like bandages in order to make myself perceptible to myself and to the world, as if I were an invisible body that could only become visible when something visible covered its surface' (Merton, 2003, p. 37). I find this a powerful image of how many of us are tempted to hide our authentic selves (and Melanie Rogers would suggest our vulnerability) by winding experiences around ourselves. Perhaps this also means distracting ourselves with the accumulation of 'stuff' (see http://storyofstuff.org). I imagine this as if bandaging ourselves like mummies, and the process of becoming more mindful, authentic and able to live with integrity as being committed to unwinding these distractions. Critical reflection and a commitment to holistic practices, which incorporate spiritual aspects of people's lives, will help with this.

Some people may criticize spirituality (versus religion) as potentially being too individualistic and potentially selfish in its most extreme versions. I hope that it is clear within the chapters presented here that this is not what any of us are suggesting. Spirituality is not merely about deeper under-standing of the self, leading to self-improvement, although spirituality and authenticity might contribute to this.

Bruce Rumbold argues for the need to position our understanding of spirituality within a broader context, respecting historical and cultural tradi-tions. This also can ensure that spirituality does not become a set of indi-vidual and idiosyncratic beliefs and practices. We may not want religious organizations to dictate and mediate our understandings of the transcend-ent, but it may also be useful to reflect upon how others have negotiated the bigger questions of life over time and in different cultural contexts. I agree with Bruce's suggestion and am currently pursuing further study about the historical and cultural impacts on Christian spirituality. I have shared some of these reflections in my chapter about the role of hospitality in the 'Rule of St Benedict' in the sixth century, which continues to have an effect in current-day dispersed communities like the one Melanie Rogers describes in Chapter 10. Maria Cheung and Lisa McCorquodale also both touch on the impact of the ancient teachings in Buddhism and Daoism on their daily personal and professional practices of mindfulness meditation.

Interconnectedness and social justice

Another way in which authors have demonstrated a focus on intercon-nectedness in spirituality is through their reflections on how spirituality and social action/social justice are intertwined. Jan Fook is the first to mention this in Chapter 2. Jan describes her commitment to social justice throughout her career, and her current engagement with Catholic social justice teaching in a Catholic university setting. She also describes the way in which critical reflection of practice can lead people to make changes to their practices to ensure they are more congruent with their values, leading some to a commitment to social action.

Fiona Gardner discusses the impact of Quaker spirituality in her life and how her first connection with Quakers was through their peace activism.

She comments on the fact some Quakers are primarily contemplative and others are primarily social activists. Cassandra Hanrahan focuses a great deal on trans-species spirituality as being committed to social justice and anti-oppressive practice. For her, spirituality is fundamentally about ethical relationships between humans and all other animals. Being aware of the interconnectedness of all beings results in a way of life committed to compassion and justice. Maria Cheung, focusing on the body-mind-spirit practices of Falun Gong, describes how her mindful meditation leads to an awareness of connection to all, compassion for all and the need to peacefully resist the injustices she sees.

Finally, Bruce Rumbold, describing spirituality as being expressed in relationships with people, places, things, and communities of practice and ideas, points towards his current interest in the conceptual framework of public health. He points out that public health perspectives remind practitioners of the contribution to health made by families, friends, neighbours and other members of local communities. He draws upon Kellehear's (2005) work on compassionate cities and communities, providing a clear and pragmatic image of how communities could integrate the spiritual aspect of compassion much more effectively. Although both Bruce Rumbold and Allan Kellehear are particularly concerned about the need for compassionate communities for appropriate and responsive end-of-life care, they are both just as concerned with public *health* as well as public *death*. They point out that we will all die, so in the meantime, 'What is a good life?' and 'What is a good society?' This is yet another excellent reminder that spirituality is about more than personal belief systems and also has a great deal to do with relationships and actions.

Conclusion

It seems appropriate to end these concluding remarks by thinking about community because none of us live, or develop ideas, in isolation. And as Bruce Rumbold points out, 'Learning communities should promote diversity – either by engaging with different communities while bringing the resources of the past into the new discourse, or ensuring that fresh perspectives and experiences are invited into continuing communities of practice. New communities bring about new experiences, fresh analyses, renewed strategy – and they also open up opportunity to reflect upon past experiences and understandings'.

I have attempted to develop a type of learning community in this book which is diverse in spiritual and professional practices, and which has been enriched by interdisciplinary influences. It has been made up of contributing authors, some of whom are in the beginning stages of their academic careers and some of whom have lengthy and renowned careers with an extensive list of publications to their names, while some of us fall in the middle somewhere. Nonetheless, we are all experienced, using Gadamer's definition of an experienced person, since we have all reflected and built upon experiences while also maintaining an interest in learning more from new experiences. We have all reflected upon and described the influences on the development of our thinking about spirituality in our personal and professional lives.

I hope we have encouraged readers to think about what gives them meaning and purpose in their personal and professional lives, and how they might continue, or develop, practices that allow for congruence across these areas of their lives. I hope they have found this book refreshing and inspiring and that it may have encouraged some to develop their own learning communities, or networks, that might support ongoing critical reflection.

References

Béres, L., 2009. Mindfulness and reflexivity: the no-self as reflective practitioner. In S. Hick, ed., *Mindfulness and social work*. Chicago: Lyceum Books. Ch. 4.

Fook, J., and Gardner, F., 2007. *Practising critical reflection: a resource handbook*. Maidenhead: Open University Press.

Gadamer, H.-G., 2000, 1960. *Truth and method*, 2nd rev. edn. Translation revised by J. Weinsheimer and D. G. Marshall, 1989. New York: The Continuum Publishing Company.

Kellehear, A., 2005. *Compassionate cities: public health and end-of-life care*. New York: Routledge.

Merton, T., 2003, 1961. *New seeds of contemplation*. Boston: Shambhala.

White, M., 2000. *Reflections on narrative practice: essays and interviews*, Adelaide: Dulwich Centre Publications.

Index

Made in the USA
San Bernardino, CA
31 October 2018